DATE DUE

FEB 28 2006	

TIME AND ORDER

IN METROPOLITAN VIENNA

A SEIZURE
OF SCHEDULES

TIME AND
ORDER

··· IN METROPOLITAN VIENNA

ROBERT ROTENBERG

SMITHSONIAN INSTITUTION PRESS

WASHINGTON AND LONDON

Designed by Linda McKnight.
Edited by Jennifer Lorenzo.
Production editing by Rebecca Browning.

Library of Congress Cataloging-in-Publication Data

Rotenberg, Robert Louis, 1949–
    Time and order in metropolitan Vienna : a seizure of schedules/ Robert Rotenberg.
        p.   cm. — (Smithsonian series in ethnographic inquiry)
    Includes bibliographical references and index.
    ISBN 1-56098-103-2
    1. Vienna Metropolitan Area (Austria)—Social conditions.   2. Vienna Metropolitan Area (Austria)—Social life and customs.   3. Time—Social aspects—Austria—Vienna Metropolitan Area.
    I. Title. II. Series.
    HN418.V5R68   1992
    306′.09436′13—dc20   91-32894

British Library Cataloging-in-Publication Data is available.

Manufactured in the United States of America.

5 4 3 2 1 96 95 94 93 92

∞ The paper used in this publication meets the minimum requirements of the American National Standard for Permanence of Paper for Printed Library Materials Z39.48–1984.

CONTENTS

· ·

SMITHSONIAN SERIES IN ETHNOGRAPHIC INQUIRY
William L. Merrill and Ivan Karp, series editors

Ethnography as fieldwork, analysis, and literary form is the distinguishing feature of modern anthropology. Guided by the assumption that anthropological theory and ethnography are inextricably linked, this series is devoted to exploring the ethnographic enterprise.

· ·

This book is about people who live in a metropolis and about what difference their living in a large city makes in how they live. Looking at the way life in cities generates shared meaning runs counter to the tradition in urban studies established by the researchers of the Chicago School, which emphasizes communities, class, and internal differentiation. Today, only the urban political scientists stress the truism that for many facets of social life, the larger the community the more important it is for everyone to know and play by the same rules. This book examines how households sometimes invent, more often react to, and always then play by, the rules. It views these rules as much more ad hoc, context sensitive, and variable than the rules of, say, municipal decision making.

Time and Order in Metropolitan Vienna deals with a European city. European life as North Americans see it through the media and through tourist experiences is not the way Europeans actually live. Some might argue that the search for common cultural features is more appropriate in Europe because of the various homogenizing features of nation, church, and language. North American cities, the argument continues, were peopled by immigrants from various parts of the world and therefore represent a far more complex, heterogeneous substratum that retards the formation of commonly shared values. This view ignores the power of the economic forces that have transformed European culture to channel people of quite different backgrounds into industrial and commercial centers. The homogeneity of European cities in general, and Central European cities in particular, is a fiction. Yet it is a fiction maintained by the metropolitans themselves as a way of more carefully delineating their own individuality, their own relative proximity to the common body of meaning. This research is a first step toward understanding this particular dynamic between self and city.

This book examines how European metropolitans define the temporal dimensions of their daily lives, as a polity and as households. This definition is not without conflict. North Americans hear of European workers winning thirty-five-hour workweeks and wonder at the lunacy of the politicians and owners of capital, as if these persons allow the trade unions to walk all over them. In reality, time is politicized in Europe far more than it is in North America. Time is part of the discourse on power there much more so than in North America. Unpacking this discourse here offers a glimpse into the meaning that people give to their lives.

Finally, *Time and Order in Metropolitan Vienna* is about the anthropology of the metropolis. It argues for a set of questions and research strategies appropriate for very large communities. Such a research effort requires new approaches. This work is an example of what such rethinking can accomplish. Time is only one mirror for reflecting the culture of metropolitans. This is the first of what I hope will be a series of books on Vienna, each offering a different mirror.

ACKNOWLEDGMENTS

Many people have contributed to my understanding of Viennese public schedules. Andrew Lass, at Mount Holyoke College, first suggested this approach to analyzing my experience in Vienna. I am grateful to the European Studies Program of the department of anthropology at the University of Massachusetts in Amherst for research support, and for the help and advice of its field directors for 1975 and 1976, H. Martin Wobst and Zdenek Salzmann. Many individuals within this program listened to and criticized my ideas, including Sylvia Forman, A. B. Hudson, James Wright, George Armelagos, Carole Counihan, Steven Sampson, Marilyn McArthur, and David Kideckel. John Cole provided advice and encouragement during the dissertation phase of this research. At the European Seminar at the Graduate Center of the City University of New York in the fall of 1978, I was fortunate to have the opportunity to develop my ideas about the relationship between history and culture in conversations with Jane Schneider, Eric Wolf, Sydel Silverman, and Peter Schneider. Ulf Hannerz, M. Estellie Smith, and Leonard Plotnicov asked the hard questions. Several colleagues made valuable suggestions on earlier drafts of the text, including Susan Tax Freeman, James Fernandez, Ruth Mandel, Larry Bennett, Steven Goldberg, James Ryan, and Mitra Emad. I am grateful for the support I received from the College of Arts and Sciences of DePaul University through a faculty summer research grant.

In Vienna, several Austrian social scientists, journalists, and government officials took time out of their work schedules to help me; this study could never have been completed without their assistance. Thanks go to Professor Dostal of the Institut für Völkerkunde of the University of

Vienna; Dr. Christian Feest of the Museum für Völkerkunde; Ing. Gehmacher and Dr. Graf of the Institut für empirische Sozialforschung; Dr. Waltraud Heindl, Dr. Peter Bachmeier, and Brigitta Kösten of the Institut für Ost und Südost Europa; Heinz Tomek and Heinz Altschul of the Austrian Presse Agentur, and Sidney Weiland of Reuters News Service/ Vienna; Dr. Theodor Prager and Dr. Mündel of the Kammer für Arbeiter und Angestellte in Wien; Dr. Berger of the Bundesministerium für Wissenschaft and Forschung; Dipl. Ing. Margulies of the Gewerkschaft der Privatangestellten; Baurat Wolfgang Bock of the Allgemeine Krankenhaus; Dr. Doris Langeder of the Postsparkasse; Dr. Renata Banik-Schweitzer and Dr. Gerhardt Meissl of the Verein für Geschichte der Stadt Wien; and the staff of the Österreichisches Statistisches Zentralamt and the Statistische Abteilung (Magistratsabteilung 66) of the Gemeinde Wien.

Six people eased my adjustment to living in Vienna. Henry and Lillian Rotenberg supported the early stages of this research, when institutional support was hard to find. Herbert Lass and Hilda Scott Lass opened their home and their hearts to me. Their experience as journalists, social scientists, and longtime residents of Central Europe was particularly helpful to me throughout the 1975-77 research period. Honza and Jola Zalud gave me friendship, support, and many friends. To these two extraordinary people I owe more than I can ever return.

The list is a long one for such a short book. I learned a great deal about cities and about the Viennese in the course of my ten-year period of research. Working with Rebecca Browning, of the Smithsonian Institution Press, and Jennifer Lorenzo was a pleasure. Their careful reading both lightened and strengthened the manuscript. Thanks, too, to the anonymous authors of Microsoft Excel 3.0, the application program that created the three-dimensional charts. Any errors that may have entered the text are my responsibility alone. Finally, a special thanks to Sonja for her patience, for her strength, and for her love in all the metropolitan regions we have lived in while this book was being written. No one could have asked for a better partner in research or in life.

CHAPTER 1

INTRODUCTION

If all the clocks and watches in Berlin would suddenly go wrong in different ways, all economic life and communication in the city would be disrupted for a long time.

GEORG SIMMEL

The Metropolis and Mental Life

With this aphorism, Simmel identifies a common characteristic of urban life. Urban settlements may exist without clocks and watches, but all possess a consciousness of time, learned and shared among the population, that is different from that of nonurban settlements. The urban order is as much a specialized development of the human capacity to define temporal patterns as it is a special use of space. While the spatial aspects of urban life have a long, rich tradition of academic inquiry, the temporal have been neglected.

Time is our invention. Like so many other aspects of culture, it is a tool that enables people to coordinate and control their joint understanding of their environment, society, and history. Anyone who has learned to live in a new city realizes that many temporal patterns so often taken for granted, such as shopping hours, traffic speed, or norms of punctuality, can vary considerably. Beyond these easily grasped differences lie even more complicated variations in the daily round: the duration of work, the rigidity of schedules, and the routine of life. This study is about how the organization of time shapes the lives of people in a city. The organization of time is not merely conventional; it is the mechanism that reproduces order in both production and consumption. It is an extraordinary instrument of power and domination precisely because it appears so conventional. We encounter the organization of time as if it were natural, ahistorical, and unproblematic. We habituate to it as we learn to live in cities. It is an essential experience of life in the metropolis.

METROPOLITAN KNOWLEDGE

Urban residents relate to time in an intensely egocentric fashion. They ignore the remarkable level of temporal patterning inherent in metropolitan life and they underestimate its constraining effect on their daily lives. They appear to be unaware of how the activities they choose to perform are timed. They see themselves exercising choice in their activities when in fact these choices are inconsequential in the face of the constraints of the city's schedule. The following riddle illustrates the difference between the perception of choice and the pattern of constraint:

> A young man has two women friends, one uptown and one downtown. To visit them, he must take the subway. This is convenient because the train lets him off right in front of their apartment buildings. He likes them both equally and usually cannot decide which one he will visit. Instead, he simply stands on the subway platform and takes the first train, uptown or downtown, that arrives at his station. After a year, he realizes that through this method he has visited the woman who lives uptown nine times more often than the downtown one. Why?

The solution to this riddle lies in the interrelationship of urban events in time from an aggregate perspective rather than one centered on the young man's activities. What schedules do these trains follow? Are the schedules regular? How far apart from each other do trains enter and leave a particular station? These clues are sufficient for the solution of the riddle, but they are not the usual considerations of urbanites toward the temporal organization of their lives. That is why the riddle can tease us. (The solution can be found in the note.)[1]

This riddle illustrates another point. As a child growing up in an urbanized region, I felt I could solve this riddle even though the closest subway was thirty-two miles away and I had not yet ridden in one. The knowledge of what subways are and how they behave in time was something I had picked up, perhaps from television or a book. Subways are a part of the knowledge that cities create and broadcast to the suburban hinterland. Subways and everything associated with them are a domain of metropolitan knowledge.

Urban environments appear impossibly complex for effective cultural analysis. The social experiences they contain seem to defy the bounded contexts that provide so much of the framework for cultural analysis in other kinds of settlements. Is there such a thing as urban culture? I believe there is. What makes it specifically urban in its content or in its scope? Two examples are shared rules for traffic behavior and shared influences on consumer taste from education and mass media. While these rules may exist in nonurban settlements, the press of traffic and the variety of public displays in cities imbue these domains with greater scope and importance. The organization of time is another aspect of human culture that takes on greater weight in the experience of urban people.

Culture refers to the assemblage of knowledge of all aspects of experience. In practice this includes everything that a highly efficient interviewer could collect from the partial understanding of individuals who live together. Such complete assemblages have never existed, although postulating their existence is valuable for understanding how social life is possible and how its features change. As an interviewer, I was rather inefficient. I collected a very small and narrowly drawn set of responses to questions about daily activities, from individuals who sometimes shared very little with each other beyond residency in the same metropolitan area. Within this small group of interview partners, I concentrated on the schedules in people's lives.

The metropolitan experience, like the experience of civilization, with which it shares many features, is itself composed of a limited number of domains. Metropolis and civilization both refer to social formations in which a small, restricted set of values forges social integration. Linguistic, aesthetic, religious, political, or economic domains of knowledge commonly become restricted for use by the institutions of metropolis or civilization. Metropolis and civilization differ in scope. Metropolis refers to integration around a central city within an urbanized region. Civilization applies to integration across regions, states, and language groups. These higher-order complexes differ from the local knowledge and understanding of life individuals share through common experience (Geertz 1983). Metropolitan knowledge is supralocal.[2] It is made up of only the domains that people who rely on the same institutions within the same metropolitan area find necessary to share. Since these institutions vary among metropolitan areas, so too does the content of metropolitan knowledge. Within a metropolis, sharing knowledge is not the same thing as sharing opinions; it is more like sharing a language. Indeed, standard languages are often the elevation of metropolitan dialects to serve the language needs of entire states. The language, like other domains of metropolitan knowledge, provides a standard, regular and predictable way for people to behave when they want to communicate. Other domains of metropolitan knowledge perform the same service when people want to travel, work, shop, or play. Metropolitan knowledge is not an intellectual straitjacket. Individuals can think their way into seeing the knowledge as institutional, just as I have tried to do here. Many have. But tens of thousands of others unthinkingly accept the knowledge as natural, producing in the acquiescence to it the regularity of metropolitan life that intrigued Simmel. This regularity need not be temporal. In many cities in the world metropolitan knowledge of time includes quite liberal parameters for tardiness. Urban life will always require some rules about behavior in time. What those rules are and how they came into being are ethnographic questions worth pursuing across the variety of cities.

An urban region is an expansive social space, often with ecologically definable boundaries, in which highly specialized activities are concentrated within clusters of dense populations. These clusters often employ people's talents to the exclusion of subsistence activities, making the population dependent upon trade with a food-producing hinterland and other regions to meet the needs of residents. The extent of this dependency will vary considerably among regions, and there are several forms this dependency can take. Such dependency forces the people of the hinterland to reorganize themselves according to the social, temporal, and spatial relations emanating from the city. Once reorganized in this manner, the social relations of the hinterland become indistinguishable from the city (Leeds 1973). This view of the scope of the urban experience suggests that the distinction between urban and nonurban in human settlements is merely an intellectual convenience.

A metropolis is a very large and dense city, often the political and intellectual capital of its state. What identifies the metropolis is a sudden and irregular shift in size and power among settlements within a region. Economic geography uses this model to describe urban market systems that are idiosyncratic and that diverge markedly from certain assumptions of economic rationality in people's use of space. Such market systems monopolize the distribution of goods and services to such an extent that the hinterland is left underdeveloped, while the central city flourishes (Smith 1976, 258-60). The region containing Vienna has these qualities.[3]

The metropolis monopolizes more than the market system. It also can appropriate meaning. Metropolitan knowledge beams outward toward its hinterland like a beacon, throwing those domains of local knowledge into shadow. Residents of localities in the hinterland recognize this knowledge as originating in the metropolis. Possessing this knowledge, they identify (or contrast) themselves with whatever virtues (or vices) they judge the metropolis to represent. Such knowledge is expansive and universal, transforming widescale diversity into a shared metropolitan experience. But it is also threatening to local identities and virtues: It attacks the security of the familiar and can easily create discomfort. Metropolitan knowledge also may arrive with an extensive apparatus of power attached to it. Thus it becomes a powerful constraint on the lives of local residents. The true boundaries of the metropolis are neither the juridical nor the economic. They exist at the point where local knowledge can successfully resist the metropolitan hegemony.

The urban order has evolved different features from the social orders of settlements. Although cities concentrate large numbers of people, urbanites know far fewer people than residents of small towns do. A city is a society of strangers that bases relations between people on universally applied rules, laws, and conventions. This separation from corporate and familial contexts as the exclusive basis for meaning produces a sense of isolation in the urban dweller. Simultaneously, it fosters a level of anonymity that can heighten self-reliance and behavioral freedom. Individuals must depend on their ability to mobilize their network of friends and acquaintances to get jobs, and on their own performance to keep them. Success creates differences in status. Status differences define differences in social power. The universally applicable rules generate their own administrations, bureaucracies, and regulatory agencies, including the features of the public schedule. The social-control actions of these agencies are often antithetical to the interest of corporate and family groups. They require individuals to modify their behavior to conform to universal expectations (Press 1979, 9-12). While this is a necessary constraint on the behavioral freedom of urbanites, it is also the source of ambivalence, resentment, and apathy. The point at which the public schedule no longer influences the organization of household activities is an important cultural boundary of the metropolis.

As the urban order develops, the boundary between it and the nonurban world becomes less clear. The urban studies traditions in geography and political science offer formal definitions of urban central places, standard metropolitan statistical areas, and juridical-fiscal units (Leaf 1983). Depending on the kinds of questions anthropologists have asked, they have found these definitions useful for locating the processes in space that are particularly and peculiarly urban. Others, beginning with Anthony Leeds (1973), suggest that the underlying institutional dependence of the urban order pervades every settlement in a region. In this view, the whole idea of the city becomes misleading. No one location, i.e., the central district, is intrinsically more urban than any other location. Since each urban region has a unique historical development, the diversity of adaptations among the locations is large.

PUBLIC SCHEDULES

Time is a powerful language in which to locate actions of many different types. Time considerations order people's lives in many different ways, ranging from biological clocks to history and genealogy. The rules for organizing activities appropriately in time are a small subset of this domain of social time. Because of these rules, we carefully measure the durations of some activities but not others. We schedule some activities as sequences but not others. We anticipate the recurrence of some activities but not others. These rules are not like laws or computer programs; they simply connect temporal dimensions to the social meanings of activities, the priorities we attach to these meanings, and the choices we make as a result of these priorities.

The urban experience of time is central to the concerns of both households and metropolitan institutions. Most urban dwellers are dependent on institutions for their livelihood, socialization of their young, and access to provisions, durable goods, and services. A temporal dimension, tempo, the rate of recurrence of entry and closure, governs their access to these institutions. The tempi of metropolitan institutions may be directly coordinated with each other or may merely overlap. The former produces a coordinated public schedule. Bock has aptly termed the latter form correlated schedules (1966, 97). What sets these public schedules apart from the daily routines of individuals is the necessity of households to enter the institutions for their livelihoods. Households need to shop, work, educate, and play but have no control over the schedules of those institutions.

The people who design the institutional schedules usually do not take the needs of dependent households into consideration. Small shopkeepers were the only example I found of schedule makers who thought about their customers' schedules. Nor are these administrators likely to consult with each other to create coordinated schedules. There are simply too many work, educational, and market institutions in a metropolis for such coordination to take place. Coordination comes about when government steps in to regulate tempi. This is most likely to occur when the demands of the various schedules have become chaotic and conflicts break out. Ordinances to control the myriad schedules tend to simplify access times and the rates of recurrence to a few easily understood time markers. Government regulation of time can begin as revolutionary action. Schedules quickly begin to rigidify as various power groupings in the metropolis use the official time markers for different purposes (Goodenough 1963; Zerubavel 1977). Once involved in the business of regulating social time, governments politicize schedules. Power groups become identified with either keeping things as they are or changing them. The government intervention in the metropolitan schedule simplifies, rigidifies, and politicizes the organization of institutional time.

Vienna lends itself to an examination of the metropolitan public schedule because its own schedule is the most rigid and constraining of any industrial city in which I have lived. Long-term visitors are amazed at the lack of shopping opportunities in the evening, the shortness of the workweek, and the dramatic differences between weekend and weekday. Like Sweden, Austria has a mixed economy with a sizable, constitutionally mandated government investment in energy, industry, commerce, and service. The Austrian government is both an employer and an advocate for the wage-earning citizenry. The period from 1959 to 1980 was a particularly active one for work-time legislation. Viennese wage-earners found their workweek shortened, the weekend extended, and their workday lengthened. These mandated changes in work time exposed the temporal linkages between the schedules of institutions and households that reveal how time is used to produce order in the metropolis. For these reasons, Vienna is an ideal metropolis in which to view the public schedule.

Civilizational ideas, such as modernism and industrialism, have slowly altered the public schedule over the last 200 years. Entrepreneurs, and later workers, erased the premodern schedule and instituted a more rigid, specialized routine in its place. At the same time, the public schedule increased in its scope, expanding the number of work, market, and administrative institutions that subscribed to industrial patterns of time organization. As the scope of the public schedule expanded, people involved in private household activities began to take increasing notice of its force on their lives.

Vienna shares its modernist, industrial organization of time with many other cities. Its particular experience reminds us that no two places respond to widescale culture change in precisely the same way. Vienna's experience was unique as the capital of an empire, Austria-Hungary, the residence of its administrative elite, and the victim of the ill-fated fortunes of the state. It is an industrial city to which industry came late and slowly. Its entrepreneurial class struggled against an entrenched absolutist bureaucracy, never quite succeeding in imposing its efficiency-oriented temporality upon public administration. Its working class developed from immigrant workers from the provinces. Industrialism ruined most of the resident preindustrial artisans and absorbed the rest into the factory system. The direction for Vienna's development and the momentum of its changes produced increasing routine and specialization of activities in time. Here, then, is a glimpse into one metropolitan future in which increasing control by individuals over the tempo and timing of their activities is traded for greater constraint on choices among those activities.

THE CONDUCT OF THE STUDY

The urban settlement poses different data-collection problems than communal settlements do. Cities contain much hidden variation in social behavior. As the center of elite activity, a city is likely to have a well-documented history. Cities have their social scientists and policy institutes, which generate valuable information. In addition, the anthropologist brings to the metropolis the same data-gathering tools developed in nonurban settings: direct observation and self-involvement in the life of the settlement over extended periods of time; attention to features of life that may reflect the broadest experiences of the population; a concern for evidence of culture change, especially in those features for which a comparative literature already exists; and finally a sensitivity for the personalities one meets in the settlement, including a desire to present their lives in the best possible light.

This study developed over a period of four research visits during which I employed various strategies for gathering data. To experience the diversity in daily rhythm that different locations in the metropolitan region might create, I lived in six different places during my fieldwork.[4] In each neighborhood I observed the rhythm of my neighbors' comings and goings throughout the day. I participated in their commuting patterns, their shopping, and their use of local recreational facilities. Learning to live by their schedule was the primary means by which I learned its features. The contrast between the Viennese schedule and the schedules I had known in the United States was sharp and clear. From it I developed the questions for my interview partners: How do you get your shopping done? What do you do for fun?

To understand the meaning that people attributed to these activities, I became acquainted with several Viennese households. I continued to meet their friends, and their friends of friends, until I became familiar with the circle of acquaintances in four separate social networks. Each revolved around a different age group—adults in their twenties, thirties, fifties, and sixties. Because social power usually increases with age in Vienna, the latter two networks tended to include people with greater responsibilities at work, higher standards of living, and more time to talk to me. They are disproportionately represented in the study. I conducted the interviews in both English and German.

The Viennese speak a dialect of German that is highly idiomatic and uses many non-German words. While I could make sense of dialect spoken in context, I needed a native, professional German-English interpreter to help me transcribe the tapes of these interviews. Some of the people I met were educated speakers of English who had spent time in Britain and the United States. Not until the last months of my initial period of fieldwork (1976) was my German fluent enough to abandon English when speaking with them.

In the early 1960s, Viennese social scientists established a practice of conducting large sample time budget studies every ten years. The Kammer für Arbeiter und Angestellte, the body of popularly elected representatives of the wage-earning population, conducted the first ones. The latest one was part of the national census. These decennial studies are each slightly different both in the way they ask their questions and in the method for reporting the results. I sought out these studies for their large sample sizes.

They provide some check on the errors of small sample research. Not having access to the original data, and agreeing with Michelson's observation that large-scale time budget studies are impossible to use for post hoc hypothesis testing (1978, 187), I have relied on these studies only as indicators of broad trends in behavior. From the studies, I adapted the set of activity categories that Viennese social scientists employ when researching time budgets. These are used throughout this study. Armed with these categories I found new questions to put to my growing circles of acquaintances. I looked for similarities between the survey categories and everyday activities by asking interview partners to list all the alternative activities available to them at specific hours of the day. This proved to be an exceedingly tedious exercise. I soon stopped using it. Instead, I borrowed a technique from nutrition research, the twenty-four-hour recall. In this exercise, I asked interview partners to recall everything they had done the previous day, from waking to sleeping, with as many references to clock time as possible. This was more successful because interview partners saw it as a test of their memories. The narratives of the recalls were not all of equal quality. As every fieldworker learns, some interview partners have better memories and are more forthcoming than others. Also, there was no way to predict whether a person's "yesterday" would be typical or not. The dynamics of my appointments with interview partners were an aspect of the research I could not control very often. Since interview partners proved to be less enthusiastic about repeating the exercise every time we talked, I obtained only a few fully developed responses. I have placed a more technical report on the interview sample in the appendix. I also discuss some additional data-gathering tools in the topical chapters.

Another important data-gathering strategy involved archival research. With the help of Viennese social historians, I enjoyed access to archives that gave a detailed picture of the particular development of the public schedule in Vienna. Two historic works in particular, Pezzl's *Skizze von Wien* (1792) and Gross-Hoffinger's *Wien wie es ist* (1832), were lengthy descriptions of the Viennese pace of life before the industrial transformation.[5] Translating them provided an effective set of comparisons that made features of the contemporary public schedule stand out in sharper relief.

My interview partners saw my research as primarily concerned with their Freizeitgestaltung (leisure activities). They considered my interest in their play flattering and sought to involve me in as many different kinds of play activities as I had time for. I was less successful in participating in their work activities. I visited the workplaces of my acquaintances at least once. I received a tour of the place and met the favorite work-mates and the managers. Because I was an educated Ausländer, a foreigner who also spoke German, I enjoyed special access to the home lives of a few interview partners, access that ordinary Viennese would not often extend to each other. Interview partners wanted to know as much about my experience of Vienna and the North American cities in which I have lived as I wanted to know about their experiences. I would eat a meal with the household, accompany them while shopping, occasionally help their children with schoolwork, walk with them in the countryside on weekends, and sometimes even live with them for short periods.

As observations and involvements accumulated over time, I began to understand the limitations inherent in doing research in an urban setting. Metropolitan fieldwork bears a closer resemblance to the archaeological dig than it does to village or neighborhood studies. Limited energy and resources permit the fieldworker to sample only a few "pits" of metropolitan experience, leaving the rest buried for future expeditions. Like the archaeologist, the fieldworker can only hope that the patterned variation among the artifacts relates to the core of the metropolitan experience.

METROPOLITAN VIENNA

Vienna lies at the point where the Danube River bends southeastward on its way toward Hungary. To the north is the Marchfeld, a grassy plain extending eastward toward the Pannonian Basin and the site of a group of northern suburban towns. To the west lies the Wienerwald, a group of forested hills that rise from 150 meters above sea level at the edge of the Danube to the Kahlenberg (484 meters). The entire city is built on two terraces at elevations of 180 meters and 200 meters above sea level. Vienna is located at the northern end of the Vienna Basin, which stretches southward, creating a flat area that now contains residential suburbs, industrial settlements, and commercial wheatfields. The basin extends to the industrial city of Wiener Neustadt 40 kilometers away. To the east extends the Lobau, a low swampland, now partially drained, created by the Danube. Beyond the river are more wheatgrowing villages and industrial developments. The current size of the city is 133 square kilometers. The population at the last census (1981) was 1,531,346.[6]

The street grid of the city is a circular web with the formerly fortified city district, the Innere Stadt, in the center. The wide Ring boulevard separates the old city from the rest of the region. A circle of small inner districts, the Vorstädte, surround the Innere Stadt. They in turn are enclosed by another circular boulevard, the Gürtel, which traces the line of the old outer fortifications. Beyond the Gürtel and the Danube River, around the outer rim of the city, lie a group of large districts. In all there are twenty-three municipal districts, each with its own history and character. Stretching from the Ring through these districts are over twenty major radial boulevards. An extensive and widely used public transportation system, including commuter trains, underground and elevated trains, streetcars (trams), and buses, services the entire metropolitan region.

Each group of districts developed at a different time and reflects different architectural styles and planning concerns. The Innere Stadt is the old walled city; its core is a Roman fortress built around the time of Christ. Churches dating to the twelfth and thirteenth centuries still stand, but the bulk of the existing buildings date from the nineteenth century. The small districts around the Ring were once autonomous farming villages that supplied the city with provisions. During the seventeenth and eighteenth centuries, these villages underwent a building boom and became the sub-

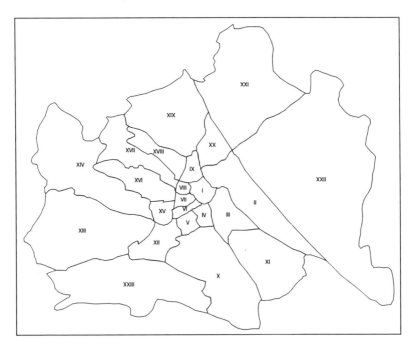

FIGURE 1: Map of Vienna and Its Districts.

urban residences of middle-class Viennese. These were also the original sites of industrial development. Eighteenth-century, two-story, open court-yard workshop buildings can still be found among the seven-story, twentieth-century apartment buildings. Some of these districts, such as Josefstadt and Wieden, were developed through imperial investment in the eighteenth century, and architecture from that time still stands (Bobeck and Lichtenberger 1978, 76–79). The larger districts were the sites of the massive influx of industry and migrant labor in the nineteenth century.

Housing has been a driving political issue in Vienna throughout this century. Before World War I, the larger districts on the boundaries of the city were ecclesiastic or aristocratic land holdings, or wheatgrowing agri-cultural villages. After the war, they were sold under forced divestiture to the municipality and to some private investors. A special tax funded a number of public-housing estates, but the majority were built through private investment. The larger districts experienced the greatest increase in housing, especially in the period between 1919 and 1934 (Weihsmann 1985). The destruction caused by Allied bombing in the closing months of World War II necessitated replacing many eighteenth-century buildings with modern five- and seven-story apartment houses. Postwar municipal housing consists of international-style apartment complexes set on open lawns. In the 1960s, municipal investment created suburban housing com-plexes and shopping centers, transforming the outer districts in one decade into important residential clusters. But the existing housing was so old that even after sixty years of municipal investment in housing renovation, 15% of the population still have no plumbing within their apartments.[7] Cur-rently, 821,175 housing units stand within the municipal boundaries. This represents a 30% increase in the number of units over the last thirty years.[8] The new housing drew residents to the more isolated eastern and southern rims of the city. This in turn increased reliance on automobiles for such activities as shopping and commuting to work, in spite of the availability of a good public transportation system, and raised the general level of traffic congestion in the city as a whole.

Green space is an important element in the shape of the city. The Wienerwald, a huge nature reserve, lies along the city's western rim. Small district parks range in size from a few house lots to an entire block. Larger parks are found around the Ringstrasse: the former imperial hunting re-serve at Lainz, the famous Prater park in Leopoldstadt with its original Ferris wheel and graceful riding paths, and the Böhmische Prater in working-class Favoriten. Scattered around the rim of the city are Klein-

gartensiedlungen (small garden settlements), also known as Schrebergär-
ten (allotment gardens). These are large, fenced-in areas containing as
many as 600 20-by-30-meter plots, on which people have built little sum-
merhouses and planted gardens.

Government service, manufacturing, finance, and commerce contribute almost equally in the number of workers employed and the value of the
activity to the regional economy (Magistratsabteilung 66 1983, 178).
These sectors also account for 76% of the jobs in the metropolitan region.
Over the past ten years, the greatest growth in both the gross regional
product contribution and in the number of jobs has been in the sectors of
finance and commerce. To reach these jobs, approximately 60% of the
employed must travel at least as far as another municipal district, 14%
must travel to the city from suburban residences, and 3% must travel from
the city to suburban worksites.[9] For those who commute across district
lines, most drive from the outer districts to the inner districts, through the
radial boulevards (Hansely and Indrak 1978, 11). The kinds of jobs located
in smaller inner districts are more likely to be in the governmental, commercial, or financial sectors than in the industrial. Industrial jobs tend to
locate in the larger outer districts (Benda 1960). Since the greatest number
of jobs are concentrated in the inner districts, the daily flow of traffic
through this circular-shaped metropolis is centripetal in the morning and
centrifugal in the afternoon.

This brief description highlights only those facts that serve as the basis
for scheduling public activities. The ideas Viennese have about what urban
life is and what it can become form the substance of the following discussion. Chapter 2 presents evidence of the changes that have taken place over
the last 200 years by contrasting two scenes of daily life in the city: one
written in 1792 and one based on my observations in 1976. This comparison identifies the issues of timing wagework, housework, meals, shopping, and play that are discussed in detail in subsequent chapters. Because
the public schedule today is primarily an artifact of legislation, chapter 3
describes the priorities expressed by the political managers who forged this
schedule. Although these politicians identified themselves and their policies with a variety of political labels, they shared a modernist perspective
toward urban life. These attitudes culminated between 1960 and 1975 in a
return of several hours of work time to wage earners to do with as they
wished. Chapter 4 explores how wage earners evaluate the meaning of
their work experiences and how these understandings have influenced their
decisions to reallocate their newly won free time. These decisions have

engendered acute schedule conflicts with other household members, especially school-age children, and institutions, especially markets. A long-simmering conflict between households and work institutions over the structure of people's movements during the day is discussed first, in chapter 5, through a reconstruction of the changes in meal-taking behavior among Viennese households. The conflicts in scheduling household shopping time and the responses of the retail merchants to the changing market behavior of households are discussed in chapter 6. Chapter 7 looks at how the changes in household schedules have changed the long-term patterns of play and caused a shift in play preferences from recreation to entertainment among the Viennese in the last few decades. The concluding chapter summarizes the Viennese experience with the industrialization of social time and suggests ways in which theory and method could be linked to generate comparable research on public schedules in other cities.

CHAPTER 2

LEARNING FROM PEZZL

It is a common observation that the lives of people in diverse cities develop different rhythms. How these differences accumulate over time, to become what Zerubavel has called the "anchor of normalcy" (1981), is a key question in the study of urban culture. To begin, we need to know more about the archaeology of urban time. Sjoberg provides only a few observations about time organization in his classic study of the preindustrial European city. He notes that time was not the scarce commodity it has become, citing indications that the calendar was a more important timekeeper than the clock. He also suggests that the lack of effective public lighting restricted many activities to daylight hours. He characterizes the work time of the preindustrial workshop as barely rational (1960, 104; 210). These hints suggest a specific kind of preindustrial city, one dominated by commercial institutions. Sjoberg leaves out cities in which ritual, administrative, military, or agriculturally oriented time organizations dominate. Vienna, for instance, was an imperial capital, immersed in the administrative relations and rhythms of metropolis and province. This fact alone provides a very different starting point from which to modernize time. The point from which a city starts to modernize is crucial to the kind of time organization we observe today.

THE CITY ON THE EVE OF MODERNIZATION

Some of Sjoberg's haziness about premodern time organization is understandable. The farther back in time one searches for scenes of daily urban life, the scarcer the information becomes. Consciousness of the daily round of activities is a feature of modernity, of that cultural style that cherishes flux and transformation over stasis and tradition. Few diarists and publicists before the nineteenth century felt that the round of activities in their cities was notable. They provide us at best with selections from their personal schedules, but without reference to the schedules of others. For Vienna, sources for the premodern organization of time are few. Herbert Matis has successfully probed the travel literature and diaries of the eighteenth century for insights into the industrialization of the region around Vienna (1968). But specific information about the organization of people's daily schedules is lacking. I found clear evidence of a consciousness of time organization only in a work written at the very end of that century. In 1792, Johann Pezzl, an essayist and publicist in the time of Joseph II and Mozart, wrote a series of scenes of city life. One of those scenes, *Tagesordnung der Stadt*, presents the earliest available picture of the daily life of the imperial capital on the eve of industrialization (1923, 222–30).[1]

Daily Schedule, 1792

It is interesting to consider how a family of more than two hundred thousand, as Vienna is today, keeps to a regular time schedule without consultation or compulsion. It is a time schedule where every hour has its own employments, uniting or dividing thousands of people among various intents and purposes. The accustomed hours may be arbitrary, but constant timekeeping creates a harmonious whole.

From this schedule derives the cycle of activity and rest, of alarm and quietude, which reigns throughout the day in the streets and courtyards.

Consider an ordinary weekday in the midst of spring or autumn. Between six and half-past six in the morning, the scullery maids tiptoe from the back doors of the houses of noble and Bürger on their way to church, still clad in their morning robes and clutching their noisy rosaries. Their lovers, the hacks, husars, butlers, and equestrians, make a point of putting in an appearance at church as well, to satisfy the needs of both their souls and their hearts. After church, they crowd the cheap coffeehouses to take breakfast. Here the girls leave their moustached suitors with a kiss.

Meanwhile, in all the major squares and markets, things begin to get lively. The women from the surrounding villages have arrived with their baskets of fruit and vegetables, milk, eggs, and poultry. Arrayed in long rows, they begin to offer their wares to the early shoppers. The same scene repeats itself at the same time on the main streets of the suburbs.[2]

A river of cooks arrive at these markets, carrying everything from garden produce to pheasants and wild hares away with them. Around eight o'clock, after the cooks of the wealthy have bought their fill, the wives and daughters of lowly clerks, artisans and officers, clad in shabby robes and with fans in their hands, arrive at the market to bargain with pride and cunning for their household provisions. One can hear the ridiculous alternations of flattery and insult. The voices of the market women are coarse and sharp, and painful to the ears. Their tongues are so voluble that many an orator would envy them. These markets bustle until ten o'clock, when the rush slowly subsides.

No noble coaches are seen in the streets before nine o'clock. Only the occasional carriage of a well-to-do Bürger or court official from the suburbs mixes with the rough wagons loaded with wood, beer, meat, and other commodities.

At half-past eight, an army of over three-and-a-half thousand men is on the move. It is an army of clerks, including battalions of secretaries, registrars, adjuncts, accountants, ingrossists, assessors, and office boys. They are followed by hundreds of coaches filled with career officers, chancellors, vice-chancellors, presidents, vice-presidents, archivists, councilors, and the higher ranks of accountants. They arrive at the State Department, the Chancellor's Office, the War Department, the Bohemian Council, the Hungarian Council, the Netherlands Council, at City Hall, at the Supreme Court, at the Mint, at the Comptroller's Office, at the Commission on Religion, on Education, on Government, etc.

By ten in the morning, the streets have become really lively. People have left work for breakfast, or the tailor's shop. The coffeehouses are full.[3]

From eleven-thirty to noon, the noble families attend church. People fill the streets to watch the parade of rich coaches filled with young girls whose gowns are pretty enough to stand the gaze of the curious, while they themselves shield their eyes from the unaccustomed brightness of the midday with lorgnettes. The popular churches are Saint Peter's and Saint Charles. The streets in front of them are always crowded with people hoping to catch sight of someone really important.

Meanwhile, all sorts of idlers and dandies appear in front of the Milanese coffeehouse. From this vantage point and armed with binoculars, they survey the daughters of the noble houses as they leave Mass.

By noon, the well-to-do send their subordinates back to the offices, while they visit their lovers or take a half-hour's walk. They do this both to enjoy the exercise and to improve their appetite.

Between twelve and one, we see many coaches driving toward Leopoldstadt. Those are the ladies of the high nobility going with their friends and children for a drive in the Prater, to enjoy the spring air and to interrupt the monotony of their days.[4]

The middle-class youths take this midday hour to stroll behind the town pier, where the view is splendid and where the vigilance of many mothers [over their daughters' virtue] has been outwitted.

The common man eats at noon. The better-off citizens and officials, who must return to their desks at three o'clock, eat at one. The truly powerful officials eat at two. Nobles eat even later.

After one o'clock there are few pedestrians on the street. The traffic is heavy with coaches fetching the councilors from their bureaus to bring them home for lunch.

By two o'clock the streets are quiet. Everyone is sitting at table, eating wholesome, filling courses, followed by a cup of black coffee.[5] Or they are lying down to aid in the digestion of the meal.

At three o'clock, the councilors are back at their inkwells.

Things start to get lively again at four-thirty. The streets fill with people, horses, and carriages. Most of them are going to work or to meetings about their work. Others are out just for the fun of it. This is the time for walks. On foot, horse, or carriage, people wander toward the town pier, the Belvedere, the Prater, the Palace, and elsewhere.[6]

Those are the people who do not have to work, like noble ladies with their friends. Their husbands will follow later. Aficionados of spectacle enjoy this parade as much as any in the theater.

After six there is much noise in the street. The offices are closing. The workers in the suburbs are laying down their tools. The beginning of the parade is near. The time of the salons is approaching. The greater portion of handworkers are finished by this hour. The open stands offering goods and the small storefronts close up shop for the day.

The army of clerks swarm into the streets. The suburbs brace themselves for the ensuing onslaught of traffic. The well-to-do seem to escape at such a gallop that the stone streets echo. They are on their way to their cabarets and clubs. The ordinary citizen drags his body to a beer hall or his neighbor's house. Increasing the muddle in those already impassable streets, those innumerable women who have been offering all sorts of goods to passersby are putting their baskets on their backs and clearing out.

If a new play or opera is opening, the clatter of coachwheels, horses' hooves, and bells over the squares makes a hellish racket. One takes one's life in hand trying to cross where the coaches converge from four directions. The pedestrian traffic at this time is so dense that walking about requires strong legs and an indifferent nose.

The tumult lasts until seven o'clock, after which there comes a general stillness. Only a few late strollers are about, and they seem lost in the wide streets.

At dusk, the willing girls of the poorer variety begin to make their appearance. The first to arrive are the ones whose clothes are too ragged to stand the scrutiny of midday customers. Their accustomed standing places are the very squares that are the busiest during the day. . . .

After nine, the noise starts again. The theaters have closed. The social clubs are shutting down. This disturbance lasts only a little while, as the coaches rush people home and the pedestrians scatter quickly.

At ten, the doors of the private houses are locked. This is an order of the police. For a city so large, with such large apartment buildings and so many inhabitants, this is certainly a good idea. Otherwise, all sorts of dubious characters, idlers, and thieves could hide in the courtyards and corridors of large houses and it would be more difficult for the police to keep law and order, a thing they do astonishingly well. On the other hand, the closed houses make life a little more difficult for the inhabitants. Anyone coming home after the locking hour must call to the porter, a not always polite servant who expects a good tip for his late-night pains. After ten-thirty, the cavalry patrols the town and the suburbs.

When one has seen the river of people busily running around the streets of the town during the day, it is hard to understand the sudden quiet that now descends. There is not a soul in the streets. At eleven o'clock, if you were to stroll across town, you would encounter fewer than fifty people as the coffeehouses and pubs empty of their last customers. I think there are two reasons for this quiet. The mass of the people who work in the town live in the suburbs and have already gone home for the evening. The ten o'clock lock law propels people home to avoid having to encounter the porter.

Just after midnight a few coaches from the big palaces drive the dinner guests home. The common citizen and his wife, asleep in their bed, are awakened by the noise, but do not mind. Many a young Viennese was conceived amidst the nightly clatter of noble coaches.

At two, the lanterns in the town are extinguished. Four hours later, at six o'clock, the same cycle will begin again: of noise and quiet, of crowds and empty streets, of work and pleasure. The cycle will repeat itself as long as Vienna is the capital of a large, rich, and powerful state, as long as it is the home of great nobles, and as long as it is the center of a large population.

In summer and winter there are slight changes. In the summer the palaces are empty; the noble families go to Hungary or to the Austrian countryside. In winter, they return. New friendships are made. People fall in love. They marry. The winter is the soul of the town and renews its life.

Pezzl has taken up a most central position from which to observe this baroque parade. It is somewhere in the middle of the central district, probably the Graben or Stock-in-Eisen Platz. From his vantage point, he hears as well as sees the rhythm of the city's activities. He is struck by the regularity of it all. The people appear to move to the wand of some unseen conductor. Even his fellow observers watching the coaches of noble families as they ride to and from their churches and palaces seem to have assembled on cue. Everything fits. Everyone has a place and a purpose. This is not merely a feature of prose, it is an accurate picture of the life of a successful administrative city, one whose very existence is tied to organizing people.

The most arresting feature of this picture of the preindustrial day is the way the work segment is broken up into three periods of short duration by the mealtimes. Two periods of two hours each make up the morning segment. Each of the morning segments is bounded by a mealtime. Over the course of the morning, the streets are quiet. Most people are indoors. Only during the mealtime do people stream from their offices. When the second two-hour period ends around noon, the most temporally homogeneous and uniform part of the day is finished.

A third segment of five, four, or three hours, depending on the length of the midday meal, occupies the afternoon. The afternoon segment has a built-in break for meetings. This segment supports a great deal more variation in the starting and stopping times of work. It puts more people out of doors. It is louder. This irregularity at first appears incongruous with the patterns established in the morning work periods. Accustomed as we are to understanding work time in terms of its duration, this afternoon segment appears to our modern consciousness as so much chaos. In the logic of an administrative work schedule, there is greater concern for adherence to a specific sequence of activities than for specific application of a fixed time duration. The afternoon can become chaotic because responsible individuals are following through on sequences of activities dictated by the morning's work. Since each sequence might require different durations to complete, the ending times for the afternoon work segment are widely divergent. For those clerks who are stuck in their offices all afternoon, closing time is 6:00 P.M. What we learn from Pezzl is that on the eve of the Industrial Revolution, administrative and not commercial functions dominated the organization of activities in the central district. This organization of time from which to start to industrialize is different from that described by Sjoberg.

There are at least three different schedules contained within Pezzl's scene: the activities of the employed, the activities of the nobles, and the activities of households. The schedule of employed people shows them going to and coming from the different work segments, eating, or taking in the pleasures of the town. We only glimpse the nobles, as their coaches take them to and from their churches, parks, and palaces. Pezzl offers no private details of the daily activities of the highborn. He discusses their household activities only to the extent that they occur in public. We learn little of what is going on indoors. What emerges from his account is a feeling for the rhythm of the daily round, the alternation of noise and quiet, that the residents share. This is the schedule of the street, the public schedule.

Compared with contemporary Vienna, this preindustrial public schedule is homogeneous. In the morning, the different kinds of workers seem to do the same things at the same time. In the afternoon, many more activities are possible. The most important variable here is class. In 1792, class determined one's social position in a highly developed hierarchy. In Pezzl's account, different classes eat their main meal of the day at different hours. Commoners, clerks, their bosses, and the nobles each begin the midday meal an hour apart. The period around midday includes opportunities for recreation, such as visiting a lover, purchasing the services of a prostitute, watching the parade of noble coaches, or going to a park. The Josephine Viennese enjoyed walking around their town and its surroundings.

Pezzl is aware of the clock time referent for most of the periods of activity he discusses. Public activities, especially work activities, are carefully noted. Household functions fit into the round so precisely that locating activities through specific clock times is unnecessary. His observations are no more accurate than the half-hour.

In Pezzl's time, clocks were in the belltowers of the churches. They rang the hours and half-hours then as they had for the preceding 400 years. Smaller clocks and pocketwatches were the expensive toys of the wealthy (Landes 1983, 130). The people Pezzl finds so nicely regulated by timekeeping possessed no watches. This reliance on clock time to structure the day shows how much regularity in activity patterns preindustrial administrative institutions created. As Pezzl notes in the first paragraph, the population was self-regulating. Beyond the precise boundaries between activities lies the discipline of monitoring one's own activities by the clock. The discipline of paying attention to the clock preceded industrialization in Vienna, just as it did in France (Le Goff 1980, 46). This does not seem to have been the case in preindustrial England (Thompson 1963).

In Pezzl, two specific features of the organization of space seem to influence the timing of activities. The first is the proximity of the home to the workplace. Most of the people Pezzl observed lived in the central district. This made the integration of household- and work-oriented activities in the same daily segment physically possible.[7] The second feature is the concentration of administrative and commercial offices within the old, walled, central district. This created noisy centripetal and centrifugal movements as people moved in and out of the city.

The people in the scene are concentrated in the central district for their work, home, market, and play activities. Very little is said about the life of the suburbs. These were separate villages lying outside the city's walls, asylums for those whose roots were not truly in the city itself. One may work in a suburb or reside there, but the central district remains the most important arena in the social environment. This spatial dichotomy was obliterated by the forces of industrialism that transformed the metropolitan area throughout the nineteenth century.

THE CITY IN THE TWILIGHT OF MODERNIZATION

In the 184 years between Pezzl's writings and my observations, daily life in the city had changed dramatically. Pezzl's scene suggests that some features of the public schedule were fixed, or at least less subject to variation than others. We can rightly assume that the lives of some residents of Josephine Vienna diverged from the norm. The schedules of households are among the most varied patterns of activity in a city. Industrial organization increases the extent to which household schedules vary. It remains impossible today to specify the public schedule with the same degree of generality or inclusiveness evident in Pezzl. If he were alive today, he would find no single position in the central district where he could sit and observe the scene.

Nevertheless, a public schedule exists in Vienna today; it is as powerful and as dominant in the lives of contemporary residents as it was during the reign of Joseph II. One must stand in many different places to observe the urban parade. Diffused through the metropolitan space, rarefied through restrictions on activities in time, and dominated by political and administrative oversight, the work lives of contemporary Viennese generate a myriad of schedules among the city's households.

To view the scene, one can sit at an outdoor café on one of the busy boulevards radiating from the central Ringstrasse. Josefstädter Strasse is a good candidate. Extending westward from the Ring and connecting to the outer belt of the city, the Gürtel, it is a narrow street between four-story buildings that house stores on the groundfloors and apartments above. Named for Joseph II, the boulevard contains many of the features found in the city at large: municipal and federal office buildings, small manufacturing sites, commercial firms and banks, coffeehouses, restaurants, cinemas, food shops, appliance stores, a major theater, intersecting public-transportation lines, a small park, medical offices, a business college, an elementary school, and a kindergarten. The residents include the employed and the retired. They live in a range of households from large to small, some with children and some without. The street is lively and full of traffic throughout the day and much of the night. I lived on Josefstädter Strasse for six months in 1976. My observations from this residence, together with my experiences living in five other districts of the city and the 1981 Federal Microcensus time budget study, serve as the basis for my account of the daily round in contemporary Vienna, with Josefstädter Strasse as the mise-en-scène.[8] Here is that scene as Pezzl might have described it today:

Daily Schedule, 1976

It is interesting to consider how a family of more than one million, six hundred thousand souls, as Vienna is today, keeps to a regular time schedule without apparent consultation or compulsion. It is a time schedule where every hour has its own employments, uniting and dividing tens of thousands of people among various intents and purposes. The accustomed hours may be arbitrary, but the constant timekeeping creates a harmonious whole.

From this schedule derive the pulses of traffic that reign throughout the day in the streets and expressways of the twenty-three city districts and forty-odd suburbs that comprise the metropolis of Vienna.

Consider an ordinary weekday in the midst of spring or autumn on Josefstädter Strasse in the Eighth Municipal District.

The day begins early. At 4:00 A.M. the lights in the apartments of some factory workers are lit as people shower, eat breakfast, and prepare for work. By 5:00 A.M., the first automobiles appear on the street as workers begin their trip to work, a journey that for some can average forty-two minutes each way.

On the street, a delivery truck has arrived in front of the corner bakery to deliver the fresh breads from the central factory. Right next door, the dairy store is also receiving its shipment of milk and cream. The bakery opens at 5:30. The milk store opens at 7:30. The rumble and bell of the streetcar, noises that will repeat at five- and ten-minute intervals until 11:00 P.M., make their debut.

By 6:00, most factory and office workers are preparing for work. Their children prepare for school. One of the children runs downstairs to buy a loaf of bread for breakfast. With the water boiling for tea and coffee, the families sit down to a breakfast of bread with jam and butter, and soft-boiled eggs.

Most of the factories and warehouses begin to pay their workers at 7:00 A.M., but they have arrived earlier to park their cars and change their clothes. On Josefstädter Strasse, workers arrive from other districts while residents of the street leave to work. Only the shopkeepers have simply to descend a flight of stairs to their workplaces. Their clerks may have farther to travel. The butchers, greengrocers, delicatessen owners, and dry-goods merchants open their shops. They open at 7:30 A.M. to a waiting group of customers, anxious to get their food shopping done before going to the office or tending to the morning's household chores.

The street is now teeming with pedestrians, autos, bicycles, and streetcars. At 8:00 A.M., an army of over four hundred thousand men, women, and children is on the move, mostly by streetcar. The children must be in school by 8:00. The adults form an army of clerks, including battalions of secretaries, accountants, account managers, filers, stenographers, keypunch operators, switchboard operators, receptionists, expediters, and operatives. They are followed a half-hour later by thousands of automobiles filled with professors, doctors, certified accountants, master engineers, master business administrators, supervising engineers, consultants, commissioners, board presidents, trustees, councilors, vice presidents, presidents, and chairmen. They arrive at the Department of Finance, the branch of the Zentralsparkasse Bank, the parliament, the offices of the Hochbau A.G. construction company, the laboratories of AustroChemie m.b.H., the warehouse of Meier's furniture company, the business offices of the Theater in der Josefstadt. The higher one's position, the later one arrives at work.

By 9:00 A.M., the streets belong to the pensioned women of the district. They walk from food shop to food shop dragging shopping carts behind them. In each store they greet the same clerks and neighbors they have known for decades. The stores are their courtrooms as they question their acquaintances for the latest gossip and opinions about the events of the times. This is information they can exchange with their close friends at the coffeehouse later that day. They buy a few ounces of sliced sausage and a bit of cheese, a half-liter of milk in case the grandchildren visit that afternoon, soup vegetables and potatoes for their supper, and a half-loaf of bread.

The electricians, gas repairmen, carpenters, and construction workers take their break at 9:30. They fill the espresso shops, pubs, and coffeehouses, to drink a beer, eat a sandwich, or have a bowl of soup. In the factories, some workers ignore the opportunity for a break, preferring to accumulate the time and leave early. Others buy a coffee in the factory lunchroom, drink it quickly, and return to their work. The office clerks, unable to leave their buildings, have their coffeebreak at their desks, sharing pastry bought at the corner bakery that morning on their way to work. At the schools, the children drink a cup of milk and eat pieces of bread with sliced sausage or cheese that they brought from home.

For the next two hours, the city is busy at work. People on the streets are going to and from appointments. The pensioned women stop and watch as a new Mercedes limousine drives by and wonder which government official is inside. In the apartments, housewives are looking after their chores. Some are washing windows, others are airing out the rooms and bed linens. Some women are shopping for food. Others may be traveling to visit a government agency, health clinic, hairdresser, or specialty shop. As noon approaches, mothers of children in elementary school begin to assemble at the front doors, waiting to walk their children home.

At noon, the pulse of traffic quickens. The streetcars quickly fill to overflowing with people who want to go home for lunch. Most workers eat lunch near their offices and factories. Some skip lunch entirely and use the time for running errands. The food shops on Josefstädter Strasse close their doors and drop their blinds for the midday pause. They will open again at 3:30 P.M. In the coffeehouse every table is occupied. The patrons will order the daily menu of noodle soup, a schnitzel and potatoes, and an optional dessert. Those with less appetite will order a pair of frankfurters, a piece of bread, and beer.

If the day is warm, people will sit on the park benches, reading the newspaper and eating a sandwich. In the flats, mothers boil noodles to mix with butter and ground poppy seeds for their children's lunch. In the offices, only the executives are still at their desks. They will leave for their midday meal at 1:00 P.M.

The machines in the factories are turned on again at 12:30. In the streets the traffic snarls as pedestrians rush to be at their desks by 1:00 P.M. They will make their bosses late for their luncheon appointments at the city's better restaurants. At 1:00 P.M., the high schools let their students out for the day. These youths quickly fill the espresso shops where they drink soft drinks, smoke cigarettes, and discuss the latest pop-music sensations. The assembly begins to disperse almost immediately. Many of them have four hours of homework ahead of them and parents who insist on diligence. The less ambitious among them spend their afternoons in the espresso shops.

Between one o'clock and three o'clock the volume of traffic slackens. The streetcars still rumble and clang their way along the tracks, but their cars have many empty seats and they appear at longer intervals. The pensioners are taking their naps. The schoolchildren are doing their homework. Only the executives returning from their luncheons drive along the streets. No one seems particularly interested in these fancy new cars now.

Things start to get lively again at 3:30 P.M. The food shops reopen and immediately fill with the older women anxious to hear any news that has circulated since the morning. They soon fill the tables of the coffeehouse for their afternoon meal of coffee and a bit of pastry.

The streetcars are beginning to fill again as the workday in the factories ends. The first to leave are women with school-age children. Many of them work fewer hours than the standard workweek and lose some benefits because of their part-time status. Other workers have skipped lunch and the coffee breaks entirely to leave work at the earliest possible hour. They go immediately to grandmother's apartment to pick up the children who have waited for them since noon. Sometimes the children have been home alone for three hours. Who knows what mischief they have gotten into.

By 4:00, the male factory workers are returning home. Some stop in their local pub for a few beers. Their talk is of sports and politics. Others do the food shopping for supper, to spare their working wives the extra burden of having to shop later when the stores are crowded.

Between 4:30 and 5:00 the offices are closing, sending that army of clerks into the traffic-choked streets and crowded shops to wind their way home. The executives are likely to stay an hour later to finish their work. Sometimes they interrupt the journey home to spend some time with friends in a coffeehouse or pub. Home life begins in earnest around 5:30 when the family prepares to eat supper together. If both adults work, and especially if they have eaten a warm lunch, supper will be fresh bread with sliced sausage and cheese bought at the delicatessen a few moments before. If one adult has time to cook, supper will be the major meal of the day, with soup, meat and vegetables, and even a sweet. More frequently, it will be made up of leftovers from weekend meals.

In the households of factory workers, the supper table is laid soon after the adults arrive home, around 6:00 P.M. Office workers eat within two hours of arriving home, around 7:00 P.M. Skilled tradesmen and executives eat late in the evening, after the television news at 7:30 P.M.

The stores close at 6:00 P.M. Food stores can stay open until 6:30. They are still crowded with customers when a clerk goes to lock the door. From 6:30 until the bakeries open again early the next morning, it is impossible to buy anything for household consumption anywhere in the city.

At this point the entire character of the street begins to change. With the local residents happily warm and comfortable at their supper tables, the restaurants, theaters, and cinemas prepare for the evening's clientele. At the Theater in der Josefstadt, the Albert Kino, the Fromme Helene restaurant, the Apollo restaurant, at the coffeehouse, and at the disco bar around the corner on Langegasse, the actors, waiters, and cooks are preparing for work. The visitors to the street's entertainments will come from other districts. The pulse of traffic that brings them to the street ends at 8:00 P.M.

The residents pay no attention. They will watch the news on television and plan the evening's activities. Children will be sent to bed early, exhausted from their homework and the tumult of chores that follow the family supper. If the television schedule offers a program of interest, the adults will watch it. Otherwise, they will plan to meet their friends at the local pub, or if the weather is nice, to drive up the street into the foothills of the Viennese Woods to a wine garden for an evening of social drinking and friendly conversation. In the homes of the educated, the evening may be spent reading. Such socializing begins after 8:00 P.M. and will continue until 10:00.

Some executives and skilled tradesmen have not yet finished their workdays. They move to their desks at home to work on papers or drive to a client's apartment to begin their second jobs for wages that will not be reported to the revenue office. Some service workers, especially the police, and medical personnel, work evening shifts. Some factories and data-processing centers also run second shifts in the evening.

At nine, the doors of the private houses are locked. This is by order of the police. Friends leaving an apartment later than 9:00 P.M. have to be accompanied by the host, who unlocks the door. All the residents have keys; none of the apartment houses have porters anymore.

Between ten and eleven o'clock, the television programs end. This is the signal for most people that it is time to go to sleep. At eleven o'clock the theaters have let out their audiences, the pubs and the restaurants are closed. The disco crowd moves on to the nightclubs in the Innere Stadt. The streetcars make their final run down Josefstädter Strasse.

When one has observed the pulsing traffic of the streets during the day, it is hard to understand the quiet that now descends. Only the occasional auto passes in the street. If you were to walk across town, you would encounter fewer than fifty people, and they would be on their way home. Sure that they have exhausted all the evening's possibilities, the prostitutes leave the doorways of the closed shops and walk quietly home.

On Friday, Saturday, and Sunday, the story is completely different. Most children, especially high-school students, are in school Friday and Saturday mornings. Their parents are busy competing with the pensioned women for the attention of shopclerks. With their daily routine interrupted by these weekend interlopers, the older women retreat to the coffeehouse or to the churches. The stores close at noon Saturday and do not reopen until Monday morning. The streets are full of automobiles and streetcars as some families head for their weekend cottages, their country relatives, or the Vienna Woods. Their excursions will include a long hike and a meal at a country restaurant. A few families will make it a point to stop at a wine garden on the way home for a picnic supper and some fresh wine. The streets become busy again at 5:00 P.M. as the families return to their apartments. Evenings are spent in the city: at the theater, the cinema, restaurants, or in the pub with friends. Relatives visit each other at home on the weekend evenings. New friendships are made. Young people fall in love. They marry on weekends. The weekend is the soul of the town and renews its life.

What is most striking in these two accounts is the similarity between the two periods in the city's history. While the contrasts show how urban cultures change, the similarities show how they are conserved. This is the strongest evidence I have found of the existence of specifically metropolitan culture. There is no way to ask the Josephine Viennese if the meaning they attribute to, say, a noble coach with curtains drawn rattling down a cobbled street is in any way similar to the meaning that contemporary Viennese give to a Mercedes limo with dark glass windows. To the extent that we can infer continuity in the structure of meaning that underlies the observable similarities in behavior, Viennese metropolitan culture seems to follow Romer's Law. That is, the changes that take place are directed at returning the people's lives to some status quo ante. In spite of the pressures of industrialism and modernism, or perhaps because of these pressures, Viennese culture changes by trying not to change.

The historical contrast here is between the premodern and the modern: between a social formation in which the continuity of the meaning of time and space is embraced and a social formation in which continual destruction and reinvention of the meaning of time and space dominate. The baroque schedule was shattered with the coming of industry. Two centuries later, these very fragments pasted together repeatedly in new patterns continue to impart their features to the public schedule.

The industrial reorganization of work embroidered upon existing time patterns as it created new ones. The length of the workday has increased. The eighteenth-century workday was six to seven hours long. The current workday can exceed ten and a half hours for some workers, although the norm is closer to eight and a half. The workweek in 1792 was six days long, producing a thirty-six-hour to forty-two-hour workweek.[9] The standard workweek in 1976 was forty hours.

Compared with the baroque schedule, the work segments in contemporary Vienna have rotated to a position earlier in the day. Many residents are on their way to work at the hour when the scullery maids would have been arriving at the market. This work segment is broken into two periods of four to five hours' duration, instead of the three segments in the baroque schedule. Mealtimes occupy the boundaries of these segments only at the onset of work and at the midday break. Having started earlier, Viennese now finish work earlier than their Josephine ancestors. The postwork segment can include housework, shopping, or social activities, as well as an early evening meal. In spite of the earlier position of the work segment, Viennese today must travel much farther to work, work longer hours with fewer structured breaks, and must consign most of their household responsibilities and social activities to evening hours and weekends.

The modern work segment is not only longer in its absolute duration but also more homogeneous in character. While at work, Viennese must sustain their attention for longer periods without the relief of social interaction or distractions of any kind. Except for those few workers whose jobs require them to work outside or to travel from site to site during the day, contemporary Viennese remain indoors throughout the two work segments. The only opportunity to walk outdoors occurs during the midday break, which is only a half-hour in duration.

There are at least four different types of schedules in the contemporary account: the activities of the employed, the activities of retired women, the activities of housewives, and the activities of children. Two of these groups, retired women and children, are missing from Pezzl's scene altogether. He provides only a few details about domestic life. The large number of retired women is a demographic phenomenon produced by the differential mortality brought on by World War II, the improvements in obstetrical care and the subsequent increase in female life expectancy, and the substantial pension benefits that allow retired people to remain financially independent.

The large number of children moving through the city is the product of compulsory education laws. The first of these laws was instituted in the same year Pezzl published his essays. The schools have proliferated as the population of the city has expanded. In 1976, the city was undergoing a baby-boom that started in the late 1960s. Thus, the movement of children from home to school and back over the six-day schoolweek was an item in the rhythm of the street that did not exist for Pezzl.

Missing from the contemporary account are the activities of nobles. World War I signaled the final erasure of a class that had been an anachronism since at least 1848. Today, a growing community of international officials and diplomats attracts the attention once reserved for the nobles, as Vienna's role as a center of United Nations activities, international arms reduction talks, and meetings of the oil producing nations brings international personalities to the city.

The contemporary public schedule is heterogeneous. In the morning, workers wake, eat breakfast, travel to the workplace, and begin work at different times. The length of the workday varies from eight hours to ten hours depending on the type of work institution and the decision of the workers. Outside workers can enjoy a different structure of the work segment than inside workers. Housewives do their housework, shop, and care for their children in different sequences. The length of the schoolday varies depending on age, and in high school it changes from day to day. Retired people seek to maintain a pattern of store visiting and socializing. They are often interrupted by housewives buying food before the stores close for the midday pause or workers hurrying to get home for supper. Shopkeepers open and close their stores at different times, seeking to maximize the number of customers.

In Pezzl's day, the timing and duration of the midday break was a class marker. The owners of property, the educated, and the nobles took long breaks, each eating their meal later and later in the afternoon. The office managers, clerks, and workers took short, hour-long breaks and ate close to the noon hour. Today, it is the relative power of an employee's position within the work organization that determines the differences in the schedule. The midday break is now less important. All employed people and property owners eat between noon and two o'clock. The beginning and end of the work segment itself is staggered. Those who work for hourly wages begin first, followed by salaried employees. Later, those who manage the time and resources of the organizations take a break. The workday ends for these groups in the order it began. The more institutional power and responsibility employees have, the later the placement of their work segments in the day.

Clocks are everywhere: on walls and desks, hanging from fine gold chains around the neck, and strapped to wrists. Radios give time checks every five minutes during the breakfast period. Children learn to tell the time at the very beginning of their schooling. So accustomed are the Viennese people to glancing at clocks while going about their daily activities, that most can estimate the time of day using clock time even when a clock is not available. As a result, the references to clock time have a quality of precision to them. Many more time boundaries are imposed by government agencies and work institutions: the beginning and end of the work segments; the midday and other breaks in the workday; the shops' opening, closing, and midday pause; the beginning and ending of the schoolday; and the apartment lock law. Through clocks, bells, and government inspectors, all the time boundaries are enforced precisely to the minute.

In Pezzl's day, contact between household members occurred more often. The notion of a distinct separation of the work site from the residential neighborhood is an artifact of industrialization. Employed members worked a short distance from where they lived and took part in the household activities throughout the day. Most meals, but especially the midday meal, were taken at home. Restaurants and coffeehouses were beyond the budgets of most employed people. The proximity of the workplace to the home gave the connecting streets increased importance. Most Viennese spent their time on the street. Mothers and children would stroll to visit the father at work, stopping to greet neighbors. The husband would interrupt work when his family visited, usually without penalty.

In the Josefstädter Strasse scene, the household is more distant. When an employed member is at work, his or her separation from the activities of the household is complete. The household is the domain of the non-working adult. Working members have only limited responsibilities there and are absent for long periods during the day. Those individuals who are in greater control of their work time, such as licensed tradesmen and executives, can be more involved with their households. I have met people in these positions who can leave work early to participate in a child's important day, or to shop for a special meal. Such involvement, even among those who control their work time, is exceptional.

The play periods of the eighteenth-century Viennese were scattered throughout the day. From Pezzl's account, it seems as if work interrupts play more often than play interrupts work. The residents make good use of their city as a playground. The maids visit their boyfriends in the coffee-houses after church. Youths stroll with their girlfriends behind the city walls. Noble families take their children to the park to play. Theaters and dinner parties occupy people in the evening. The many long meals through-out the day bring people together socially in an atmosphere of pleasure and conviviality. In contrast, the contemporary working people relegate play periods to the evening hours. Time free from household responsibilities is spent in front of the television, a less social, more passive, contemporary equivalent of the eighteenth-century theater. The workday is bereft of play for workers, except for the occasional card game. An executive might choose to use discretionary work time to play, if the opportunity seems important enough. The work schedule constrains most wage earners from all possibilities for play during the work segment.

The eighteenth-century worker enjoyed an eight- to nine-hour sleep segment, which may have included, as it does today, reading, talking, sex, thinking, listening, or child care, besides actual sleep. For residents of the central district, the sleep segment was interrupted by the midnight noises of nobles' coaches. This segment has shrunk over the last 200 years. Today, employed household members manage to sleep six to eight hours. The demands on their lives have required people to exchange private time and sleep for more waking hours that can be sold for wage labor.

Pezzl saw the primary variations in the daily rhythm of the city as seasonal. In the contemporary schedule, the primary variation is weekly. Weekday schedules are different from weekend schedules. The weekend is a twentieth-century time artifact produced by the reduction of the standard workweek to six days. On weekends, the influence of the public schedule on the lives of householders is greatly reduced, only the market and school schedules remain from typical weekday constraints. The suspension of constraint frees households to engage in activities now crowded out of the weekdays: household chores, shopping, socializing, recreation and entertainment. Activities once integrated into the everyday rhythm of baroque Viennese life are now disjoined and redeployed to weekends.

The most striking difference between the eighteenth-century city and the contemporary one is the loss of the rhythmic alternation of quiet and noise in the streets that is the hallmark of a homogeneous time organization. The coming of industry dismantled the 1792 schedule. Today the activity in the streets is an unbroken stream of automobile traffic, delivery trucks, ambulances, and pedestrians, from six in the morning until well after midnight. Only then is the city quiet. I remember walking up Mariahilferstrasse, the Fifth Avenue of Vienna, at 1:30 A.M., after a party at a friend's apartment. As I walked past the dark department stores, the prostitutes walked ahead of me, looking back over their shoulders for a taxi on the deserted boulevard. The only sound was the click of their heels on the sidewalk. The windows of the ancient apartments above us were dark. The modern city was finally quiet.

CHAPTER 3

MODERN TIMES

One idea inspires this whole book; namely, THAT THE WHOLE BASIS OF THE VIEWS OF ARCHITECTURE TODAY MUST BE DISPLACED BY THE RECOGNITION THAT THE ONLY POSSIBLE POINT OF DEPARTURE FOR OUR ARTISTIC CREATION IS MODERN LIFE.

—OTTO WAGNER, *Die Baukunst unserer Zeit (1914)*

Our understanding of the potentialities of the present is entirely dependent upon our view of the past and future, and vice versa. To be aware of time at all is to be aware of its passing. When I focus on the immediate moment, whether it's an hour, a day, a month, or a year, as it recedes into memory, I am present-oriented. When I concentrate on the accumulation of moments in memory and project the promise of even greater accumulation in the future, I am past-oriented. Yet the two orientations are not equally powerful maps of time in all societies or, for that matter, in all domains of action. One mode will dominate, creating a temporal style that governs the language of time in that society or in that action domain. In the Viennese discourse on public schedules, the present dominates the past. This feature of Viennese metropolitan knowledge links it with other industrial cities and with a temporal orientation called modernism.

Modernism is a category of intellectual convenience. It describes a particular orientation toward social change. The term is useful for discussing the historical experience of the past few centuries in Vienna and in other cities transformed by the powers of industrial capitalism. Yet modernism never did anything; it was planners, industrialists, and political activists who did things in the name of modernism, or "modern life." Modernism was never a concrete program, like communism, socialism, or fascism. Lacking a clear manifesto, people who called themselves modernists often reached different conclusions on the same issue. Modernists and their antimodernist opponents coexisted in positions of power in Vienna for a long time. The debate between these diametrically opposed interpretations of the value of experience in solving the problems of modern times irrevocably changed the nature of urban life in the city. As the quotation from Otto Wagner reveals, modernists are conscious of their departure from the past.[1]

In the modernist orientation, tradition is suspect, or at least less desirable, in comparison with new models for action. This is the case even when the new models contain historical components. "To be modern is to find ourselves in an environment that promises us adventure, power, joy, growth, transformation of ourselves and the world—and, at the same time, that threatens to destroy everything we have, everything we know, everything we are (Berman 1982, 15)." This potential for both unbound greatness and unmitigated disaster arises from the priority that modernists give to the immediate present. By consciously rejecting past values, relationships, and meanings as ultimately dubious, modernists run the risk of creating a weightless system of values. In such a system, social actors who can deploy the most concerted expression of power will reshape society to suit themselves. Everything is open to change. Everything from the organization of city streets to the fundamental relations between men and women is malleable and plastic. With nothing in the past to stem their ambition, such actors can produce the extreme political positions and social atrocities so common to the nineteenth and twentieth centuries.

Marx draws our attention to the increasing frequency of acting according to what is personally convenient instead of what is socially appropriate. In the *Manifesto* (Marx and Engels 1974, 70) he accused the bourgeoisie of creating a society in which "all fixed, fast-frozen relations, with their train of ancient and venerable prejudices and opinions are swept away, all new formed ones become antiquated before they can ossify. All that is solid melts into air, all that is holy is profaned, and men are forced to face with sober senses the real conditions of their lives and their relations with their fellow men." The product of modernism over the last 200 years, whether in the arts, the economy, or in social programs, is always a greater consciousness of social relations as the source of meaning.

With urban modernism, the product has been greater consciousness of the urban social order. Three examples of how Viennese modernists shaped the consciousness of the Viennese population can be found in urban planning, industrialization, and politics. Each of the modernists viewed his domains of action as inherently plastic and malleable, and each contrived to fix his energies to the needs of the present. As one example, industrialists—the epitome of modernists—manipulate factors of production, including their employees, to reduce the cost of production. These industrialists focus their efforts on gaining a specified return on their investments and make decisions without regard to long-term planning or to the nonwork lives of their employees. As a second example, the actions of urban planners virtually reshape social space. Modern architects are more likely than their traditionalist colleagues to redesign existing urban spaces, disrupting patterns of movement and social interaction. As a third example, political modernists set the agenda for governmental action with the city as if it were constantly in crisis. Impelled by the terrifying social problems they see around themselves, these activists are willing to regulate and politicize previously private relationships in the name of equity. They may encourage alterations in institutions that have remained unchanged for generations. Because of the scope of their activities, modernist industrialists, architects, and politicians have a great impact on the metropolitan knowledge of their urban communities.

INDUSTRIALISM

Industrialism refers to the modernist program of transforming work institutions and economic relations. Most of the globe has experienced this transformation over the last 200 years. Because of it, the spatial and temporal relations of workers to their materials, as well as the value of work, have changed. Industrial entrepreneurs reorganize production. They localize resources and tools in space. They try to intensify the work efforts of others within specific periods of time. They invent a new kind of labor—management. Unlike the guild masters, managers control access to the materials and tools but not necessarily the skills and knowledge to use them. The focus of the manager's efforts is to reduce production costs relative to the final price of the finished product. Workers earn wages for the time they participate in the productive process, rather than for the completion of any particular product (Braverman 1974, 83–123). Thus industrialism applies to the management of work organizations in general, including service professions, and not only to manufacturing.

Industrialization replaces the existing pattern of work. How quickly this occurs, what aspects of the preexisting work organization are retained, and what effect the reorganization has on the existing social organization vary considerably from place to place. The Viennese industrial experience is different from that of England or North America. One historian (Rudolph 1973) has described the pace of the transformation as leisurely. It certainly occurred late compared with other areas in Europe, and even compared with other parts of the Habsburg Empire (Berend and Ranki 1965; Klima 1974; Kisch 1981).

Much of the early managerial activity concerned the relations between machines and the people who tended them. In a broad sense, technology can be any artifact, material or social, which people use to shape their environment. In and of themselves, the artifacts tell us little about the quality of the lives of the people who use them. The influence of a particular technology on social life can be understood only when we observe its use in a living context. This use is not inherent in the tool. The values of the people who possess the tools determine appropriate use. Values that determine the appropriate and inappropriate use of the technology are the base from which a community constructs its relationship to new technology. Such was the case with the industrial innovations. What was revolutionary about industrialism was not its new technology but its new, modern technical values. These swept out all existing ideas about the use of workers and tools, and replaced them with ideas that flourished in the present.

The Austrian technical order is similar to that in the rest of the industrialized world. Where the Austrian experience differs is in the preconditions of industrialization. These initially included an entrenched, threatened aristocracy and eventually came to include a very strong trade-union movement. Central European industrialization, including the Austrian experience, dates to the mid-eighteenth century in the countryside. The large migration of workers to the metropolis began in the mid-nineteenth century. These migrants were disciplined industrial workers who came from factory jobs in the smaller regional towns of the Habsburg Empire, not from farms. They migrated because their employers moved their factories closer to important marketing and transportation centers and took the best disciplined workers with them. For this reason, the costs of worker socialization in Vienna were far less than they were in the United States (Rodgers 1978, 66; Rotenberg 1987, 136–37, 140). In the nineteenth century, this managerial community created factory conditions that were similar to those in the United States. Managers used both piece-rate wages and systematic substitution of technology for skilled labor to reduce the work experience to the least engaging parts of the production process. Work shifts began before sunrise and ended long after sunset. Workdays were so long in the 1830s and '40s that the rate of marriage among the immigrant worker communities fell (Ehmer 1980, 129).

The workplace in Vienna has become an important arena for the struggle between modernists and antimodernists of various stripes over the last 200 years. The factory owners and managers carried the banner of modernism first against the entrenched customary work culture of the urban guilds and privileged charter companies, and later against the agriculturally oriented aristocracy. The trade unionists used the rhetoric of modern life to undermine these same industrialists. They accused the manufacturers of supporting antisocial wage and work-shift policies that were destroying the quality of urban life.

MODERNISM IN URBAN DESIGN

The defensive fortifications surrounding the circular city were razed in 1857. The open space between the central district and the populous suburbs became the broad, curving Ring boulevard, containing most of the buildings housing the major political and cultural institutions of metropolis and empire: the city hall, the university, the parliament, the emperor's palace, a miniature cathedral, museums, schools for fine and applied arts, the police and defense departments, the stock exchange, the national theaters and opera, and privately owned banks, hotels, and palaces.[2] The Liberal power block planned and implemented the project, known as the Ringstrasse. The planning and design of these buildings glorified the values of the entrepreneurial class, liberalism, and modernism. As Schorske has shown, each building subordinated the practical objectives of architecture to the symbolic function of representing the values of the emerging modernist program. This project aimed to polish the city's image, which was tarnished by decades of aristocratic neglect (1981, 25–26).

The design of each building borrowed from the historical style of the period in which its functions were the freest from political influence. One architect built the parliament in Antique style. He reasoned that since

Greece was the birthplace of democracy, its architecture would inspire democracy in the empire. The parliament served first as the meeting place of the Imperial Diet. This was not truly a democratic institution; the deliberations of its provincial representatives were only advisory. Another architect built the city hall in North German Gothic style, to inspire the municipality to recapture the independence it had once enjoyed. This sentiment was appropriate for a time when its elected Bürgermeister, Karl Lueger, was denied elected office twice because he represented a political position the emperor didn't support. Still another architect built the university in Renaissance style. He felt that style best represented the moment in history when intellectual pursuits were most free from political interference. The professors were imperial appointees.

Although the effect of the historical design was to heighten consciousness of the past, the planners' intent was to use the past to draw attention to the present and future. For this reason, the Ringstrasse movement was both tentative and unsatisfying. It delivered its message of political resentment toward absolutism and the need to steer the city toward a liberal future, but its historical models were elitist and inadequate. The values of the commercial classes in the 1880s bore no more relationship to those of the gothic Bürger than those of the current aristocracy bore to the manorial lord's. Nevertheless, the Ringstrasse project signaled a break with the style of the immediate past (classicism); all future efforts at urban design would have to take its measure.

The Ringstrasse liberated architects to explore alternate models. It sparked a debate within the architecture schools over what style was appropriate for the contemporary conditions of life—a very modern argument. Camillo Sitte and Otto Wagner staked out the two competing positions. Sitte (1909, 2) held that a city "must be so constructed that it makes its citizens at once secure and happy. To realize the later aim, city building must be not just a technical question, but an aesthetic one in the highest sense."[3] To reach such a goal, the entire direction of urban development would have to be reversed. Rather than reject the historical style of the Ringstrasse, Sitte wanted to make its influence more complete by recreating the unplanned, inefficient, but socially comfortable spaces: the enclosed square, the public forum, the open marketplace, and the wandering street. Sitte saw the urban consciousness as already in a state of revolt against the increasing scale of life. He wanted to establish principles of design that would create humane public spaces for people to live and work in. Many of his ideas turn up a few years later in the sociology of Georg Simmel. Simmel's use of the current psychological conditions of life as the criteria for design is modern. He remains the type of modernist who looks to models of the distant past to fulfill the present conditions of life.

The one theorist who divorced himself completely from historical models was Otto Wagner. In his textbook (1914, 11–12), Wagner asserts that "the whole basis of the views of architecture prevailing today must be displaced by the recognition that the only possible point of departure for our artistic creation is modern life."[4] For Wagner (1911, 39), this modern Baukunst (art of building) must "do justice to the colossal technical and scientific achievements, as well as the fundamentally practical character of modern mankind." These new architectural forms would celebrate the frenetic, ambitious city life he saw around him. His buildings would be objects of use, not objects of study. They would convey the messages of the industrial technical order that were already establishing themselves as metropolitan knowledge: efficiency and practicality, rationality and thrift. These were the values that he saw in the current conditions of Viennese life.

Wagner won the debate. Named professor of architecture at the school of fine arts, he also served as city architect during a period of intensive infrastructure improvement under both Liberal and Christian Socialist municipal governments. Wagner reshaped Vienna with his aqueducts, rebuilt the Danube canal, and constructed the underground and elevated city railroad system. His apartment houses and office buildings, and especially his Church of Saint Leopold at Steinhof, are models of art nouveau design. His students carried on into the building boom of the 1920s. Wagner's success in applying expressly modern forms to programs of urban design helped to legitimize this style of architecture.

In giving physical expression to the modernist program, urban planners and architects legitimized the priority of using modern solutions to treat modern problems. By establishing this perspective as a theme in urban design they brought the modernist program to the consciousness of the Viennese public. More than any other social actors, the planners saw their task as one of educating the public through the powerful medium of art. In doing so, they reinforced the posture of modernists in government and industry. They also forged a link between modernism and the Viennese urban identity. That link is even stronger today than it was at the turn of the century.

POLITICAL MODERNISM

The experience of almost a century of living under a moribund Habsburg political establishment provided the impetus for embracing modern strategies. Beginning with the reign of Maria Theresa in 1740, the Habsburg Empire became increasingly centrist and absolutist. This political ideology reached its peak under the regime of Metternich and rigidified to obsolescence under Franz Joseph. At the municipal level, under Karl Lueger, and at the national level, under Viktor Adler, a modernist political action program began to evolve. With the dissolution of the empire in 1919, the proponents of the modernist program reached the height of their power.

The first impulse toward political modernism can be traced to a new consciousness of authority that evolved in the late seventeenth century. In the mid-seventeenth to mid-eighteenth century, German tragic drama portrayed political leaders not as the mythic exemplars of virtue, as they were in Greek and Roman tragedy, but as historical actors clothed only in personal virtue. The dramas show this armor to be consistently inadequate. The dramatists saw leaders weakened by relying on past models for dealing with current political problems, the so-called "state of emergency," and strengthened by following models for action based on personal virtue. The heroes destroy themselves and their kingdoms when they fail to see political conditions as they really are. These works circulated widely throughout the German speech community. The Viennese theaters of the 1700s tended to play these dramas as satirical comedies (Benjamin 1977, 69). Some of the best-known comedians of the period, like Josef Anton Stranitzky (Hanswurst) and Gottfried Prehauser, built their considerable reputations with these satires. The message was not lost on the Habsburg emperors Maria Theresa and Joseph II, who controlled the city throughout the second half of the eighteenth century. Viewed today as reform emperors, mother and son focused their attention on the conditions of life of their subjects. They passed many laws aimed at improving the health, living conditions, educational levels, security, and quality of life of subjects from middle-class urban merchants to agricultural serfs.

These reforms, like French Republicanism, were particularly threatening to the landed aristocratic class. When the aristocrats regained control of imperial policy after the death of Joseph, they supported reactionary edicts that restored many traditional restraints. During the Revolution of 1848 the stifled commercial and working classes of Vienna showed their rage. Long suppressed by the absolute control of the emperor, these groups began to struggle for self-expression and against traditional authority. They formed political parties: the Liberal party for the larger commercial operators, the Czech Nationalist party for the Czech-speaking majority in Bohemia and Moravia, the Pan-German party for the German minority in those same areas, Zionism for the Jewish middle class, the Christian Socialist party for the small shopkeepers and skilled tradesmen, and the Social Democratic party for the thousands of foreign factory workers who had flooded the metropolitan region throughout the nineteenth century. Each party promised to fulfill the agenda of its constituents for improvement in their current living conditions. Each party practiced political modernism for their benefit. By World War I, the Liberal and Christian Socialist parties had left an indelible mark on the shape of Vienna through urban planning.

Nineteenth-century Austrian Liberalism shared many general philosophical principles with German Liberalism, but the political conditions of the two countries were different. Sheehan (1978) has described Central European Liberalism as a family of ideas incorporating notions of constitutionalism, individualism, and progress, through which a noncorporate *Öffentlichkeit,* the politicized public, struggled to depose established corporate power structures, especially the administration that linked absolutist aristocratic interests with the Church. What made this political movement different from the liberal movements in the Atlantic States and North America was that it drew its adherents from more than a single class. Aristocrat and Bürger alike rebelled against the economic stagnation of absolutism.

In Vienna, Austro-Liberalism embraced a wide range of participants, including progressive aristocrats, such as Eduard Taaffe and Count Leo Thun, and Jewish intellectuals, such as Freud. The party wanted to create a climate in which the impediments to industrial development that landed aristocrats and proguild bureaucrats had created in the first part of the century were removed. It derived the greater part of its strength from industrial entrepreneurs of both the middle and aristocratic classes. The party was stridently anticlerical because the Church, a landowner of enormous power, inevitably sided with the aristocracy in questions of economic policy. The party favored the emancipation of Jews from political and economic restraint. It attracted large numbers of Jewish activists to its ranks, including the journalists Moritz Benedikt of the *Neue Freie Presse* and Moriz Szeps of the *Wiener Tagblatt,* the leading liberal organs. Austro-

Liberal political control did not last as long in Viennese municipal government as it did in the imperial government.

The most effective Liberal politician in Vienna was the Bürgermeister Cajatan Felder, who held office between 1868 and 1875. It was Felder who commissioned the building of the new city hall on the Ringstrasse. He also added to the Ringstrasse mystique by underwriting the construction of the Stadtpark and the central market (Landstrasse). Under his leadership, the city purchased the huge central cemetery from private ownership. Felder's administration improved the quality of life in Vienna through large engineering projects, including the regulation of the Danube to prevent flooding and the construction of a 150-mile-long aqueduct to supplement the city's water supply (Johnston 1972, 64).

Christian Socialism was a reaction to the anticlericism and Jewish toleration policies of the Austro-Liberals. Karl Baron von Vogelsang, a Prussian whom the archdiocese invited to Vienna in 1875 to edit the Catholic newspaper, wrote its program. Vogelsang's socialism bore no relation to that of Marx or any of the other nineteenth-century socialists. Instead, Vogelsang wanted to substitute Christian ethics for capitalism. He was less concerned with restoring economic or political rights than he was with restoring the independence of family action and the hierarchical social structure of medieval society (Johnston 1972, 59). Production would be organized along family lines with workers and management sharing in the profits. These family industries would then be linked into branches and ultimately into a chamber of industry. Skilled craftsmen would be required to join a guild that would limit the number of masters and apprentices. The economic program, together with a vituperative rhetoric of anti-Semitism, was attractive to many German-speaking, working-class Viennese who resented both foreign workers and capitalists.

The most effective Christian Socialist politician was the Bürgermeister Karl Lueger. He carried out a version of municipal socialism in which natives, especially native shopkeepers and entrepreneurs, could be protected from foreign monopolists. He differed from Felder in his efforts to strengthen those municipal institutions that helped the lower middle classes. During his term of office (1897–1910), the municipality appointed Otto Wagner as its city architect and commissioned him to build the rapid-transit system and to rebuild the bridges over the Danube canal. The city also took control of the gas companies, a savings bank, an insurance company, and a retirement insurance company, extending inexpensive policies to ordinary wage earners for the first time. It electrified the streetcars, landscaped the parks, and passed the first store-closing ordinance, a law that banned retail activity on Sunday. The legacy of both Felder and Lueger is the activism of the municipal government throughout this century, which regards the quality of life as something it can shape through legislative action.

Political modernism is the application of this confident activism to political problems. Its adherents appropriate the values of the current conditions of life as the primary criteria for further developing municipal and national life. All the political parties that developed in the wake of imperial absolutism were politically modern in this sense. They examined all institutions for ways in which they constrained the aspirations of the political community. While this strategy borrows from the tradition of social positivism articulated by Saint Simon and Comte, political activism took on a very Austrian character by the turn of the century. The instigators were the Austro-Marxists, especially those within the Vienna Section of the Social Democratic party.

The Austro-Marxists were a group of intellectuals and leaders of the Social Democratic party, founded in 1888 by Viktor Adler. Their socialism diverged from that of the Second Socialist International and its theorist of international socialism, Karl Kautsky (ironically, an Austrian). As a variety of Marxism, Austro-Marxism was moving in exactly the opposite direction from Lenin and the Bolsheviks. Where the Leninists sought confrontation and revolution to transform society, the Austro-Marxists sought conciliation and the slow but steady development of the just society. This willingness to conciliate with the hated Liberals and ethno-nationalists of pre–World War I Austria earned the Austro-Marxists the opprobrium of even the more moderate members of the Socialist International but worked to their advantage in Vienna.[5]

Like Wagner, the Austro-Marxists embraced the current values of their city as the givens from which the new metropolis must develop. Their willingness to inspect all institutions for fossilized attributes was signaled by Viktor Adler's famous comment on the Austrian bureaucracy: "Absolutismus gemildert durch die Schlamperei" (absolutism mitigated by slovenliness). Both the commercial and working classes could benefit from more efficient government, and Adler committed the Social Democratic party to a program of reform and reconstruction. Taking control of the municipal government in 1918, initially in coalition with the Christian Socialists, the party ruled for the next sixteen years.

The alienation his more radical fellows feared as the most destructive force in social life never troubled Max Adler, the social theorist of the group. He sought to draw a parallel between Kant's concept of mind and Marx's concept of society by urging workers to forge a personal connection to the current conditions of life, embracing existing options on their way to creating new ones (Johnston 1972, 111). For Adler, the role of the party was to remove any impediments that might stop people from developing their personalities, to provide a synthesis of individualism and socialism. Under his influence, the social policies of the party, especially in the areas of work, health, family life, education, and housing, sought to bring to the working classes the same freedom of individuality that the commercial classes had enjoyed.

Otto Bauer, the political theorist, reinterpreted the national struggle of the ethnic groups within Austria-Hungary as disguised class conflict, a position that socialists could claim after 1918 had enabled them alone to foresee the collapse of the monarchy. A devotee of progressive legislation, Bauer wrote many bills in the 1918–20 period that reduced tensions in the workplace and improved the quality of life for working people. These included an eight-hour workday, minimum paid vacations, public access to health spas, resettling of farmers, and guidelines to make labor negotiations more orderly and workers less prone to strikes. For him as well class struggle meant the liberation of individuals so that they could pursue the cultured leisure that was once the province of the wealthy.

The principles of political modernism articulated by these early theorists of Austrian socialism still dominate the Social Democratic party. When I arrived in Vienna in 1975, a common piece of political advertising appeared on a border skirt around the roof of each streetcar waiting booth. The white-on-red letters proclaimed the current election slogan of the majority Social Democratic party: *Mehr Freizeit, Mehr Urlaub und Eine gute Zukunft* (more leisure, more vacations, and a good future). The slogan was a reference to the reduction in the standard workweek and increases in the number of paid vacation days the party had won for workers over the past decade. The worktime issue is perfect for an Austro-Marxist. It removes a constraint from the prevailing conditions of life, allowing wage earners to realize greater freedom of individual expression in their nonwork lives—the "better future." The program is even within the strategy of building socialism through conciliation with class enemies, since the authority of the employer to decide the conditions of work remains unchanged despite the worktime reductions. Only the period during which that authority applies was redefined and delimited.

This philosophy of conciliation after World War II is known as the *Sozialpartnerschaft* (social partnership). This refers to the meetings of the *Paritätische Kommission*, whose four members include the federal chancellor and the heads of the trade-union council, the chamber of commerce and industry, and the farm council. At these meetings, economic policy is reviewed and potential price and wage problems are identified. Through this review, compromises can be reached before public conflict occurs.

A brief review of the political conditions in Austria between 1945 and 1955 explains how this industrial syndicalism evolved. The four Allied powers divided Austria and Vienna, as they did Germany and Berlin. As these powers competed to influence the future political direction of Austria, the Social Democrats found that Soviet patronage for the Leninist Communist party of Austria was eroding its base of support within the trade-union movement. As the opportunity for the return of sovereignty approached, the Social Democrats formed a coalition with the Austrian People's Party, or *Österreichische Volkspartei* (ÖVP), a party usually identified as conservative and closely tied to the Church. The party represents elements of the commercial and agricultural interest groups that rejected fascism. The intention of this coalition between socialists and liberals was to rebuild the capitalist industrial structure of the country. It remained in power until the mid-1960s, and successfully undermined the support for the Communist party by winning many social and financial concessions for working people in the new capitalist order. The cooperation between the organization of industrialists and trade unionists continued during the 1960s. Between 1966–69, the People's Party had a parliamentary majority. In the 1970s the Social Democratic party held the majority.

The Paritätische Kommission worked out the policies for reducing work time without reducing wages throughout the postwar period. The Paritätische Kommission was a government within a government. Born out of the need to undermine the appeal of the left-wing socialist agenda of the Communist party, it established its own momentum as a force for change. The social partnership is an artifact of political modernism in both its form and its actions. In form, it represents a deliberative policy-setting commission that is focused on present-day conditions. In action, its pronouncements tend to seek compromise and establish industrial peace in spite of the inequality in economic relations that remains in the society. Each compromise is a new and unique formulation. Since the parliamentary delegations of both the People's Party and the Social Democratic party hold an overwhelming majority of votes, any compromise reached by their representatives within the Sozialpartnerschaft is readily enacted into law. The purpose of having the federal chancellor, the head of the government, sit on the commission is to ensure that the necessary votes to approve the compromises will be forthcoming.

The Sozialpartnerschaft benefits both factions. The industrialists win by focusing attention on the need for negotiation in wage policy, while price policy remains decentralized and non-negotiated. While price controls are in place for certain food items and for rents, no other prices are regulated. This allows industrialists to recover surplus value through price increases when the parliament enacts increases in the wages, or work-time concessions. This policy has not resulted in significant price inflation. During the 1970s, Parliament carried out the largest work-time reduction measures. It was also a decade when the rest of the industrial world was experiencing substantial inflationary spirals due to energy price increases. With the reductions in the standard workweek and the global economic climate, Austria's inflation rate averaged around 3% per year![6] The industrialists can profit from the strike-free, strife-free workplace that a conciliatory trade-union movement makes possible. The trade unions win by showing their members they can get work-time concessions from employers. The workplace politics of the Sozialpartnerschaft led to a substantial increase in the standard of living of Austrian wage earners without incurring additional cost to investors or owners of enterprises.

The Austro-Liberals, Christian Socialists, and Austro-Marxists forged the modernist political program in Vienna. Like the thousands of unnamed industrial managers and the star architects of their day, they wanted to uproot the resistance to change of the prevailing political and economic institutions. The revolution in the organization of time in the nineteenth and twentieth centuries takes its meaning from the historical trajectory of the city itself.

Where to start discussing the history of a specific place is always arbitrary. The sections that follow provide a summary of the city's development and the changes in the structure of the work schedule from Pezzl's time to the present. Since the focus of this study is the restructuring of work time during the last three decades, the early periods of the city are given very cursory treatment. Once the modernist's program begins to assert itself in Viennese life, details about specific conflicts and legislation take center stage.

THE ORIGINS OF THE CITY

People inhabited the high ground among the streams that drain the western slopes of the Wienerwald throughout the Central European neolithic age. Although the Danube was a major trade route throughout the Bronze Age, no permanent settlement developed in this area. Travelers left the river and turned eastward to avoid the swamps on the east bank and the steep hills on the west bank. The first settlement followed the establishment of the Roman fortress Vindabona in the latter half of the first century A.D. It was the home of the Thirteenth Legion, and later the fourteenth and tenth legions. The fortress attracted a sizable civilian population, which established a town on the east side of the fortress. Villages to the south and west also began to grow in response to the economic stimulation provided by the legions. The fortress was destroyed by the Germanae in 167. Marcus Aurelius recaptured and rebuilt the fort in 180. In the third century, it was one of the more important forts along the Danube. The surrounding region prospered from the money sent by Rome to strengthen the garrison. The first evidence of Christian converts occurs in the fourth century. Non-Roman soldiers, especially Goths and Alani, maintained the garrison at this time. Toward the end of that century, Roman power in the region waned. The fortress was sacked and destroyed soon after 400. Continuous habitation of the settlement after the fall of Rome was due to the importance of its marketplace to both the immediate region and the growing east-to-west trade along the Danube (Neumann 1958, 267).

It is impossible to figure out the languages spoken by the inhabitants of the area after the collapse of Roman hegemony. Records during this period of widespread movements in Central Europe are very difficult to find. Archaeological evidence places Lombards in the area in the sixth century, before they invaded Italy. Place-name analysis suggests that the farming population around Vienna included both Germanic- and Slavic-speaking people. In the period between 400 and 600, both groups were converging on the area from different directions. The southern Germanic-speakers were probably in place a few years ahead of the western Slavic-speakers. Their advance halted when they encountered Slavs in the Alpine foothills to the south, and Ostrogoths and Danubians in the Danube Valley to the east.

The Turkic-speaking Avars conquered the territory sometime after 600. They reduced the entire population in the area to agricultural slaves.

Large numbers of southern-dialect Slavic-speakers settled there immediately afterward, probably as additional slave labor. The Avars established a system of military vassalage that prevailed until it was replaced by manorial contracts under the Babenberger in the eleventh century. Political integration of the Avar state was prebendal. Vassals, known as Ringer, received control over taxes from agricultural areas in return for military loyalty to the Avar chiefs. The Ringer were little more than gangs of toughs. Wealth came from taxing the peasantry. Patronage of a market center conferred prestige on the local chieftain, and Vienna's attractiveness as a safe place for Danubian traders to stop continued throughout the period. The conditions of the slave peasantry were intolerable. Under the leadership of a Frankish merchant named Samo, the slaves revolted against the Avars and their Ringer in 626. The revolt crumbled with Samo's death and Avar control of the area went unchallenged until the rise of the Kingdom of the Franks. Charlemagne led three invasions into Avar territory (791–796) that succeeded in destroying a number of fortified towns, killing off a few Ringer, and upsetting the economic basis of the Avar occupation. By 800, the Avars retreated from the Danube Valley. By this time, the Slavic- and German-speaking populations had merged and the language of the peasants probably included a German-Slavic-Turkish pidgin. Magyars expanded westward to fill the gap left by the retreating Avars. Their advance was stopped at Lechfeld in 955 by a Frankish vassal, Otto I of Babenberg. His victory established the region around Vienna as the Eastern March of the Holy Roman Empire (Ostmark, later to become Österreich), the first line of defense against the eastern infidel.

Under Babenberger control from 976 to 1247, the city and its immediate region enjoyed an economic boom. The Babenbergers sponsored a sizable resettlement of German-speaking peasants from Bavaria (Lohrmann 1981, 117). These farmers increased the labor force and revived the agricultural production that had languished since the retreat of the Avars. Craft workers, commercial traders, and long-distance traders began to settle in the city for the first time (Petermann 1927, 46). The knights of the First Crusade passed through Vienna. The granting of a staple charter in 1221 acknowledged the commercial importance of the city. Staple rights gave cities some degree of self-government for the purposes of administering long-distance trade. The charter established a city council of twenty-four men and provided for one hundred notaries who could establish standard weights and measures and witness contracts. The city's Bürgermeister, originally the chairman of the finance committee of the council, was first elected in 1282. The council controlled the court for settling trade and property disputes, administered warehouses and hostels, and regulated the flow of traffic within the town and at the river port. The charter codified the customary procedures for conducting trade. Any trader who wanted the services of the city's councilmen or notaries had to unpack his goods and either sell or bond them. In this way, a chartered town located on an important transportation route, like Vienna, could benefit from long-distance trade that might otherwise bypass it. This enabled Viennese merchants to accumulate prestige and capital.

In 1245, the Church of Saint Stephan received the patent to become a cathedral and a bishop was installed. The cathedral would become the symbol of the political and intellectual importance of the city. The increasing power of Roman Catholicism in the city coincided with the passing of control over the Eastern Reich to Rudolph of Habsburg in 1282 (Kann 1974, 5). Under his descendants, the family's power would expand until it controlled most of Central Europe. Rudolph and his descendants made Vienna residence, administrative capital, and ceremonial center of the Habsburg Empire. Habsburg domination of the city lasted until 1919.

The fourteenth century marked the initial period of Viennese mercantilism. The major trade routes shifted from the east-to-west axis of the Danube Road to a north-to-south axis that linked Central Europe with Venice and Trieste through the Alpine passes. Viennese merchants opened trade relations with Venice through the Habsburg possession of Carinthia. The fourteenth and early fifteenth century saw the economic power of the city soar. After being conquered by Matthias Corvinus (1484), the city lost its staple charter. Its eastern location removed it from the mainstream of European trade for almost fifty years (Thompson, J. W. 1965, 197). The revival of Hungarian silver and copper mining under the direction of the Augsburg-based Fugger Corporation, coupled with the election of Maximilian of Habsburg as Holy Roman Emperor, revitalized the city in the sixteenth century (Ehrenberg 1963). Under the reign of Maximilian's nephew, Charles V, and the growth of Spanish power throughout the sixteenth century, Vienna also prospered.

THE PUBLIC SCHEDULE IN MERCANTILE VIENNA

Mercantile Vienna was a production center as well as an important grain- and meat-trading center. Crafts that used precious metals and agricultural products were particularly important. Both kinds of materials moved westward from Hungary. By the end of the fifteenth century, Vienna had 110 guilds with particular emphasis on the textile, metalworking and food-processing crafts. The development of a technological sense of time occurs in the city during this era. Precise clocks began to replace churchbells in the fourteenth century. Within the city, the fixed durations of commercial time organization included the bonding period for staple goods in warehouses, the winter closing of mountain passes to Italy and France, the due dates of bills of exchange between traders, and the length of time people and information took to travel to distant cities and markets in various seasons.

Traders organized the mercantile craft production through the *Verlagssystem,* or "putting out" system. They would supply raw materials to a group of workshops. The *Verleger,* or supplier of the raw materials, had exclusive rights to market the finished goods. He tried to manipulate the time it took to turn raw materials into finished goods. Workshops that wanted the patronage of a ready supplier of raw materials would commit themselves to fulfilling the contract within the stipulated period. Although the guilds promoted the control of craftsmen over production, patron-client relations between trader and workshop undermined this control. Independent guild workshops were converted into subcontractors for powerful traders.

When the urban guilds rebelled against the ever-increasing time constraints imposed by the traders, or when their production costs began to rise, the traders bought from peasant producers in the countryside.[7] Operating under either the Verlagssystem or the *Kaufsystem,* in which the peasant supplied the raw materials, the merchants maintained a stable and well-organized production ensemble. The Kaufsystem insulated the merchant from the peasant producer.[8] Since the merchant had not invested in the raw materials, he had no stake in the time it took to finish the product. In the manorial economy, peasant production was under the control of the local lord. He absorbed peasant craft production as labor service (Kriedte 1981). With the expansion of markets in the sixteenth century, peasants commuted their traditional labor service and land rents into cash payments. This enabled them to market their household production directly through the Kaufsystem to raise the cash.

The merchants could escape the costs of the guild system by employing peasant producers, but this was a limited strategy. Manorial organization precluded any large-scale development for two reasons. First, the estates could not afford to support nonproducers without sharply reducing the income of the local lord (Bloch 1961, 443–46). Second, manorial production involved contractual relations between lord and peasant that specified the quantity but not the quality of the products exchanged for use rights and protection. There was little basis for insuring market-quality products (Schlumbohm 1981, 96). For these reasons, merchants found little support from the local lords when they tried to intensify peasant production. When they could not deal directly with the peasant producer, the quality of the goods produced was poor.

These conditions tended to force the traders back into the city and the guild workshops. In the seventeenth century, grain prices were particularly depressed. Many estates did not produce enough grain for peasants to meet their cash rents (Slicher von Bath 1963). The availability of cheap peasant labor for craft production all but bankrupted the urban guilds. In Vienna, craft production fell to the extent that most guild workshops disappeared (Tremel 1969, 260).

THE PUBLIC SCHEDULE UNDER ABSOLUTISM

With the guilds seriously weakened, the initiative for control over work time in the city passed back to the imperial court and its clients. Demand for Vienna's crafts, including textiles, metalworking, and woodworking, began to revive within the empire in the early 1700s. To meet the demand, the emperor would grant special, limited chartersuniversal to entrepreneurs to set up and run workshops for periods of ten to fifteen years. The charters freed the manager from guild restrictions on hiring and workshop organization, including traditional workday standards. Known as the privilege system, these charters set a precedent for a nonguild organization of production in the city that would eventually provide the basis for the first factories.[9]

In the War of the Austrian Succession in the 1730s and the Seven Years War in the 1740s, the empire lost its most important industrialized linen manufacture, mining, and metalworking region, Silesia, to Prussia, a rival with one-third the treasury and one-sixth the population. The aristocracy realized that without secure control over the emerging industrial capacity of its many provinces the independent future of the empire was in doubt. This sparked two bouts of reform aimed at ensuring more central control over aristocratic landowners and marked the beginning of the period of Austrian absolutism. Vienna felt the reforms most keenly. They included posting officials loyal to the empress in every regional town who would report on the activities of the local squirearchy as well as oversee tax collection. The reforms also included the creation of a plenary council that could overrule and impose sanctions on the local lords; set limitations on the labor services the lords could require of their peasants; increase taxes; and organize emigration from more populated rural regions to the less populated areas of Transylvania and the Banat. Joseph II, the empress's son, undertook the second wave of reforms, which continued the absolutist and centrist policies. They included the disestablishment of the landowning prerogatives of the Church, the abolition of censorship, the establishment of secular educational institutions, merit-based civil service (monitored by secret inspection police), suppression of the councils of landowners, a conscript army of 300,000 men, and the outlawing of urban guilds and corporations to spark competition. In 1781, the emperor formally abolished serfdom and labor service. For the city of Vienna, the reforms meant the formal destruction of guild control over craft production and the removal of restrictions on migration and occupations (Anderson 1974, 318–19).

After the death of Joseph II, the new ministers systematically reversed the reforms. Too many interest groups had seen their power and prestige threatened. The landowners, the guilds, the Church, and the emergent nationalists in the provinces viewed Josephine centralism with contempt. Joseph's successor reinstituted the status quo ante, stopping short of renewing serfdom.[10] This was the time of the French Revolution. Fears among the aristocratic elite of nascent republicanism in the urban elites forced the emperor to keep those features of absolutism, namely the bureaucracy and its secret police, that could protect the institutions of empire. This period of reaction is known as the *Vormärz*, because it ended with the March Revolutions of 1848.

Under absolutism, the thousands of bureaucrats brought to the city to organize and centralize the affairs of the empire resolutely imposed an administrative organization of time on the commercial city. In the countryside, the reforms could be resisted by powerful lords. In Vienna, their implementation was very effective. The well-defined regularity of life described by Pezzl was already well established under Maria Theresa. By the end of the century, the administration had coordinated the various schedules of the city into a precise sequence. The morning market, the midday meal, the rigid boundaries between workday and evening, the lock law, and the cavalry patrols all show a careful and bureaucratic approach to regulation of life in the central city. Pezzl credits the return to power of the Church with the guarantee of a free Sunday for all workers, the first evidence of an administratively enforced weekend in the history of the city (1923, 220).[11]

A characteristic of administered organizations of time is the decentralization of control over sequences in nonadministrative activities. The administration oversees sequences only to the extent that they require coordination. In Vienna, this decentralization gave each district (if walled) control over its gates, the location and duration of farmers' markets, lock law, curfew, and the shifts and rounds of district watchmen. In 1800, nine villages ringed the central, walled district. Each had its own district council to administer these schedules and timetables. For example, the lower part of the seventh district, called the Spittelberg, gained an international reputation for the laxness of its late-night closing ordinances, allowing pubs and brothels to remain open all night. In the neighboring eighth district, greater interest by church and crown created a very regulated rhythm, in which the sidewalks were rolled up at 9:00 P.M. (Brandstätter, Treffer, and Lorenz 1986, 234).

The administration of work time was also decentralized. The government reorganized the guilds into three categories: police guilds, which were closely regulated by government officials (*Polizei*) and included professions dealing with foodstuffs for direct consumption, book publishers (censorship), health care, and shopkeepers selling direct to the public; self-regulating commercial guilds, which could decide work standards without interference from the administration; and so-called "free" professions, which included unskilled or semiskilled workers like seamstresses, shop clerks, and beggars. To regulate work time, the administration passed ordinances to close shops at certain hours or days for an entire district. In police guilds, it could directly proscribe the specific work hours. The store-closing ordinances constrained, but did not directly control, the commercial guilds and free professions. The privilege-charter workshops could not be regulated at all.

Not everyone in the imperial administration was content with the independence of the commercial guilds. Proguild and antiguild interest groups competed to direct the government's industrial policy. The proguild group included the older class of urban merchants who feared that loss of guild control over production would undermine quality and Vienna's share in the marketplace. The antiguild forces represented the growing number of provincial industrialists who sought to move their operations into the metropolitan areas of the empire. They found employing guild craftsmen expensive and unmanageable. The privilege charters were too few and confined to the manufacture of a few specific goods. The antiguild groups were the first modern industrialists. They sought what they called industrial freedom, in which they could set up any factories they wished, unhampered by guild regulations.

Under Joseph II, many commercial guilds disbanded and the number of privilege charters increased. Under the reorganization of the guilds during the Reaction, the number of privilege workshops declined and a moratorium was declared on the building of new factories "within four miles of the city walls (Haüsler 1980, 104)." Neither interest group could impose its point of view on the administration until 1849. The first phase of industrialization was an amalgam of increasing industrial work organizations and administrative intransigence in the control of the public schedule.

THE FIRST PHASE OF INDUSTRIAL TRANSFORMATION

The stalemate between the proguild and antiguild forces guaranteed that Viennese industry would fall behind that of other European metropolitan regions. In addition, the anti-industrialism of the Austrian Reaction created a period of lethargy from which the economy was slow to recover. Meissl has identified four specific effects of the failure of the administration to establish a consistent policy during this period (1980a, 104). First, traders turned away from urban production to increased use of the rural Kaufsystem. This delayed the need to centralize production in many crafts until the middle of the nineteenth century. The high profits from decentralized production proved a hard habit to break; even when investors built factories in the city, much of the production remained home piecework.

Second, the lack of an administrative policy kept a capital market for smaller firms from developing in the city. Lending banks funneled investment to the provinces where factories were already established. This resulted in a preponderance of large, specialized factories taking hold in Vienna, limiting future growth and flexibility.

Third, these large industries were energy- and capital-intensive. They required mostly semiskilled labor. Because of the guild monopoly over even semiskilled labor in the city, this labor could be found only in the neighboring provincial towns. As a result, the few large Viennese firms slowly moved out. This left the remaining industrialists with a diminished power base and strengthened the obstructionist tactics of the reactionary aristocratic and guild interests. This steady movement of firms toward the suburbs is evident from addresses of exhibitors at the Viennese trade fair over the decade 1835–45. Their locations are increasingly suburban and exurban (Meissl 1980a, 80).

Fourth, workers, whether they were guild or home pieceworkers, were reluctant to exchange their autonomy for the discipline and production rates of the factory. Therefore, those factories that survived the anti-industrial climate of the city had to import their disciplined work force. These migrant workers were cultural outsiders, as well as competitors who took work away from long-term residents. Over the thirty-eight-year period of the Reaction the total population grew at a fast 2%/10% per year; the immigrant portion accounted for 95% of the total growth.

The organization of work time offered by these factories was substantially different from that of the guilds. Industrial time was under the control of factory managers who stripped workers of the freedom to control the duration of the workday, sequence of tasks, and pace of work activities. Under guild organization, workers could control duration by taking traditional breaks at mid-morning, lunch, and mid-afternoon. The week was five days long, with Sunday and Monday given over to church and play.[12] The guild craftsmen did forego these traditional durations when the deadline on a contract neared. In the factories, the duration of work was an unbroken shift of as many as sixteen hours, seven days a week. In the workshops, the practice of completing one product before beginning another controlled the sequence. Each artisan experienced the work effort as the finishing of individual items. The factory manager experienced the work effort as participation in a process without regard for the completion of any one item. In the guild tradition, the fixed duration of the contract allowed the rhythm of work activities to vary. When the contract first began the pace was slow, and it speeded up as the deadline neared. In the factories, the pace was as constant as possible.

The migrants filling the suburban and exurban factories had never experienced these guild work standards. Their work socialization experiences had been in peasant villages and mill towns in Lower Austria, Bohemia, Moravia, and Styria. In 1765, Maria Theresa founded a series of textile schools in areas of high rural unemployment, which would provide useful work skills for ''idle youths, but also for adults, especially soldiers, women and children (Haüsler 1980, 38).'' Such schools would teach skills as well as work habits, such as the authoritative role of the factory manager, the relationship between wages and work, the difference between industrial and manorial work organization, the sin of absenteeism, and the discipline of work time.[13] Unlike the native Viennese, the immigrant worker in Vienna's factories was already well acquainted with the new work standards.

In the new factories, the workday in winter began at 4:00 A.M. and lasted until 8:00 P.M., and in summer it began at 5:00 A.M. and lasted until 9:00 P.M. This workday was probably shorter than the amount of time a homeworker would have to spend to earn the equivalent wage. Factories hired children and women because they were less likely than men to rebel at the artificial and sometimes arbitrary authority of the factory manager (Ehmer 1980, 122). If demand for goods should slacken, as it did in the depression years of 1835–45, some of these pliant workers could be laid off while others worked longer hours. The duration of the workday in early industry was solely at the discretion of the factory manager.

As the number of factories in the suburbs increased, the living standards of the immigrants fell to new depths. Analysis of demographic data from the period shows that factory employment tended to undermine family life. The annual marriage rate was lowest among residents of the factory districts, while the number of children born out of wedlock was the highest. The successful families were the ones employed in decentralized occupations, such as homework or odd jobs (Ehmer 1980, 120–26).[14] The extreme length of the factory day did not provide sufficient time to maintain viable households (Glossy 1919, 68–70; Haüsler 1980, 51; Rotenberg 1987).

The March Revolution of 1848 marked the end of this initial phase of industrialization. It involved all the major conflicting subgroups and resulted in a new alignment of forces in the city. The urban elites revolted against the centralism of the aristocratic Reaction, successfully imposing a liberal ideology on the city's government, and occasionally on the empire as well, for the next four decades. Industrial interests, together with nationalist groups, succeeded in breaking the absolutist policies. Aristocratic power was in decline as reforms eradicated the last vestiges of serfdom. In the provinces assemblies formed. In the factory districts, the pent-up frustration and anger over the scale of the exploitation produced a revolt not unlike the English Luddite actions of twenty years earlier (Haüsler 1980,

50). Workers burned factories. They sabotaged machines. They hunted down factory managers and killed them. Skilled workers in the central districts and the new immigrant factory workers began to recognize their common interests. Out of this *Maschinensturm*, the modern Viennese workers' movement was born.

The birth in 1848 of both the managerial-class movement (liberalism) and the working-class movement (socialism) signals a new phase in the development of industrial control of time organization. The administrative control of centralism was in decline. Further developments in the public schedule would result from the competition between liberalism and socialism over issues of work time. The single most important of these issues was the manager's control over the duration of the workday.

THE CONSOLIDATION OF THE INDUSTRIAL SCHEDULE

The period between 1848 and 1890 was one of Liberal ascendancy. After the emperor had intervened directly for a decade to keep them out of office, the Liberals took control of Vienna in 1860. Their control of the city council reached its peak with the administration of Felder (1868–75). This was the period of the Ringstrasse, the development of the broad boulevard circling the central district. With the closer connection among the districts, a municipal identity began to grow. Residents viewed public health, housing, street maintenance, and sanitation as the concerns of the municipal government. Both population and the number of industrial enterprises doubled between 1848 and 1890 (Magistratsabteilung 66 1912, 45; Meissl 1980b, 174). By 1890, all but three of the present municipal districts had been incorporated.[15] By providing municipal services in the factory districts, the city relieved the industrialists of that responsibility. This made locating industries in the city cheaper and more attractive. The Liberal party's policy was to create an environment that was as conducive to industrial development as possible.

The government abolished all guild regulations limiting commercial development in 1859. Instead of the traditional division into police, free, and commercial trades, the new trade organization provided for only two: free trades, requiring only formal registration of members, and commercial trades, for which the government retained regulatory oversight. The commercial trades, which declined in number from 1802, included the building trades, bookselling, and food processing. The free trades could hire and train their members and compete with each other to produce similar goods and services.

The Liberal power block was not entirely responsible for the slow but steady growth in the industrial base. The removal from power of the old guilds, the elimination of aristocratic blocks to progress, the growth of the railroads and similar infrastructure developments, the sacrifice of two entire generations of workers, and the growing availability of venture capital were the result of imperial and not Liberal policy. Nor can the Liberals be blamed for the slow rate of growth through the latter half of the nineteenth century.[16] English and French firms had grabbed Austrian markets in Eastern Europe during the Napoleonic years and held on to them, limiting the outlets for Viennese production.

The Eight Hour Day movement spread from England to Vienna in the 1880s. The Liberal position was that there should be no regulation of work time by the government. Any change in the workday would reduce productivity and injure Vienna's ability to compete in international markets, reducing jobs and profits for the entire city. The Social Democrats pushed government intervention for three reasons. First, workers needed to be protected from the physical dangers of operating machinery while tired. (Eventually, workers' social and psychological well-being also became an issue.) Second, shorter shifts would reduce unemployment by forcing employers to hire more workers to maintain the same level of productivity. Since employers were unlikely to reduce the length of shifts, government should regulate work time and thus reduce the social costs of unemployment. Finally, greater free time would enable the province-born worker to acquire and appreciate the benefits of metropolitan living, including education, recreation, entertainments, and participatory politics. It was doubtful that the Liberals would enfranchise the working-class majority. For that reason, government should step in to ensure that the working class had the same benefits of democracy that the industrialists enjoyed. The terms of this debate have remained relatively unchanged (Haas 1979).

The actual length of the workday differed from trade to trade and often from factory to factory. As early as 1848, for example, workers in the elite, skilled fields of machinemaking and locomotive building had won a ten-hour day. The reason was that their English counterparts had won that ten-hour limit two years earlier. Viennese workers benefited from the local industrialists' efforts to prevent a massive drain of skilled labor to England. For the less skilled trades, work time remained unregulated and highly variable. In small factories (under twenty employees), the workday ranged from twelve to sixteen hours in 1848. In sugar-processing factories, the day was between twelve and fifteen hours long. In the garment industry, people worked a consistent fifteen to sixteen hours a day. There were no vacations, and days-off for Sunday or holidays depended on the religious convictions of the factory owner (Bach 1898, 248).

THE FIRST MODERN INDUSTRIAL SCHEDULE

The first major involvement of the state in worktime regulation was the Industrial Order of 1859 (Mischler 1905, 210). It concerned child and adolescent labor and only affected enterprises of more than twenty employees. The act excluded children under fourteen from night work. Adolescents between fourteen and sixteen could not be forced to work that shift, but they could do so if they wanted (Mischler 1905, 210). Although limited in scope, the order set the precedent of state intervention in this area of industrial organization.

Leaders of working-class movements began to focus increasingly on government intervention in industrial life. The 1867 constitution aided in this effort by guaranteeing the rights of assembly and association. Workers' parties and trade unions formed throughout the period of 1865–1914. In spite of their rivalry for members, each party included provisions for the ten-hour day, the reduction of shifts for women and children, and a minimum age of fourteen for factory work (Klenner 1952, 55). Some of these positions were won by indirect means. For example, in the early 1870s, mandatory education lasted to the fourteenth year, effectively limiting the age of entry into the factories. In 1870 the courts recognized the right to strike, although the police and militia continued to ignore that right for another two decades.

The problems of life in the workers' districts came into sharper relief during the depression and unemployment following the market crash of 1878. An 1883 conference sponsored by the newly formed Chamber of Workers drafted a program that reduced the workday for adolescents under eighteen, ensured a ten-hour day, six-day week for all workers, and guaranteed free holidays (Deutsch 1908,119). Miners won a ten-hour day the next year. In 1885, Parliament enacted the New Industrial Order, giving workers in factories employing more than twenty people an eleven-hour day and a six-day week. The eleven hours did not include breaks from work. Other workers still worked twelve hours a day. The textile industry, with its twelve-hour shifts, was exempted from the order, as was the glass industry, which continued to operate on an eighty-four-hour workweek. The order also established a woman's right to a four-week, unpaid leave after giving birth. As progressive as this Liberal-sponsored legislation appears, it was rarely enforced (Zeisel 1971, 37–38).

In 1890, the first May Day demonstration took place in Vienna. The most prominent issue was the demand for an eight-hour day. The industrialists had procrastinated so long in meeting the workers' demands for a ten-hour day that the trade-union councils had decided to raise their demands. An experiment with a nine-hour shift in 1893 led to strikes and machine sabotage as managers tried illegally to reduce wages for the hours not worked. Some trades, the building trades in 1894, for example, used the strike mechanism successfully to reduce work time (Klenner 1952, 194).

Enforcement of the existing regulations was sporadic. A brickmakers' strike in 1895 protested seventeen- and eighteen-hour days and no free Sundays, conditions which had been banned ten years earlier. This lack of enforcement led to the 1895 Holiday Closing Law, which closed factories on Sundays and holidays. In 1899, the ordinance was extended to warehouses and retail shops, except food shops that remained open on Sunday mornings (Ministerium für Soziale Verwaltung 1968, 48).

The period from 1895 to 1910 was particularly productive for trade-union agitations and strikes. These led to direct negotiations with state authorities, bypassing the industrialists entirely. It was the era of the *Kollektivverträge* (collective contracts), in which a trade union would conclude a work agreement directly with the government. The contracts would ensure industrial peace for some years. In practice, only a third of the contracts resulted in reduced strikes, and all were met with resistance by managers on the factory floors. Parliament ratified the contracts and they had the force of law. In 1905, ninety-four separate contracts were put into effect. By 1907, there were sixteen hundred. The state had found its vehicle for dealing with the conflict between workers and management.

The standard workday described in these contracts varied widely from factory to factory and office to office. The range was between eleven hours a day and nine hours a day. The mother of one informant, Heinz Ritter, once told him that as a young apprentice in a retail shop before World War I, she began work at six in the morning and finished cleaning up at ten o'clock at night, hours after the shop had closed. This was probably the worst work schedule in the city at the time.

The actual work times for Viennese industry between 1890 and 1907 reveal an interesting pattern. The more the particular industry relies on a few skilled workers, the shorter the workday. On the other hand, the more the industry relies on many unskilled workers, the longer the workday (Meissl 1980b, 189). The first type of industry, typically represented by metalworking factories, was more likely to be located toward the center of Vienna. The second type, represented by textile factories, predominated in the suburbs. The proximity of a pool of skilled labor to the political activity of the central city made these workers more aware of the gains of union organization. The outlying textile factories were politically and socially isolated. It was harder for unions to organize them. As outlying firms became more capital intensive and required more skilled labor, they had to hire more politically conscious workers. Their work forces became unionized and the length of their workday eventually declined.

The process of establishing a viable work schedule, which began with the events of 1848, culminated before World War I in a work force convinced of its power to control conditions in the workplace. In the period that followed, the power to dictate the public schedule would alternate between the socialists, who initially took power in the city after the war, and the Liberals, whose base of support drifted to the right with the anti-socialist policies of its fascist wing, the Christian Democrats and the National Socialists.

THE FIRST REPUBLIC AND THE THIRD REICH

The events of the first half of the twentieth century completely changed Vienna's economic and political direction. Before World War I, the conflict between industry and the trade unions was mediated by an imperial administration. At best this administration played the role of disinterested arbitrator. At worst it operated against the best interests of both sides. After the war, there was no imperial administration. The empire flew apart. Vienna became the oversized capital of a country one-ninth the size of its prewar dominion. The conflicting parties in the control of work time found themselves confronting each other for the first time without the benefit of a referee.

Vienna's industry was intact after the war, but reparations imposed by the Allies taxed the industrial capacity to its limit. The population of the new state was 23% of the former empire, but its access to what were once domestic sources of raw materials and markets was now restricted. Its trade relationship to those new states was weak. Fearing a threat to their newly won independence, Czechoslovakia, Hungary, and the Balkan States were reluctant to become too dependent on trade with Vienna. Middle-sized industries dependent on these markets went bankrupt. The reduced access to raw materials threw the food-processing, textile, and metalworking industries into a five-year recession (Schilder 1921, 45–47). Only small handicraft and luxury goods industries retained their markets.

To deal with the economic decline, the First Republic passed several laws to protect employment and stave off massive depression. These included a prohibition against laying off workers, an order for manufacturers to increase their work forces by 20%, and a reduction of shift length to eight hours. When these laws expired in 1928, the strains imposed on inventories, inflation, and debt resulted in an economic collapse (Hertz 1970, 142). The experiment with legislating economic policy had won many adherents among the trade unionists and the general population. The Social Democratic party was the party most closely identified with this legislative strategy. It enjoyed a majority control over the city government and a powerful block of votes in the national parliament. At the national level, the party would not gain a majority in Parliament until 1970. Except for those years when it was hounded from power by the fascists (1933–45), the party dominated the work-time policies within the city throughout the century.

At the time of the economic collapse, Viennese workers enjoyed the highest wages, the most comprehensive insurance programs, the newest housing, the best health facilities, and the best child care and education of any of the industrial centers of the former empire. The length of the work shift was eight hours and the workweek was six days. Beginning in 1928, Austria also had the highest unemployment. Figures assembled by Hertz (1970, 138–54) show that Austria's unemployment problems penetrated deeper and lasted longer than those of any of its chief international competitors throughout the 1930s. Forty-five percent of workers were out of work in 1934. The many women seeking work to help increase their depressed household income added to the unemployment problems.

In spite of the surfeit of qualified labor, the workers who managed to hold on to their jobs saw the hard-won forty-eight-hour workweek erode gradually. The report of the inspector of industry in 1930 cites instances of illegally lengthened workdays (Klenner 1952, 911). Efforts to get industrialists to hire part-time workers (i.e., less than forty hours per week) caused workers to bid against each other for lower wages. Even so, only a fifth of those employed in 1930 were part-time workers (Zeisel 1971, 72). The period was one of retrenchment from the work-time policies of the 1920s. Armed with the power to withhold work, the industrialists reestablished their control over the public schedule.

This shift coincides with the ascendancy in 1932 of the Austro-Fascists. This party was not affiliated with the NSDAP, but represented a coalition opposed to the socialists, including industrial interests. A civil war between these political ideologies began in 1927, broke into open warfare in 1931, and culminated in the banning of the Social Democratic party, the Communist party and the National Socialist party in Austria. The Austro-Fascists declared a state of emergency, dissolved the parliament, and suspended civil rights. The eight-hour day was rescinded for retail shops. The overtime premium was reduced from 50% of normal wages to 25%. Holiday time had to be worked the following week. The forty-four-hour weekly limit for women and workers under sixteen was lifted. The government revoked the collective agreements. It declared the trade unions illegal, and replaced them with trade councils whose policies were consistent with the interests of the industrialists (Zeisel 1971, 75–76). If the pendulum of power had swung too far in the direction of the trade unions after World War I, in 1934 it moved too far in the direction of the industrialists.

In 1938, Germany annexed Austria into the Third Reich (*Anschluss*) and staffed Austria's government institutions with German and Austrian members of the National Socialist party. The occupation ended the period of retrenchment in work time in Austria for two reasons. First, the Reich granted workers in the new territories the same rights as German workers, which had a different historical development from those of the Austrians. The control of work time was placed within industry-specific councils made up of representatives of labor, industry, and government. The second reason was World War II. At the beginning, the typical workday was shorter to ensure the greatest productivity. The Ordinance of September 4, 1939, guaranteed extra pay for overtime, Sunday and holiday work, and the night shift. Although the guarantees temporarily diffused the discontent of workers, they were short-lived. The Reich revoked them on November 11, 1939, and reinstated the conditions in effect before September 4th. By the end of the war, the workweek had increased to sixty hours (Marschall 1957, 24).

THE SECOND MODERN INDUSTRIAL SCHEDULE

Unlike the conditions it faced in 1919, the government after World War II was burdened with a severely damaged industrial base. The city, as well as the entire country, was occupied by the armies of the Allies. Domestic work policies during this period had to satisfy the interests of the Soviets, the British, the French, and the Americans, as well as those of the trade unions and industrialists. The issue surfaced again when local control over internal affairs returned.

During this period, trade-union interests controlled work policies. The industrial interests had lost power because of the destruction of the factories. Without factories, their ability to create or withhold work was restricted. The Allied occupation forces wanted war reparations. They saw a weakened industrial faction as one way of lowering Austrian resistance to their demands. The Soviets also felt a political kinship with working-class parties and supported their policies, especially within Vienna.

The initial burst of legislation included the reestablishment of free holidays (1945), paid vacations (1946), renewed protections for women and children (1947), and the establishment of a nationwide collective agreement on the forty-eight-hour normal workweek (1949), the first collective agreement to be ratified since 1928. In 1950, Parliament agreed to develop a new set of policies for determining future changes in work-time laws. This last action proved the most significant since it established the authority for future work-time reductions by the federal government (Zeisel 1971, 86–87).

With the industrial base of the city slowly rebounding and the worldwide economy returning to normal after the postwar recession, this was a period of relative prosperity for Vienna. It was also the first period to resemble a normal peacetime economy since before World War I. The dissolution of the empire, the Great Depression, the German Occupation, World War II, the Allied Occupation, and the industrial rebirth were in the past. No further strains in the economy would occur until the late 1970s.

During this period, the political control of the country rested with a coalition between the Social Democrats and the People's Party. It was under this power-sharing arrangement that the greatest government involvement in work time occurred. This resulted in the eventual creation of a two-and-a-half-day weekend, a doubling of paid vacation time, and the reduction of the workweek to forty hours. Although these reforms originated with the socialists, most were enacted by a coalition government. By the time the Social Democratic party won a majority of seats in Parliament (1970), all the major work-time legislation had already been enacted.

The basis for this cooperation between industry and labor in the Second Republic was the Sozialpartnerschaft. Reminiscent of the industrial councils formed by the Nazis in the early stages of the war, the Sozialpartnerschaft would meet to decide how potentially volatile problems of economic policy would be solved. Two postwar facts of life made it possible to seek compromise before an issue erupted into open conflict. First, leaders of industry and the trade unions had finally come to respect each other's power. Over 150 years of direct conflict had shown that neither side could accomplish its goals against the opposition of the other. The idea of the partnership offered to both sides the opportunity to implement part of their programs at much lower cost and within reasonable amounts of time. The Sozialpartnerschaft sharply reduced the amount of work time lost to strikes. Second, the State Treaty, through which sovereignty returned to Austria, included several provisions that nationalized basic industries and established the government as an employer and as a competitor for industrial capital. These nationalized industries included the major steel, mining, oil, and energy-producing facilities plus control through stock ownership of many manufacturing and service industries (Tremel 1969, 414–27). With this treaty, the federal government became a major figure in the battle for industrial peace.

The debate over work-time policy resumed in the same year that sovereignty returned and the Second Republic of Austria was established. In 1955, the industry that had previously proved the most resistant to government intervention, the bakery industry, was enjoined from forcing its workers to work weeks of more than forty-eight hours. In a more comprehensive move, all workers gained a full hour of rest during the workday, of which half was paid and therefore counted toward the weekly total. Because of this manner of treating break time, the actual workday was longer than the paid workday.

In 1956, workers in dangerous employments won a forty-hour week. Also in this year, the question of the constitutionality of the government's authority to set national work standards, such as limits to the workweek, reached the *Verfassungsgerichtshof* (constitutional court). The court upheld the government (Zeisel 1971, 88). Throughout this year and the next, a variety of manufacturing and service-oriented trades won individual collective contracts reducing their workweeks to forty-six and forty-five hours. Pressure to shorten the forty-eight-hour week for all workers was mounting (Österreichischer Gewerkschaftsbund 1956, 77).

The year 1958 was particularly important for work-time reductions. Unregulated professions won contracts that permitted workers a free day off every other Saturday. This resulted in an average of forty-five hours over two weeks: forty-seven and a half hours in the first week, and forty-two and a half hours in the second week. Miners and automobile workers won a forty-five-hour workweek in their collective contracts (Österreichischer Gewerkschaftsbund 1958,14). In 1958, a new store-closing ordinance (*Ladenschlussgesetz*) was passed that reduced the workweek for store clerks. These new ordinances created a free afternoon by closing stores on Thursday afternoon. The number of hours a shop could open to the public shrank by an hour. General merchandise shops now closed between 6:00 P.M. and 7:30 A.M. These restrictive store hours benefited the clerks by placing maximum limits on the length of their workday (approximately ten and a half hours; Österreichischer Gewerkschaftsbund 1958, 20–38). The public viewed this ordinance as a positive improvement in the working conditions of the least skilled and least organized workers in the city.

In 1959, a national collective contract on work time reduced the regular workweek for all workers to forty-five hours. The total included breaks, although only half of the break time was paid. Overtime began with the first part of the forty-sixth hour. "Time and a quarter" would be paid for the first two hours. After the forty-eighth hour the worker received "time and a half." This collective contract also increased the minimum wage for both hourly and piecework workers (Österreichischer Gewerkschaftsbund 1959, 90).

This was the first attempt at work-policy planning at such a national level since the 1920s. It was only possible because of the Sozialpartnerschaft. The intermediate premium between the forty-sixth and forty-eighth hour of overtime is an example of working out the implementation problems ahead of time. Paying only half the break time is another example. With these compromises, the representatives of industry could encourage the support of their colleagues. The provisions of the contract were sufferable, while rejecting them might mean a return of the expensive class warfare of the 1930s (Geissler 1959). The ratification of this contract is a measure of the maturity of the political process within this state. Since the increments were small enough to be tolerated without an appreciable drain on capital, the industrialists were willing to concede work policy to the trade unions.

In 1963, warehouse workers took the lead in a renewed attack on the six-day week. By arranging their forty-five hours into ten-hour days, they could free their Saturdays and Monday mornings (Österreichischer Gewerkschaftsbund 1963, 8). This short-week pattern remains in many workplaces today. It represents an effort to concentrate work activities into longer durations over fewer workdays, postponing nonwork time to an extended weekend. To keep the workday from becoming so long that productivity suffers, the workweek must constantly be reduced to satisfy workers' demands for longer weekends. Why the workers chose to expand their free time at the end of the workweek instead of dividing it proportionally across the week is the central question in understanding Viennese metropolitan understandings of the meaning of time.

By 1968, the question of further reductions in the workweek surfaced again. A referendum in early 1969 produced over a million popular votes for a forty-hour workweek. The Social Democrats made the reduction of the workweek their central policy issue for the upcoming parliamentary elections. As articulated in an article in the party magazine, support for reducing the workweek stemmed from four contemporary conditions of life among wage earners. First, work methods and productivity demands generated increasingly stressful conditions under current shift durations. This adversely affected worker health. Second, automation created a rapid shift in the occupation structure, especially among technical workers. People needed more free time to retrain. Third, every third worker was a woman holding down two occupations, i.e., as wage earner and as housewife. Finally, every fourth worker was a commuter in a region slowly being strangled by traffic and pollution (Solidarität 1970, 8).

Parliament ratified the new collective agreement in September 1969. It produced a stepwise plan to implement the reduction to forty hours over a five-year period. The first reduction to forty-three hours started in 1970. In 1972, the week was further reduced to forty-two hours. The final goal of forty hours was reached in 1975 (Österreichischer Gewerkschaftsbund 1969, 5). The 1969 law differs from the 1959 law in several ways. It does not include the pauses in the weekly count. A paid eight-hour day is in reality a nine-hour work segment. Exceptions to the work limits are pro-

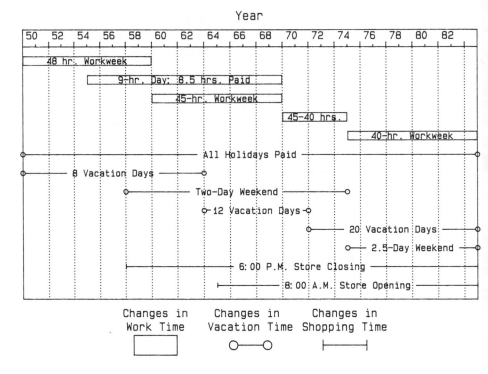

FIGURE 2: Changes in the Public Schedule in Vienna, 1945–1985.

vided for very dangerous occupations (lower limits), or where the public interest is endangered (hospital workers, police, and firefighters, for example). Also, the law superseded any previously won contracts by individual trades, even if they were more advantageous (Weiszenberg and Cerny 1970).

The agreement was ratified in December 1969, closing a decade that had seen a 15% reduction in work time. After this, industrial interests began to resist further reduction. Attempts to write contracts for thirty-eight-hour weeks succeeded in only a few of the highly skilled trades. At the end of the 1970s, trade unions began discussing the possibility of a thirty-five-hour week. The political will for a national accord on the reduction of the workweek was simply not there. Social Democratic power began to erode in the early eighties. The party formed one coalition with the right-wing Freiheitliche Partei (FPÖ), the Liberal Party, in 1983, and another with the Volkspartei, the People's Party, in 1986. Still, work-time reductions continued to be written into the collective agreements between individual trade unions and their employers. For example, the printer's union won a contract for a thirty-five-hour week in 1982. At the time of this writing, most of the manufacturing unions with sizable memberships have won contracts for thirty-eight-hour weeks. A summary of all of the postwar changes in standard work laws and store-closing ordinances is displayed in figure 2.

This review of the economic and political history of the city shows that the particular features of a public schedule in a city are a product of the modernist program of reshaping society to deal with the present-day conditions of life. There were periods in Vienna's history when a daily routine was widely shared among the population (late 1700s). There were also periods when each district followed its own schedule without regard to its neighbors' routines (1848–90). The difference between these periods lies in the priorities of the interest groups controlling the economy at the time. A high degree of uniformity exists when the political control is unified and centralized. Dividing that control among competing groups, dispersed through the territory, results in a highly varied public schedule. In this way, the public schedule of a metropolis mirrors the political economy.

CHAPTER 4

TIMING WORK

Der Berliner lebt um zu arbeiten.
Der Wiener arbeitet um zu leben!

The Berliner lives to work; the Viennese works to live!

This saying often prefaces Viennese explanations of their attitudes toward work. It means that work holds no intrinsic value for the Viennese. The Calvinist work ethic as it exists in contemporary industrial societies— the denial of idleness as the devil's workshop, the positive social contribution of wealth, or hard work as the reflection of self-worth—is absent. Individual Viennese I have met express ambition and the pride of accomplishment. Still, ambivalence about work is a prevalent attitude.

The following poem, *Der Arbeitsmann,* written by Richard Dehmel in 1905, describes this ambivalence in concrete terms:

Wir haben ein Bett,
Wir haben ein Kind,
Mein Weib!
Wir Haben auch Arbeit,
und gar zu zweit,
Und haben die Sonne,
Und Regen, und Wind,
Und uns fehlt nur eine Kleinigkeit,
Um so frei zu sein, wie die Vogel sind,
Zur Zeit![1]

Here the poet treats Arbeit (work) as one of the things that one needs to live a complete life, in addition to children, home comfort, and access to nature's beauty. What is missing is that particular kind of freedom, which birds appear to have, to stop, to fly, to call, to rest whenever one wants—the freedom of control over time. Work is a necessity but also an impediment to living. To work at living, rather than to live for working, is to pursue the elements that make life satisfying.

What is work? According to Marx it is any activity that transforms nature. This begs the question of how different societies understand nature or its transformation. Societies with wage labor, like Vienna, associate the category, work, with any activity that earns money, including *Überstunde,* (overtime) and *Pfuschen,* (a dialect term for moonlighting). For them nature includes the forces of production, the work institutions, and the wages. The transformation is the participation of the wage earner in the production process.[2]

Wage-earning activities do not exhaust the possibilities. Most industrial economies have barter systems, a black market in services, or "second economies" that develop outside of state control. In Vienna, such activities come under the category of Pfuschen. Some work activities for children are unpaid training in work skills and work discipline. School-children engage in *Hausübungen* (schoolwork), when they come home from school. Schoolwork is work. The views of nature and transformation remain the same, but the workplace and type of payment vary.

If unregulated second economies exist, third economies are possible as well. These are the goods and services that relatives and friends exchange in generalized reciprocity. These activities earn neither wages nor the return of services. Instead, they engender a generalized assurance that the receiver of the "gift" will meet the future needs of the giver. Household chores are *Hausarbeit* no matter who performs them. Housework is work.

Helping parents plant a garden (*Gartenarbeit*) or babysitting a friend's child is also work. These particular transformations are not viewed as work by the Viennese. Social scientists call them *ausserberufliche Verantwortungen*, (non-work-related responsibilities). I have never heard a non-social scientist refer to these activities with this formula, or even to refer to them as a group. They are clearly not viewed as work, except in an ironic sense.

Of these different kinds of work and nonwork, wage-earning work is precisely regulated by work contracts and federal standard work-time laws.

It is this regulation that households confront as they try to organize their lives. The wage-earning segment is a long, unrelentingly inflexible part of the individual's schedule. Workplaces and households are an average of forty-two minutes apart. For these reasons, the timing of wage-earning work is the most powerful constraint in the organization of household life.

THE CHANGING WORK SCHEDULE

Work schedules are the product of political struggles, managerial oversight of the production process, and workers' choices. Through political struggle, worker choice plays a more important role than managerial oversight. The work schedules in force in Vienna today reflect this shift in the locus of control in several ways. The variety of possible work schedules—ten-hour days and four-day weeks, nine-hour days and four-and-a-half-day weeks, and eight-hour days and five-day weeks, not to mention fortnightly and monthly work schedules—all testify to the power of worker choice. All that is required to change from one work schedule to another is for the workers in a factory to vote to have the kind of schedule they want written into their work contract. If business considerations or manufacturing costs exclude some schedules from consideration, that is negotiated first. At the time of the factory-level vote, the schedule that receives the largest support among the rank and file is the one written into the contract for a period of up to five years. Mixed schedules and "flextime" are possible in only a few industries.

Each sort of schedule has a different appeal, depending on the conditions of work and of the household. Four-day weeks are attractive to people who prize weekend recreations, but the long ten-hour days reduce the opportunity for housework and shopping during the week. Shorter work days are available for people willing to work five-day weeks, or part-time, but this schedule reduces the length of the weekend. The extreme positions of those who prefer the longest possible days and those who prefer the longest possible weeks cancel each other out. The work schedule that the majority supports optimizes both workweek and workday.

The workweek reductions from forty-five hours in 1961 to forty-three hours in 1970, forty-two hours in 1972, and forty hours in 1975 continued a trend in government activism toward work life that was established after World War I. Parliament implemented the 1970, 1972, and 1975 reductions, in particular, by allowing each work institution, or in some cases each industrial group, to determine the reduction strategy best suited to its work conditions and workers. The reduction strategies from this period, therefore, reflect the organizational concerns of worker households more directly than the more centrally imposed 1960s reductions and reorganization. The reductions of the 1970s show workers trying to coordinate their work schedules with other household members. In these decisions, we can observe the hierarchy of values through which the wage-earning households in Vienna gauge their time.

In the 1970s, efforts to close an office or factory early on Friday afternoon were the most common change in work schedules. A mixed strategy of reducing the length of both the day and the week was the second most common change. A small fraction (6%) opted to begin the workdays an hour later in the day. Another fraction (2.6%) wanted their lunch breaks extended, providing a longer midday break, which is reminiscent of the preindustrial pattern. Seven out of ten Viennese workers had some reductions in the length of the day. Only 20% of the work force cut these hours from the end of the week. The reductions affected different kinds of workers in different ways. Men gained four hours, while women gained three hours. Retail clerks, who work Saturday mornings, developed a strategy of accumulating reductions over two weeks, taking an entire day off every second week (Lamel 1976, 93).

Five different strategies emerged for dealing with reductions: workers shortened the number of workdays per week; shortened one workday per week (usually Friday); took the same reductions on each workday; took different reductions on different workdays; or accumulated reductions over work periods longer than a week. In the initial stage, two-thirds of Viennese workers, including both salaried and hourly-wage workers, chose to shorten their workdays to leave work earlier. Over half the work force supported either increasing the weekend or disproportionately reducing Friday hours. Shortening the workweek to four long days is evident in only a small fraction of work institutions. One institution in ten favored averaging reductions over periods longer than one week.

In the final phase of the reductions, fewer institutions decreased the length of the workday. Both types of Friday reductions were also less common. Still, the weekend continued to increase. For example, three in ten work institutions adopted variable workweeks based on longer averaging. One in ten institutions moved to ten-hour days and four-day weeks. Neither of these last two strategies were particularly popular initially. The pattern of preferences in 1970–75, then, was to reduce the workday first, and then reduce the workweek.

This worktime reduction involved no reduction in take-home pay. This was possible because work breaks during the shift were no longer fully paid. Since 1959, employers had paid workers for only one half-hour of their required hour of break time. This changed to a variable formula in the 1969 national collective agreement, the basis for all local contracts. For example, workers with a forty-five-hour week were paid for one hundred minutes of nonworking time, about twenty minutes per day in a five-day week. This also counted as part of the forty-five hours. Additional break time was unpaid. It served only to increase the length of time spent at work. Under these conditions, the costs of additional break time lay entirely with the workers. The work- time-reduction laws used these formulas as the model for calculating break time in the reduced workweek (Dorner 1975, 8). The 1970 reduction to forty-three hours excluded three-fifths of the one hundred minutes of break time from the standard workweek, thus reducing the paid workday by one hour and twenty minutes. The law first took away sixty minutes of paid break time per week and then gave back eighty minutes through the reductions. The net change cost the employers only twenty minutes in wages. In effect, the accounting department had to absorb only a 1% decline in workweek productivity, while the workers had to absorb a 60% decline in break time.

In 1972, Parliament cut another hour from the standard workweek, and again the calculation of breaks changed. This time employers paid only one-fifth of the required break time (twenty minutes). The net reduction in the wages employers paid was forty minutes. If workers wanted to keep the same amount of break time, they did so at the cost of a longer workday. In 1975, the formula increased to account for two-fifths of the break time (forty minutes). This was a challenge to the employers' accounting departments, since the net change now was a two-hour-and-twenty-minute reduction for workers, at no change in take-home pay. The first two stages had benefited employers, cushioning the economic impact of the reductions. The final stage benefited workers. It enabled them to win back some of the paid break time lost earlier. Through the 1970–75 period, the paid workweek decreased by five hours, but the length of time workers actually spent at work decreased by only four hours (Kinzel 1969, 28). The net effect of the reductions still favored the employers.[3]

The calculation of breaks favored workers who worked as few days as possible. Every day worked meant at least forty minutes of unpaid time at the worksite. Reshuffling hours to make four days of ten hours each enabled workers to spend at least three-quarters of an hour less at work per week. Sometimes enough spare hours accumulate during the week so a worker can leave before lunch Friday, saving him or her from taking the fifth lunch break. The "pull" of household activities for a longer weekend balanced out the "push" of break-time costs. The result was a city-wide trend toward longer workdays and shorter workweeks.

DISTINCTIONS AMONG WORKERS

Two-fifths of the population work. Their work schedules profoundly constrain their lives. One-fifth are pensioned or disabled. Their daily schedules vary depending on their social networks and household size.[4] One-fifth are children. Their daily schedules revolve around a six-day schoolweek. One-fifth are dependent homemakers. Ninety-eight percent of these are women whose schedules revolve around those of their employed spouses and school-age children.

In the literature of Austrian social science, employed people are distinguished as *Arbeiter* (workers), *Angestellte* (employees), or *Freiberufler* (independent professionals). The distinctions between worker and employee are similar to the distinction between blue-collar and white-collar workers. That is, both Arbeiter and blue-collar workers work in raw-material production, manufacturing trades, and construction, while Angestellte and white-collar workers usually are service workers and managers. There the comparison ends. The categories have different status values in Austria than they do in English-speaking countries. For example, an apartment-house janitor is an Angestellte, though he may wear "blue" coveralls while working at his job. The Austrian categories offer more precise distinctions than the equivalent English terms. The real differences among Arbeiter, Angestellte, and Freiberufler are twofold. They include the level of education required for entry-level jobs and the time period for computing wages. The state education system determines the credentials for the categories of workers. Arbeiter are not required to have any schooling beyond the ninth grade. In many cases, they acquire work training in an apprenticeship. The trade unions administer admission to an apprenticeship program in mining, construction, or factory work. In the fashion of the old guilds, they set the number of apprenticeships available each year, the level of pay for apprentices, and the course of the training. Many apprenticeships require young people to finish technical school before they begin.

The Arbeiter category is not completely homogeneous. Some Arbeiter are referred to as *Facharbeiter*, skilled workers. These individuals have graduated from a *berufsbildende höhere Schule*, a trade school in which they have learned enough of the engineering that underlies their trade to operate an independent craft. They may hold the title of "Herr Ingenieur" in the formal setting of the workplace. Facharbeiter are considered highly disciplined workers, specialists who have a high level of commitment to their trade. Many have taken state licensing exams in the various fields of engineering and are legally responsible for their workplace decisions. Such workers take on the most expensive or dangerous jobs.

Angestellte is a very broad category. For that reason, employees display distinctions between education levels as often as possible. Their educational background determines their qualifications for entry into job tracks, each of which has a different potential for future earnings and responsibilities. This great mass of middle-class, white-collar workers is ranked by educational decisions made when most of them were ten or twelve years old. This is the time when exams and evaluations track the weaker students away from highly competitive educational opportunities. This system of examination and evaluation continues to shift the children into various school tracks, or out of school entirely, until a clear hierarchy of achievement emerges in each cohort by age sixteen. At the bottom are employees and office workers who have had the minimum required education through age fourteen, the so-called *Lehrabschluss*. These are the warehouse workers, retail clerks, housekeepers, truck drivers, typists, and sanitation workers. On the next highest rung are people who have finished a comprehensive high school. They are more likely to be hired into job tracks in which they can eventually assume supervisory positions over those who left school early. On the next level are graduates of specialized programs in so-called *allgemeinbildende mittlere Schule*. These schools offer a commercial education similar to that offered at comprehensive high schools in England and the United States. They stress skills in office management, accounting, and design. These programs of study are popular, and their graduates have little difficulty finding employment. On a higher level are graduates of the so-called *berufsbildende mittlere Schule*. These are similar to the allgemeinbildende mittlere Schule but offer more technical courses and certification in clerical, educational, and technical skills. The graduates of these schools fill the thousands of clerical and supervisory positions.

Finally, there are those who attend the *Hochschule*. These include universities, technical institutes, and music, design, and business academies. They require a *Matura*, a diploma from a *Gymnasium* or similar allgemeinbildende höhere Schule. This is a college-preparatory school that includes grades five through twelve. If children are not academically prepared to enter the Gymnasium at age eleven, they can still attain a Matura, but must do so by taking extension courses as young adults. Those children who enter Gymnasium by age eleven are on a "fast track" for managerial positions. The course of study must include Latin for the universities and mathematics for the technical institutes. Hochschule graduates are honored with a variety of titles: *Diplom Kaufmann* (abbreviated as Dipl.Kfm.; a master of business administration); *Diplom Ingenieur* (abbreviated as Dipl.Ing.; a master of science in engineering); *Magister* (abbreviated as Mag., the ordinary university diploma, equivalent to a master of science degree in the philosophical faculty, but also awarded in law and theology); and *Doktor* (abbreviated as Dr.; a university dissertation in philosophy, law, medicine, or theology). When these graduates work in government offices, additional titles accrue, such as *Baurat* (supervising engineer), *Stadtrat* (city councilor), *Magistratsrat* (commissioner), *President* (chairman), or *Hofrat* (imperial court councilor, an honorary title). All of these are titles of address in the workplace. They have a long tradition. Many of the occupational titles mentioned by Pezzl in chapter 2 are still in use for this upper echelon of government workers. Academic and administrative titles can be combined if the individual also has teaching responsibilities. The academic ranks of *Primarius* (department head; in medicine, the head of a clinic), *Ordinarius* (full professor and holder of a chair of learning; usually someone who heads an institute), and *ausserordentlicher Universitätsprofessor* (professor representing a discipline that does not include a chair of learning) encompass people who practice various arts and sciences but also train others.

The Freiberufler are simply those who work on a fee for service basis, including doctors, master plumbers, lawyers, and architects. This work category requires a license and entails the responsibility to work within codes of standard practice. These codes are more pervasive than one would expect. Free professions evolved from the police guilds of the early nineteenth century. The practitioners were officers of the state, policing the conduct of their professions as well as themselves. Just as all lawyers in the U.S. are officers of the court and responsible for upholding the laws regardless of their personal preferences, so in Austria, all free professions are responsible for upholding the legal requirements of their professions. Every architect is simultaneously a federal building inspector, though professional inspectors are available. Every master auto mechanic is simultaneously a motor vehicle inspector, although inspection stations exist and periodic inspections are required.

Arbeiter and Facharbeiter earn hourly wages, while Angestellte receive monthly salaries. Professional associations set fees for the free professions. Whether a job is filled by Arbeiter or Angestellte depends on social evaluations of relative skill, commitment, and prestige, on the one hand, and legal concerns of juridical culpability and tenure protections (*Pragmatisierung*) on the other. Austrian work force statistics are announced using these categories. When people identify each other in conversation, one of the important features of personhood is a work category, with its implied status and educational attainments.[5]

The distinctions here are not class so much as *Stand* (estate). Members of each estate have clearly defined qualities but do not have a consciousness of an identity of interests among themselves and against all others (Thompson, E. P. 1963, 212). A socialist consciousness pervades the society to such an extent that anyone who works for wages to survive, regardless of educational achievement, is a worker, and anyone who derives income exclusively from property is not. When the Viennese identify someone as "ein Arbeiter," "der Herr Ingenieur," "die Frau Professor," or "der Herr Stadtrat Univ.Prof. Dipl.Ing.," the identifications refer to the educational distinctions within the working class. The Viennese conflate educational attainment, or as Pierre Bourdieu would say, "cultural capital," with social power (1984). Educational attainment only partially maps the social reality of the power to control work time. Only the highest category of Angestellte control their own work time throughout their adult lives.

THE HIERARCHY OF TIME VALUES

I will discuss eight schedules I collected during 1976. They do not represent every possible schedule. I offer none for elites, night-shift workers, guest workers (*Gastarbeiter*), tourists, pensioners, or students, to name just a few of the residents who contribute to the overwhelming diversity of metropolitan schedules. These eight schedules are, I believe, indicative of the activity patterns of employed persons and their households. I selected interview partners who were verbally inclined and interested in talking to me. These eight were selected from sixty-five interviews.[6] They represent the fullest and most cooperative accounts. The selection is biased toward moderate-wage-earning households. Still, the responses are representative of the schedules of all men and women in these occupations.

The eight individuals who discuss their work schedules here vary considerably in age and work experience. I conducted the interviews in early December. Three interviews are with housewives. Four of the five employed informants were over fifty years old. They have since retired. These introduce another bias into the impressions the reader may form. The schedules of older, fully socialized workers represent the greatest amount of flexibility and control the various work organizations can tolerate. By the same token, if these are the most flexible work schedules in each category, comparisons among them should yield even sharper contrasts.

The first of these schedules belongs to a fifty-eight-year-old factory foreman whom I will call Johann Ulrich. He is an Arbeiter who earns an hourly wage and must record his hours by punching a card on a time clock. He has a middle-school education and completed an apprenticeship in shoemaking. He is married and the father of two adult children. His wife, who is German, does not work outside the home. He has worked for his present employer for twenty-three years and is close to retirement.

The factory where he works lies a few kilometers outside the political boundaries of the city in a new industrial park. He lives in a city district at the other end of town and must drive across the city when he commutes to work by auto. This commuting distance is much longer than average. His factory manufactures chemical products for the cosmetic industry and employs thirty people. Half of these workers are in the production side, while the other half work in research, development, and management. The workers belong to the chemical workers union. Herr Ulrich is the *Betriebsrat*, the union shop steward, and he must often stay late to take care of union business. At work, the managers call him simply Herr. His position in the factory is that of master mechanic, a position that carries some of the responsibilities of foreman. He describes his typical day as follows:[7]

It is always the same for me. At 4:00 A.M. I get up and by 4:20 I am under way to work. I start work by 4:45 and will not leave the factory again until 4:30 in the afternoon. I might leave earlier, but I am also the Betriebsrat and there is always union work to do after the work shuts down for the day. My first task in the morning is to look after the machines. The routine hardly varies from day to day. When a machine breaks, I fix it. I have a sideline, too: In the morning I make sure that all goes smoothly when we start up. On the whole there is not much to say. It is always the same, except when it snows. Then I have to do some shoveling. And you must be there. Really there, so that everything works right.

At 9:00 A.M. we take a breakfast break for fifteen minutes. I am never hungry, so I stay with the machines. We break for lunch at noon. It lasts for half an hour. There is no afternoon break, because everyone wants to leave early. The women leave at 3:00 P.M., but the men stay until 4:15 P.M. The factory closes at 4:30. I go home to my family where there is always something to do. I even repair shoes and make things around the house myself. On Saturday, sometimes I go to work, but when I'm at home there is always something to do—painting and so forth. I'm preparing a garden. I know something about horticulture. Then we plan to go to the wine garden [Heurigen] and something happens that prevents us from going. There's always something.

Generally speaking, it's nice to work here. The management is easy-going. And every fourth Saturday I have things to do for the trade union. With all that, I have a pretty full life. When I'm free on Saturday, I'm together with my children and we go skiing.

My wife prepares dinner everyday at six sharp. Exactly when I come home, she begins. At exactly 6:00 P.M. the food is on the table. You could set your watch by it. This is the big meal of the day for me, and it takes about half an hour to eat it. After dinner we watch television. In the summer we might go for a walk. Last evening I cleared snow until 11:00 P.M., but normally I go to bed at 9:00. If there is a nice film on television, I might stay up longer. On Friday and Saturday night, I usually stay up until the television ends. I've always liked television. We've had a set for nineteen years. That's longer than anyone I know.

Johann Ulrich's day reflects the primary fact of the industrial transformation of urban organization: the separation of work time-space from living time-space. He leaves the house soon after rising and remains at work for twelve hours. He knows this is uncommonly long because of the extra responsibilities he takes on. While at work, his diligence and attentiveness are remarkable. He ignores opportunities for breaks to remain at the machines. Herr Ulrich is a fully involved industrial worker. He works to serve the machines. They determine both the pace and sequence of his working activities. When he returns home, he takes on the additional work of his free-lance shoe-repair business or tinkers around the house on do-it-yourself projects. While admiring his energy and ambition, one cannot help but also note that his choice of activity after work is another form of work, moonlighting in shoe repair.

Supper is a pivotal activity in the organization of his day and marks the beginning of his recreation activities. It is at this point in the day that his schedule and that of his wife begin to coincide. After supper, the joint schedule continues: taking a walk with his wife, or relaxing and watching television together. Work time is clearly separate from play time. The 9:00 P.M. bedtime allows four hours of play and seven hours of sleep before the next day begins at 4:00 A.M. He works for twelve hours, plays for four hours, and sleeps for seven hours.

Johann's diligence and commitment to work activities was responsible for his elevation to foreman and his election as shop steward. Not all workers share such commitment. Workers who punch time clocks often feel caught between the necessity to work and the burdensome demands of the work schedule. Mired in attention-demanding, repetitive, boring tasks, they possess the least control over the pace of work. To find meaning in such conditions, the worker must take pride in the work organization itself, not the products of the work. It is this loyalty to his small factory that Johann expresses, loyalty that has won him extra responsibility and higher wages.

The following schedule comes from Johann's brother-in-law, work-mate, and car-pool partner, Erwin Walter. Erwin has a middle-school education and served an apprenticeship as a tailor. He is referred to simply as Herr. At age 53, he has worked for this factory for twenty years. His wife is unemployed. While Johann and Erwin have worked together at the same factory for the same period of time, Erwin's responses to the demands of work and household are quite different from Johann's.[8]

I get up at 3:30 A.M. and make my breakfast. That's why I get up so early. It takes ten to fifteen minutes to make breakfast. Then I shower. After this I read the paper for fifteen minutes. It's nice and quiet in the morning and I enjoy the time by myself very much. At 4:15, I leave to fetch my car-pool partner. We arrive at the factory by 4:45. Work begins at 5:00 A.M. I begin my work by turning on the steam boiler for heat and preparing my machines. They must be ready to start the filling process, and that goes on until 4:30 P.M.[9] Practically, I work straight through, often with no break in the morning. In the afternoon, things ease up a bit. The most important work is in the morning. Everything must be in order so that everything is filled up, and the boiler is ready for the next day. I leave work at 4:30. It takes about half an hour, sometimes longer, sometimes shorter. I live in the Sixteenth District.

I eat supper as soon as I get home. I often skip lunch because I am trying to lose weight. For that reason I am quite hungry by five. Sometimes I do some food shopping before going home. Sometimes I have some union work or meetings. Then I get home later. In that case it is closer to 6:30 before I eat. Then I can turn on the television to see if there is anything interesting to watch. If not, I have several photographic hobbies including developing my own color slides and movie film, and film editing. Sometimes I read, or if the weather is nice, I look after my car. That's another of my hobbies.

We finish at noon on Friday. I go home to do some shopping. It is quicker at noon because there are not so many people. We do quite a lot of grocery shopping. I buy my beer. My wife says that's my affair. After shopping, I help my wife with the housework. Then we visit friends, or I look after my suits because I'm a tailor by profession. Earlier, I found a lot of extra tailoring work, but not now. My wife didn't like it. She's a hobby tailor and when there is something she can't quite manage I help her out. I go to sleep around 9:30 or 10:00 every weeknight. Of course, on weekends, it's a bit later.

We used to see films a lot, at least twice a week. But now we go less because of television and because the films are not as good as they used to be. We have a big circle of friends, and therefore we are never bored. People invite us here and there. Often we go on holidays together with friends. Most of my friends are teachers. They usually have longer holidays and can start ahead of us. Often we arrange to meet them at a particular resort in Spain or Turkey. I'm not so keen on wine gardens. I don't like wine. I do drink it if we have company, but I'm more of a beer drinker. Occasionally, we do go to them.

What would I change if I could? A lot, but most of it is connected to money and you can't do much about that. I have no control over my daily schedule. I'm fully occupied the whole day with my work. At 3:00 P.M., it's finished. After 3:00 or 3:30, I stop. I take a shower and change. Then I have to look over the whole factory, making sure that all the machines are off and the place is locked. That lasts until 4:30. One has to be careful because accidents have happened and these are security measures.

Since they commute back and forth together, Erwin works the same long workday as Johann. Both seem to devote their attention to the needs of the machines they tend without seeking to impose their own pace or sequence. But the differences in the attitudes of the two men toward control over time are striking. Erwin recognizes the lack of control the work shift creates. He does not seek extra tasks or take on additional responsibility, like his brother-in-law does. He is satisfied to fulfill his duties reliably.

The two men are different in their nonwork activities as well. Erwin gives up sleeping time at both ends of the day to have more time for himself. In the morning, he rises half an hour earlier to enjoy a simple breakfast, a shower, and the morning paper. In the evening, he has his hobbies of photography and auto care, in addition to television. Both men have the same twelve-hour work segments: 4:30 A.M. to 4:30 P.M., and the same amount of nonworking time as well: eleven hours and fifteen minutes. Johann uses seven of these for sleep, while Erwin uses less than six. The difference in their waking day is only an hour. Still, that hour is significant. It is 10% of the day remaining after work.

Those few Arbeiter who can control the pace of their work have a greater mix of activities during the day. In comparison with the work segments of factories and offices, the schedules of plumbers, carpenters, electricians, delivery drivers, and others who must move from place to place to do their work seem to have survived from an earlier public schedule. Yet, their schedules, too, are the contemporary products of the industrial organization of time. The following schedule of a thirty-year-old gas appliance repairman illustrates this.

Born on a farm a hundred miles from the city, Werner Tuzzi and his wife, Maria, moved to Vienna seven years before this interview so he could take a job with a gas appliance firm. He has a trade-school education, specializing in plumbing and mechanical engineering. He served an apprenticeship in gas-appliance repair. He is an Angestellter and earns a monthly wage. He is referred to as Herr Ingenieur. His wife was a kindergarten teacher. She has quit her job and is raising their infant daughter. At the time of this interview, Werner and his colleagues were under contract with the city to replace the fittings in the gas appliances of residents so they could burn a cheaper variety of natural gas. His current work activities include going from apartment to apartment replacing the fittings. The work is somewhat risky. He describes what he did yesterday as follows:[10]

> I got up at 6:00 A.M. and made myself tea. That's all I have for breakfast. It takes about ten minutes for me to drive to the office. I have to be

there by 7:00, but I'm usually fifteen minutes early. I like to get there early because it gives me time to straighten out the orders for the next day. I try to arrange the work in two-day segments, so I only have to go to the office every other day. Also, the earlier I get in and out of there, the less I have to put up with the Upper Ten Thousand. Understand me? I don't need them. I arrange my orders and I go out. Then I eat my real breakfast. I go somewhere where I can sit down, like a coffeehouse, and I have a good coffee and something to eat. At 8:30 or 9:00, I'm ready to start.

I work with two or three other guys. We drive to a district and divide up the apartment buildings. Each man takes two or three a day. The first day it's always a matter of changing the gas stoves and the heaters. Now we are working in the Seventeenth District. It will take another two years to finish the whole city and the suburbs. Otherwise people would get cold. Yesterday was a first day in the district. The first thing I did was change the fittings in apartments in the Seventeenth District. It took a half-hour to get there in the traffic. I completed five customers in the morning.

I go to lunch when I'm hungry, not at a specific time. Yesterday I went at 12:30 for a quick one. I really only took a snack. It all depends on how I arrange the day. I do that on my own. I see immediately how much work I've got to do. I like to get most of the day finished in the morning. If the work is easy, I can finish it quickly. Then, I get to lunch early and stay longer. There is good work and bad work. Yesterday was a bad day. All the appliances were old ones and difficult to change over. Old people live in those flats and they don't like to buy new things. They make do with what they have. Often I have to come back. I know what to expect, of course. We have computer readouts of all the appliances and what spare parts we should bring with us. Sometimes, I've been to the flat before. The more I get done on the first day, the less I have to do on the second day. I'm my own man then and no one watches me. It's possible to do everything the first day and nothing the second, but no one does that. At least, not very often.

I had a schnitzl for lunch. Supper is the big meal of the day for me. I prefer to eat in the evening. I have more time. I don't have to think about anything and can relax. The work is really stressful. For example, during the day I drink only nonalcoholic drinks. You are always with people who are offering you something to drink. If you had a beer at every second door you would be so drunk you wouldn't know what you were doing. Our work is very dangerous. Working with gas always is. You can't make a mistake. With one leg you are already in court. You are the last man and that's hard to take sometimes. If I make a mistake there is no insurance. I'm only insured for property damage that occurs when it's not my fault. That's why I don't drink during the day.

Sometimes I spend two hours at lunch. Yesterday, I spent only one and a half hours. As I said, it depends on how I arrange things. I can have three hours for lunch, but then I have to work later in the afternoon or the next day, and I prefer to do it the other way around. I try to do all the work the first day and take it easy on the second. Even on the first day, I like to have my afternoon light so that I can have a coffee around 3:00 P.M. Most of the afternoon work involves return calls to adjust something or other from a previous visit. That kind of work is much less risky and more comfortable. Then, I'm under less stress and I can say to myself, today everything is going smoothly.

After lunch yesterday, I went back to work around 1:00 or 1:15, and I worked until 6:00 without stopping. I got home about 6:30. I have to work ten hours a day, but only four days a week. Friday, Saturday, and Sunday I'm off. I didn't have to go back to the office after my last job. When I leave the apartment I'm working in, I can manage things just as I like them. I'm my own master. There is no one saying, "you have to hang around the office until six or seven." It's my own affair. If I wanted to work until 9:00, I probably would have nothing to do the next day. But no one would do that. It never gets boring, because you are always with people and not stuck behind a machine somewhere. When I get home, I eat supper, watch television and go to bed around 10:00 P.M. Occasionally, I read, but never in bed. I consider 10:00 P.M. to be quite late and I'm usually very tired by then.

The really good times happen when the appliances are easy to fix. Then, I'm finished early. Sometimes it means a three-day workweek. I can go to the pub with my mates and play cards or billiards. My wife has the best day of all because she's at home. Then you really are your own master and can do whatever you please. Of course, there is cleaning, but if one says, "today I won't clean the flat," nothing happens. Or if one does nothing at all, that's okay too. Then, she just takes the little girl and goes for a walk, and if she doesn't want to cook she eats something cold.

Superficially, Werner Tuzzi's day has the same kind of internal segmentation common in 1792. It shows a less complete separation of work and nonwork. Mealtimes, of which he has five, are the primary structural elements in his work schedule. He has much greater control over the pace of his work activities than do Johann Ulrich or Erwin Walter. He understands this control in terms of independence from the bureaucratic authority of the bosses. He has only a few minutes of contact each day with his managers, whom he refers to as the "upper ten thousand," a phrase once reserved to refer to members of the Austrian nobility. Although his employers are themselves middle class, he views their potential control over his life with the same antagonism that the non-noble classes felt toward the nineteenth-century nobility. He talks of self-control, self-mastery, and denial of outside authority. He brags about how well he can manage his time to reduce his work to the absolute minimum.

His working conditions vary from apartment to apartment. Ostensibly, his work involves replacing a fitting in each gas appliance, but as he notes, these appliances often are in need of adjustment. The variety of appliances makes his job more complicated by sometimes requiring a return visit. Since he is working with a highly explosive material, he must consider that every time he walks into an apartment, one error could kill him. He works a ten-hour day in a four-day week. However, the actual time spent in the apartments amounts to no more than five or six hours. The rest of the time he is either driving, eating, or playing cards with his workmates.

His afternoon activities seem particularly confused. Werner moonlights in the afternoon. Moonlighting is, of course, illegal in the eyes of his employers and his trade union. But Werner's participation in this unregulated economy is traditional for the service trades. In fact, so many gas repairmen are involved in this system-wide conversion that few are available to respond to ordinary service calls. He visits private customers to fix their appliances while he's still on the city's payroll.

He has solved his ambivalence toward work by controlling it as completely as possible. When I asked him how he could improve his workday, he specifically rejected the suggestion of a shorter workday. The ever-increasing control that his work granted him was sufficient. Instead, Werner spoke of having to deal only with newer and more easily serviced appliances. In other words, he was so in command of his work life that only the quality of the individual challenges he faced in the different apartments remained.

Werner's schedule is not an archaic holdover from Pezzl's era. It is produced by the same process of industrialization that produced the schedules of Johann and Erwin. The three schedules juxtapose the centralized workplace with the decentralized one. In the centralized workplace, the machine determines the pace of work. In the decentralized schedule, the worker determines the pace. In the centralized, the separation of home from the workplace structures the schedule. In the decentralized, it is structured by mealtimes. Yet all are schedules of industrial organization. Werner's work represents the very necessary function of the mobile troubleshooter, the skilled worker who is too expensive to be employed permanently by the households who hire him to fix their machines. The smooth operation of these electrical, plumbing, mechanical, and environmental appliances is necessary to free greater numbers of household members for wage-earning work. If the schedules of technically skilled workers like Johann and Erwin were less rigid, they could replace their own fittings, and Werner's work would become superfluous.

The duties found today in commercial and administrative offices are similar to those of the office clerks described by Pezzl. The commercial work segment is the product of the same rationalization processes experienced in factories. The differences lie in the more complex interrelationships of people and machines in the office. In fact, a significant portion of office work requires social involvement.

Brigitta Hartinger works in a government agency. Her daily schedule is quite similar to that of other office and clerical workers I knew. She is married and has two adult children. She has a high school education, but her war experiences and lifelong commitment to education have given her the linguistic, historical, and literary knowledge of a college graduate. She is an Angestellte and receives a monthly wage. Her husband is a factory worker and shop steward, like Johann Ulrich. In her late fifties at the time of the interview, she was the senior secretary and chief librarian for a research institute, a position she had held for fifteen years. Her schedule reveals a remarkable degree of flexibility for a centralized work institution. Here she relates what she did yesterday:[11]

> The day begins for me at 6:30 A.M. By 6:50, I'm dressed and ready for a cup of coffee. Yesterday, the cleaning lady came after breakfast. We always have a cup of coffee together and gossip a little. She has worked for us for nearly ten years and we always talk together for a while when she comes. So yesterday, I was a little late. My husband took me to work by car. We leave at 7:50 and I arrive at the office by 8:15. I am usually alone until 10:00 A.M. I have lots of tedious work to do at this time, including filing and updating the library holdings. Since I'm alone, the tedious work goes faster and I can always interrupt it for other things or a few phone calls to friends. Yesterday, Paul came in early to talk over a few personal problems. I spent half an hour with him because everyone else seemed to be late. Even the young secretarial assistant called in sick.

At midday I decided to shop for Christmas presents instead of eating lunch. We had made a list the evening before, so I decided it was a good time to look over the prices in the various shops. I didn't buy anything. The break lasted from 12:30 to 1:05 P.M. Afterwards, I went back to some typing. Then, I was interrupted by Dr. Wolf, who wanted to discuss some of the internal problems we were having at the office. This was not a personal conversation, but part of my job. He was quite exhausted from a meeting he had just left, so I made coffee for us. We usually have two breaks, one at 10:00 A.M. and one at 2:30 P.M. Since everyone was late yesterday, I hadn't bothered to make the morning coffee for myself. But when Dr. Während came in, he was so tired, I put some coffee on right away.

I finished work at 4:30 P.M. I had an appointment with an acquaintance. We had met in Paris some years ago and hardly get a chance to see each other, even though she lives here in Vienna. I took a tram to get to her apartment at Mariahilferstrasse. At that hour, you can imagine how crowded the trams were. I arrived there at 5:15. We drank a coffee together and talked over all the things that were happening in our lives. We talked a lot and I didn't get home until 7:00 P.M. Once home, I made myself a tea and ate some bread and butter in bed while watching television. My husband came home and we talked a bit. I read, smoked some cigarettes, drank another cup of tea, and looked over my supply of wrapping paper and ribbons for the presents I intended to buy. I was tired and wanted to go to sleep, but there was a very interesting political discussion on television. We watched it and got very angry. We both called the station after it was over to voice our disgust with the position one of the government advisors took. By then it was already 11:30 P.M. and I went right to bed.

I didn't do any housework yesterday because the cleaning lady was there. Usually, I wash clothes in the evening and do a bit of cleaning up in the kitchen. My husband is very good about helping with housework. So we hardly ever get behind.

The marvelous thing about my work is that I have so many different things to do. I can always switch over to something more interesting when I finish the really tedious stuff. There are always file cards to do, which is tedious, but I can also do a lot of cataloguing.

In spite of the centralization of work activities in the office, Brigitta's schedule exhibits the same control over the pace of work that Werner Tuzzi had. This is due primarily to the small size of the workplace and the lack of any real managerial presence. Fräulein Neubacher, an office clerk with only a few years' experience, spoke of a great deal more pressure from management to get things done. For Brigitta, however, issues of productivity never arise. She knows what has to be done and structures her time accordingly.

This woman has solved the problem of the ambivalence of work by structuring her time around social encounters. Her two-hour work periods punctuated by breaks of differing durations are typical of commercial office workers. Her food breaks are of little importance unless they involve the possibility to interact with others. She is willing to take work time to discuss both personal and professional problems. She sees such conversations as potentially part of the work. She never really knows until the conversation begins. Through her socializing on the job, she commands the work segment while operating within its rigid boundaries.

Brigitta's control arises from her long tenure on the job. The first few years of clerical work are marked by rigid schedules and close managerial oversight. Over time, the clerk's control over the pace of the job increases. Years of filing and organizing the essential information for an office's functioning empower the clerical workers. They become the only ones who know where everything is. As managerial oversight declines, the clerk becomes increasingly flexible about the placement and duration of breaks.

The managers of factories and offices impose on themselves the discipline required to get the work done. In the case of a trade-union official I interviewed, this meant taking on regular work activities at home in the evening. Nearing the end of his career at the time of our interview, Ernst Schönthal had been an activist in union activities since the end of World War II. His intelligence and dedication had earned him a position of power within the trade union second only to the union's president. As are most executives, he is an Angestellte with a monthly wage. A university graduate in the Faculty of Philosophy, he is entitled to use the title of Herr Doktor. His role in the organization involves policymaking. He is called upon to develop the trade union's response to current social issues. He never knows from day to day what issues might arise to draw his attention away from his planned activities. He and his wife have no children. She, too, has an executive position within one of the government ministries. Ernst's schedule reflects the flexibility and self-control that managers retain in their work activities. He describes what his day was like yesterday:[12]

> I got up as usual at 5:45. When I get up, I already have a newspaper, so I start to read it. I usually have five minutes of physical exercise, but I didn't feel well. My wife made breakfast. I left home at 7:30 and arrived

here for an 8:00 A.M. appointment. That lasted until 9:30. Then I made some telephone calls and dictated one or two letters. I went to a dentist appointment from 10:00 to 10:45. Then, I had a meeting with one of our research teams. That lasted until just before 1:00 P.M., when I left to visit my wife in her office. I stayed until 2:30 and then returned here. I had my lunch here in the office. That took about half an hour. I usually don't eat lunch since I'm trying to lose weight. Yesterday, I decided to have something for this headcold.

The afternoon was just routine work: telephone calls, reading reports, and so on. At 4:00 P.M., I had coffee and some pastry in the office. I continued working until 6:00 P.M. when I expected my English secretary. She called to say she couldn't come so I wrote some memos and went home. I left at 6:30. At that hour, it takes me about twenty minutes to get home. Usually I leave much later because I have reports or English letters to write, or I just clean up. I can arrive home anywhere between 6:00 P.M. and 9:00 P.M.

Yesterday I was home early, while my wife arrived late. I watched some television and waited for her to arrive. There was a discussion that interested me. Then I watched the news. During this television show, my wife arrived. We had dinner, which is usually the biggest meal of the day for both of us. This was at 8:00 P.M. Then we chatted for an hour and at approximately 9:30, I went to my desk and started working on some research reports that had arrived during the day. I went to bed at 12:30 and fell asleep as soon as my head hit the pillow.

Yes, of course I'm exploiting myself. I would say it's the kind of job I'm doing that involves so many more things. I just came in yesterday and said I had a new idea for organizing an international conference. Should I start it at all or not? I've gotten to the point where I have to look carefully at whether I can start something new or not. But that's the work. There's no structure to it. You have to do the job as you see it. Of course, this is not very representative of the work life in this society. I think most people would be happier if they could work as I do. No two days are alike, but every day has the same general structure. And yesterday, there was no particular feeling of success. I would like to say that every day held its own little success, or a new idea or a good start. But it was just an average day. Nothing particular happened.

What seemed to be fixed work segments in the schedules of the first four workers become movable and flexible periods of time in the schedule of this executive. He can move among a variety of desks, work odd hours unhampered by trade-union regulations or overtime quotas, create non-work segments at will (e.g., going to the dentist, visiting his wife's office), and reorder work priorities to meet unexpected problems. My observations and discussions with four other executives and commercial managers indicate that this flexibility in work schedules is the norm among this group of employees.

The executive schedule is the product of that period in the latter half of the nineteenth century when managerial roles originated. Before that time, managers were considered merely exemplary workers. The organization of their work lives paralleled that of the people they supervised. The role then shifted to that of autonomous problem-solver. The work schedule of the new manager now had less in common with workers. Today the executive retains the freedom to leave the office at will. At other times, the work revolves around specific problems that often require work at home. The industrial reorganization of work developed around the ever-increasing separation of work and nonwork activities in space and time. The managerial role represents a further evolution of the increasing separation of work time from work space. In this sense, the executive can never really leave the office.

Ernst solves the problem of ambivalence by making an intellectual commitment to his work. This transforms it into a fuller life experience. The separation between work and nonwork becomes blurred. The satisfaction he takes in new ideas, quiet successes, and worthy challenges is at least as meaningful as the joy he takes in travel and in maintaining a network of friends on five continents. This attitude is completely different from that of the previous four workers. In those cases, the work remained wholly other, and meaning derived from what the worker could control or add to that work. In Ernst's case, he has identified himself with the work so completely that the boundary between his work and his life no longer exists. For him, his life is meaningful to the extent that his work is successful.

He is completely aware of and comfortable with this fact. He also recognizes that his relationship to his work is both rare and enviable. To work as he does means to be so committed to the goals of the work organization that they become one's own goals as well. This might be possible in an organization like a trade union, where political idealism can serve as a basis for the commitment. In ordinary capitalist enterprises, identifying with the goals of the organization without at the same time participating directly in its profits is unthinkable. Johann is an exception. In his case, the commitment developed over the long term as his skills and diligence were rewarded with increases in wages and responsibilities. Aside from managers and executives, the only other workers who can completely identify with the goals of their work organizations from the onset are homemakers.

These solutions to the problem of ambivalence toward wage-earning work are not the only ones possible. There are hundreds of variations in the patterns of working to live. Some people have specific activity foci in their lives, such as weekend cottages, garden plots, sport clubs, or travel clubs, which consume substantial amounts of their nonwork time and involve their entire households. Another possible solution equates work with life goals. Among those who see their work this way are artists, musicians, scholars, journalists, teachers, attorneys, physicians, politicians, consultants, and philanthropists, to name only a few. Each of these professions becomes life-fulfilling through quite different achievements. In a similar vein, the solution of Werner Tuzzi, to restructure the work experience independently of the interests of his employers, is available to other unsupervised tradesmen and salespeople. The solution of Brigitta Hartinger is to treat the job experience as if it were essentially social in nature, and to structure work between social encounters.

These solutions imply different degrees of control over the pace of work. Werner Tuzzi and Ernst Schönthal are the most active in structuring their work activities from day to day. Johann, Erwin, and Brigitta are the least active. The contribution that increased control over work pace makes to the meaning of work varies even from Ernst to Werner. For Werner control is a concrete sign of his freedom from oversight, the retention of dignity, and the maintenance of a self-image of competence, trustworthiness, and self-discipline. For Ernst, control over work pace is required to take advantage of unforeseen contingencies and opportunities.

Those who have the least control over their work pace are confronted with the full constraint of industrial work segments. Johann and Erwin take pride in those adjustments of attitude that reduce their feelings of powerlessness. They focus their search for meaning and control in the non-wage-earning activities in their lives. Brigitta also has adjusted her attitude to reduce potential conflict. Her social interactions at work reduce the social distance between herself and the figures of authority, humanize them, and ultimately raise her to a level of social and political equality with them.

The industrialization of work creates new meanings for the work experience. The most industrialized of workers in an industrial city are those with the least control over the pace of their work. They are the ones for whom the constraint of the work segment is the most thorough and complete. The least industrialized workers are those with greater control

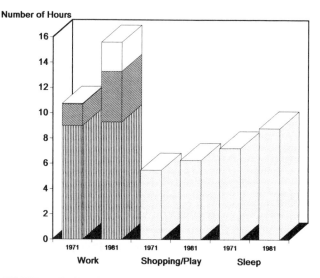

**FIGURE 3: Redistribution of Activities Following
Reductions in the Standard Workweek, 1971 and 1981.**
Source: Mündel et al 1979; Simhandl, Riess, and Riha 1984.

and the opportunity to find meaning through work activities. Their work experiences have a lot in common with preindustrial experiences, in which one's work and one's life were more fully integrated. The political efforts to reduce work time directly benefited the individuals who were not in control of the pace of their work. Because such workers are the most numerous in Vienna, the program was popular. Reducing the standard workweek extended the more meaningful nonwork activities and reduced the amount of time spent under the authority of others.

In solving their problems of ambivalence, workers have to consider the schedules of the other members of the household. Households contain non-wage-earners, especially children and their mothers, who have their own framework of meaningful activities. They represent the most consistent and powerful alternative to the values revolving around working outside the home.

WORK IN THE HOME

In this century, the number of two-wage-earning families has been relatively high in Vienna. The married women who stay home are almost always raising children. All of the women I spoke to felt that they would return to wage-earning jobs at some point in their lives. They view their work in the home as directed toward their young children. They place great importance on being as completely involved in their children's education and social development as possible. The following responses of home-based women, each with a working spouse and children of different ages, describe the experiences and perceptions of home workers.

As Werner Tuzzi noted in his account, his wife was in complete control of her time the minute she gave up her job and began to care for their newborn daughter. The first schedule is hers. Born on a farm a hundred miles from Vienna, Maria Tuzzi came to the city with Werner only a few years ago. She was not brought up in the rhythms of city life, but learned to live her life by them as an adult. Before giving birth to her two-month-old child, she was a kindergarten teacher, a job that required her to work only during the morning. She expects to return to her job when the child is six months old. Here is her account of what she did yesterday:[13]

I got up at seven o'clock and made breakfast for the baby and myself. I had to make a short trip to the bakery because we were out of bread. That meant getting the baby dressed. We bought the bread and then returned home for breakfast. By this time it was already eight o'clock. Then I began to tidy up a little, until about 9:00. I washed the floor in the kitchen and entry hall, made the beds, vacuumed the rugs, and not much more than that. That took the hour. Then, I began to get dressed to go downtown. I went to the city's Department of Families to apply for mother's aid. Before leaving, I had to spend some time getting all my documents in order. I wanted to pick up my wash package.[14] While I was downtown I did some shopping. I arrived back home at around eleven o'clock. It was nice weather, so I played with the baby in the yard. We were out there for almost an hour. Then we came up and prepared lunch. At about ten past twelve, a woman friend came by to drop off a carriage she was lending us. She stayed for twenty minutes but didn't eat with us. Then you called to say you would visit today. Finally, I ate my lunch.

After lunch, the baby and I took our afternoon nap. I woke up at two-thirty, but the baby slept until three. I dressed her and we went shopping for clothes. We didn't get home until 5:30 or even 6:00. I can't remember exactly. I started to prepare dinner and did a load of laundry. Just some small things that could be done by hand. I never wait dinner for my husband because he never comes home at a regular time. I put the baby to bed at 7:15 P.M. After that I did some crocheting and watched television. I think I fell asleep in front of the set. I remember the sports report and at least half of *The Streets of San Francisco.* I woke up at 9:30 and got dressed for bed properly. I was asleep when my husband came home.

The infant's schedule dominates this young woman's day. Mealtimes, naps, shopping trips, and household chores take place between the infant's demands for care. The meaning of her work comes from the constant care required by the infant. The public schedule is present in the form of the hours during which the bakery, clothing stores, and family agency are open. She says she always shops in the morning for food, because that is when the foods are the freshest. She eats breakfast around 7:30. She eats her main meal as close to noon as possible. Her supper at 6:00 P.M. is in the same position as supper in the households of workers who eat as soon after arriving home as possible. She eats all three meals with her daughter, but without her husband.

Maria's husband is disengaged from the household. He leaves early and arrives late. While he has the flexibility to return home if needed, he has no regular household responsibilities in his daily round. She eats at noon, but not because it is customary. She still clings to her previous work schedule as a kindergarten teacher. In that schedule work activities (food shopping, cleaning) take place before lunch, while lunch itself signals the end of the workday. Play activities (taking a walk, clothes shopping) take place in the afternoon. She need not worry about preparing meals for Werner; she does not expect to see him during the workday. The impact of her husband's schedule on her day lies in his sustained absence.

The next household schedule belongs to a woman who also has chosen to stay home for a few years while her two daughters, ages six and three at the time of the interview, are young. Born in the city, Johanna Bettauer is well accustomed to its rhythms. She holds a doctorate in a social science, but had not taught or conducted research from the birth of her first child through the time of this interview. If she worked outside the home, she would have an executive schedule. She intends to return to work when her daughters are older. She resents not being able to have both the fulfillment of professional work in her life and the satisfaction of raising her daughters. Her husband Christoph is a professional social scientist as well. His executive schedule allows him to become involved in household activities during the day. The following is a description of Johanna's day:[15]

The children woke up at 6:30 A.M. I heard them, but we stayed in bed until seven. My husband prepared breakfast while I dressed the children and made the beds. We ate breakfast at 7:20. I think it took us half an hour. I pushed my husband and older daughter out the door to work and kindergarten, and then cleaned up the kitchen. The plumbers arrived to do some work in the apartment we are renovating upstairs, and I went up to talk to them. At 8:00, I came back down to dress my younger daughter. That took half an hour because she kept running away from me. I swept the floor and straightened up the children's room. I cleaned as much of the bathroom as is ever possible to do.

My husband returned at eight-forty with the milk he had promised to buy before going to work. He left again immediately. I went in to wash the dishes from breakfast, then changed my mind. In the meantime, the younger one had made a mess of her room and I had to clean it up again. At 9:00 A.M., I put the finishing touches on some dolls I was sewing for Christmas presents. My daughter interrupted me at 9:30, so I read to her and we played on the floor. At 9:45, I dressed her and we went to buy a birthday present for my older daughter. Before leaving, I checked to see how the plumbers were doing. Then there was a phone call. That took three minutes. Finally, I got the stroller and we left. By 10:10, we had arrived at the market, and bought the present in a shop nearby. I also bought some eggs. It was a nice day so we walked to the kindergarten and arrived at 11:30, just in time to pick up my older daughter.

By 11:45, we were back home. I started making lunch while the children played. I usually make our supper at lunchtime to avoid having to be in the kitchen when my husband gets home. I started making lunch while the children played. The children did eat at 12:30, but I didn't have time. I put the dishes in the sink, on top of the breakfast dishes, but didn't wash them.

By 1:00 P.M., the younger one was asleep, and the older one and I started to bake a cake together in the kitchen. We were interrupted by the electrician, who had come to install an appliance upstairs. After that, the cake was finished and put in the oven to bake, while the two of us painted pictures together. At 3:00 the cake was ready. It fell apart as I took it out of the pan and every effort I made to put it back together only made it worse. We gave up and I went in to wake my younger daughter. That was at 3:20 P.M. Things were not going well. The younger one was in a bad mood after her nap and I had to spend some time quieting her.

Then I went to the kitchen and threw together another cake. For the rest of the afternoon, I played with the kids, knitted, read newspapers, and washed the dishes.

My husband came home at his usual time of 6:00. At that moment I was watching the children watch television while sitting in their chairs. I always watch them to make sure they don't fall over. My husband entertained the kids while I threw dinner together. After some crying and complaining by the children, I managed to get everyone together for supper at 6:35 P.M. I didn't eat because the younger one was creating a mess with her milk. At 6:55, my husband's aunt arrived and visited with the children until they went to bed at 7:30. My husband undressed them and put them down while I entertained the aunt.

The children were asleep and the aunt had left, the dishes were washed and the cake was finished, all by 8:10. My husband and I chatted for about ten minutes before he left to work on a project he was finishing at his office. At this point in the day, I can finally do something for myself, even if I'm usually too tired to think. I began to plan the birthday party for the next day. I had to decide what book should I read. I thought about what I might sew next. Finally, I decided to make Christmas presents. I made two dolls and knitted a cap. Then I took a book to bed. I finished reading at 10:45. When my husband came home at 11:15, I was just falling asleep.

As in the first schedule, much of the day is structured around the unpredictable demands of child care. Johanna's husband's schedule is important in defining the middle segment of the day. She feels she must have her cooking, cleaning, and child care under control by the time he arrives for supper. One of the children goes to kindergarten, which adds another externally imposed set of time boundaries to her day. In this case, the school schedule divides the day in half. Throughout the day, plumbers and electricians, following schedules like Werner Tuzzi's, arrive and depart. In between, she oversees their work. Johanna's lively children demand a great deal more of Johanna than Maria Tuzzi's infant requires of her. Christoph participates in the child-care activities when his work schedule allows. This enables Johanna to complete her housekeeping responsibilities, and still have enough drive to make Christmas presents.

Frau Doktor Bettauer's day reflects the commitment and activism that professionals bring to their work. But in her case, this drive to succeed is applied to the problems of running a household and raising her daughters. For her, the meaning of her homework transcends caring for her daughters.

It involves doing everything well. And the frustration she exhibits at various points is similar to the feeling professionals have when facing a crisis or making disagreeable decisions. She needs to challenge herself each day to accomplish more at home. The professional adjustment to the ambivalence of work does not end when she suspends her involvement in the executive schedule.

The third schedule is that of a woman who was never employed. Married to a journalist with an executive schedule, Margareta Koblischek has two children, ages eight and thirteen at the time of the interview. The older ages of her children enabled her to control a greater portion of the day for her own needs. Here she relates what she did yesterday:[16]

Yesterday, I got up a bit earlier than usual, about 6:30. Seven is a more typical hour for me to get up, but yesterday I needed more time to get ready for my gym class. I dressed by seven and got the children ready for school. We had breakfast together and I quizzed my son for the natural history test he had that day. Around 7:35, they both left for school. They must be there punctually at 7:45. Then I aired the children's rooms. When I have nowhere to go in the morning, I can stay in my nightgown, but yesterday I got dressed to go to my gym class. I left for the class at eight. I was back home by 9:15.

On the way home, I did some shopping for milk and bread. I do my major shopping once a week, so during the week I only have to buy bread and milk. I had put some curtains in the washer before I left and now I took them out and hung them up to dry. I woke my husband at 9:30 A.M. and made breakfast for him. We chatted a little. Then he left for work. By then it was 10:00. I talked on the phone to my girlfriend awhile. My mother had given us two bushels of apples and I spent the morning sorting them and cooking some of them down into applesauce. At 12:10, my daughter came home from school. She had arranged to have one of her friends visit in the afternoon. I called the girl's mother to make sure it was okay. We chatted together about the girls and their progress in school. In the meantime, my son came home. That was at 1:00. His school schedule has two kinds of days: "one o'clocks" and "two o'clocks." Yesterday was a "one o'clock."

I prepared lunch for us between twelve and one. We had soup and some sweetened semolina porridge. At lunch, I talked to the children about their schoolday. We finished at 1:45 and I cleared the dishes. The children did their homework and I ironed the curtains and rehung them. My daughter's friend came over at 2:30. When my son finished his homework, we left for the orthopedist. He was having inserts made for his shoes. The girls stayed in the flat. We left at 4:00 and were home by 5:15. Then I made everyone a snack of cocoa and sandwiches.

At six, my son walked the young girl home, while my daughter and I prepared dinner. At 7:00 my daughter had her bath and I washed her hair. My son had to memorize a story in English so I practiced with him. Then, my sister-in-law arrived for a short visit because she wanted to borrow a camera. I gave it to her but I couldn't show her how to use it. Her visit lasted only fifteen minutes. My daughter went to bed, and my son and I watched television together. The program lasted until nine o'clock. Then, I went to bed and read a little. By 10:30, I was asleep. I'm a light sleeper, so when my husband came home at twelve, I woke up.

My mornings are quite different every day. I'm not the type of house-wife who has a schedule that Monday is for window cleaning, Tuesday is for shopping, Wednesday is for visiting, and so forth. I clean windows when I feel like it. There are so many who keep Monday for cleaning the flat or washing, and who have Friday for shopping. I do that too. Friday morning. That's the only day I reserve for my household, per se. Otherwise, I do what I like. Generally the afternoon belongs to the chil-dren, more or less. That means I arrange my time around the children. I love to spend time with the children. The whole afternoon means from the time they get home from school until 7:00 P.M.

As with the first two schedules, Margareta Koblischek's day is not very rigid. Her gym class, her children's school, her husband's work, doctor's appointments, and mealtimes are boundary markers in the house-hold's day. She does not have the drive to organize and produce that Johanna Bettauer has. Nor is her day so specialized and centered around the needs of her children, like Maria Tuzzi, she wrestles with the problems of housework and child care in ways that will grant her the greatest flex-ibility. The schedule balances housework with socializing so that through-out her day people are coming and going. By rejecting the schedule of housework activities, she projects her personality on her household. She dedicates her afternoons to her children, from whom she derives enormous satisfaction. Their return to the household after school is a very important marker in her day. It is more important than the return of her husband. He is almost entirely disengaged from the household.

There are, then, two kinds of time in the lives of urban households. One kind concerns the self-determined durations and sequences of activi-ties within the household itself, like curtain-washing or cake-baking, through which the various needs of household members are met. The second includes the structures of timing and tempo imposed on household members as they affiliate themselves with public institutions. The schedules of housewives change when the outside commitments of household members separate them spatially from the household in new ways. As children grow, they spend ever greater portions of their day at school and outside the house. Traditionally, the work schedules of husbands have removed them from the household. In most cases, boys are not socialized to do household activities at all. Those few married Viennese males who cook, clean, or care for children learned to do so as adults.

There is no sense of powerlessness, relations with authority, or temporal constraint in the responses of the housewives. There are temporal boundaries. The regulated work schedules of their spouses structure the timing of food preparation, for example. These are only one of a set of schedules with which housewives must contend. Others include the opening and closing of stores and markets, schools and day-care centers, agencies and clinics, plus traffic and recreation.

These boundaries are not constraints in the same sense as the beginning and ending times of the wage-work segment. The work segment constrains the worker in space and restricts the choice of activity. The time clearly defines the activities. They are fully contained between the two time markers. The schedules of housewives include time markers that order the continuous interaction among children, spouse, relatives, and friends. As a result of the passing of the time marker, people are either now available or no longer available for interaction.

CONFLICT AND CHANGE IN HOUSEHOLD TIME

The greatest force for change in household schedules arises from those members whose activities are outside the home, rather than those who work in the home. One example that arose during my fieldwork concerned the conflict between teachers and parents of school-age children over the appropriate use of the children's time on Saturday morning. The adults wanted to use the newly won time free from wage labor for family recreation activities. However, schools required children to be in school Saturday morning.

The school schedule was virtually unchanged since Pezzl's day. The empress Maria Theresa initiated universal education in 1771. The six-day school schedule was progressive for its day. The schoolday was structured around the morning chanting of the office in the monasteries, beginning with Lauds and continuing to None. When secular clocks replaced the monastic bells, these hours defined the segment between 8:00 A.M. and 12:30 P.M. That became the school schedule. Younger children have a shorter day.[17] As they graduate from Kindergarten to Volksschule to Hochschule or Gymnasium, the schoolday becomes longer. In the 1970s, parents who were themselves just beginning to enjoy a five-day workweek demanded a reduced five-day schoolweek so that families could spend the entire two-day weekend together. Here is how Margareta Koblischek saw the problem:

> Our family is not really affected by the five-day workweek, because my husband always goes into the office for a few hours every Saturday and we can't leave Friday evening to go anywhere for that reason. So I don't really care if the children are home Saturday morning or in school. But there are a lot of people who say they could make better use of their weekend houses if the children were free Saturday. Others say that the children should be in school Saturday to leave them to do their housework in peace. I think it is very hard to coordinate the children's activities when they have a free day from school. One goes to see the grandmother. The other is off playing football or invited to friends' houses and no one is around the house. If the children had Saturday free, these problems would only increase and it would mean more work for me, as the mother. So if it were up to me, I'd like to keep the six-day schedule.

Some other parents agreed with Margareta, but they were in the minority. Most parents saw the six-day schoolweek as an inconvenience. The strongest opponents to the reduction of the schoolweek were the teachers. They felt the shorter workweek impaired their teaching plans because it gave the children too much time off from homework assignments. Individual educators saw their system as competitive with the best in the world and felt that the sixth day gave them an edge. Members of the teachers' union were against the reduction. The changes in the teachers' work schedules would be a major dislocation in their lives. They felt that the increasing resemblance between the schoolweek and factory and office schedules would deter many excellent people from entering the teaching profession. The "mornings only" schedule attracted people because it allowed them to retain greater control over their nonwork lives. This was particularly true of women with school-age children. The teachers' schedule was one of the few work schedules in Vienna that allowed a mother or father of school-age children to earn a full wage and still be home with her or his children for the entire afternoon.

A solution to the impasse was reached in 1979. It allowed the parents' association of each elementary school to vote on the length of the school-week instead of having the education ministry impose a single schedule nationally. This seems to have worked well. Many parents have agreed to retain the six-day week while others have voted for a five-day week. Gymnasium and other college preparatory schools are exempt from this voting and retain their six-day week.

The school schedule conflict is an example of the kinds of conflicts workers face as they try to resolve the ambivalence they feel toward the meaning of work through household and family activities. Similar conflicts occur with shopping and recreation activities. Changes in the timing of meals during this century also may reflect longer-term adjustments to the increasing rationalization of the work segment. The next three chapters address these conflicts in detail.

CHAPTER 5

TIMING FOOD

The responses to the reduction in the standard workweek are evidence of the common ambivalence toward work. However, the degree to which workers are conscious of this ambivalence varies. As in all industrial societies, some individuals strongly resist social constraints, while others are more accepting, or more apathetic. Only when faced with the unique situation of having to reallocate time originally committed to work do the Viennese reveal the degree of constraint in the public schedule. *Mahlzeiten* (mealtimes) are a more conspicuous feature of metropolitan life. All households prepare, consume, and clean up after meals daily. How often households have meals in the course of the day will depend upon the different schedule constraints of individual members. In other words, the number of mealtimes will depend on the number of time slots that other activities make possible. The conventional timing of meals is conservative and changes slowly. Thus, any alterations in the number and menu composition of meals indicate long-term changes in the articulation of households to the public schedule.

Mealtimes are convenient labels for naming times of the day. The five traditional names for meals in Vienna, *Frühstück, Gabelfrühstück, Mittagessen, Jause,* and *Nachtmahl,* also refer to those segments of the day that begin with that meal.[1] When people greet each other during the midday period, they say *"Mahlzeit"* instead of *"Guten Tag"* or *"Grüss Gott."* While this literally means mealtime, it has the same connotation as *Guten Appetit. Vormittag* and *Nachmittag* refer not merely to before noon and after noon, but specifically to the period before the midday meal and after the midday meal. Those executives who control their work time sufficiently to schedule lunch meetings usually must specify the clock time for the beginning of lunch. As Ernst Schönthal's schedule revealed, Mittagessen can start as late as 1:30 P.M. for some people. Appointments are made among friends to begin or end at the customary time of one of these meals. Brigitta Hartinger met her friend for a Jause, but returned home in time for Nachtmahl. When Margareta Koblischek's morning gym class ended, she and her friends ate a Gabelfrühstück together. Business appointments or work schedules are never described in such terms. Thus, the Viennese sustain the older pattern of recognizing five mealtimes by the timing of their social activities. Few households actually eat five meals. The names are remnants of an earlier organization of time destroyed by industrialism. How this happened provides another illustration of how the public schedule penetrates and constrains the organization of activities in the household.

As Pezzl's scene revealed, morning activities preceding work were far more important under administrative treatments of urban time than they are today. The midday break was long. It constituted a period when the household could assemble. The period after 4:30 was a time for relaxation and recreation, as mothers and children strolled through town to meet the working father as he left the office. Much has happened to rearrange family life in the ensuing two centuries. More children are at school, and the schoolday has increased in length. More women work, even if they are married and have children. More workers work farther from their homes, making returning home for lunch difficult. The workday begins earlier in the morning, limiting the possibilities for household activities. The work activities have become more concentrated, with fewer breaks, making workers more tired and less active after work. In each of these changes, the public schedule has created constraints on the pattern of activities within the household, forcing it to evolve a new, compliant pattern. The changes that have occurred in mealtimes reflect this new pattern.

MEAL-TAKING CROSS-CULTURALLY

The number of mealtimes people employ is highly variable, and there is no evidence to suggest a universal norm. Laboratory research has shown that humans tend to eat something every hour and a half if provided with foods and no external expectations or constraints on eating (Oswald, Merrington, and Lewis 1970). Primates in natural settings appear to eat constantly (Thorington 1970). All societies seem to allow two different modes of taking nourishment. Either we eat as individuals, without regard for the eating schedules of others, which I call snacking; or we painstakingly coordinate the preparation, presentation, and eating of food, so that two or more people can eat together, sharing the same rhythm. This planned, social eating I call a meal.[2]

Mealtimes are those parts of the day that the community conventionally sets aside for its members to gather and share a meal. The mealtime conventions of societies appear highly variable. In postcontact North American Plains Indian societies, meals were not held on a daily basis but were reserved for special ritual occasions (Lowie 1935; Catlin 1857). The East African, cattle-herding Nuer gathered together for food before the cattle left in the morning and after they returned in the evening (Evans-Pritchard 1938). The Hungarian peasants of the nineteenth century ate three meals during the busy days of summer and two meals during the shorter and quieter days of winter (Fél and Hofer 1969). In the main, both ritual considerations and ecological factors determine when the extra effort to mount a meal is appropriate in nonurban societies.

The kinds of foods eaten can also define a meal. Among the Bemba, millet porridge and an accompanying relish or stew are prepared only when the household intends to eat as a unit. Otherwise, individuals snack on sweet potatoes. The Bemba take their single daily meal only after the day's work is completed. When meat is available or when there are guests to impress, two meals are sometimes served. When the women who must prepare the porridge and relish feel themselves overworked by their gardening responsibilities, no meal is prepared. This suspension of the household meal-taking routine can last for two or three days. During this period, the household simply snacks on sweet potatoes (Richards 1939).

The Bemba experience underscores the variety of meal-taking behaviors that can occur within a conventional pattern. Mealtimes may be named events in the daily schedule, but actual eating behavior can be quite different from the ideal. The Viennese I knew recognized five meals but ate all five only on very special occasions. More commonly, people ate one meal and two snacks, or at most three meals. When the conventional expectations are as far out of line with real behavior as eating in Vienna appears to be, the underlying reason is usually rapid institutional change. For Vienna, that change centers around the postwar transformations of the public schedule. These late developments in the organization of the city's time constrained people from returning to a five-meal pattern after the return of economic stability in the 1950s.

THE FIVE-MEAL PATTERN

Retrieving information about meal-taking experiences of the past is quite difficult. Ethnohistorical sources sometimes pay attention to mealtimes but rarely discuss the meal's content or the social arena in which the eating takes place (Pezzl 1923; Gross-Hoffinger 1832). An authoritative cookbook based on historical principles has recently become available (Maier-Bruck 1975). It is particularly informative about traditional menu contents and preparation times. One can occasionally find references to meal-taking in memoirs of Viennese writers and publicists (Barea 1966; Groner 1965; Leitich 1941). In addition to consulting these, I interviewed three people. One, the gas repairman Werner Tuzzi, still eats five meals a day. The other two informants were older, lifelong residents of the city. Dr. Friedrich Leischner was in his early seventies when he spoke with me about the meals in his upper-middle-class household before World War I. Frau Irena Riedl was in her late eighties when she remembered the meals of her working-class Viennese childhood at the turn of the century. Agreement between the accounts, the quality of detail of these memories, and the ability of both informants to contrast their early household memories with meal patterns of the 1920s and 30s, when postwar scarcity and the world economic crisis affected all households, convinced me of the validity of these childhood images.[3] The following is a synthesis of those accounts.

The food complex of Vienna belongs to the European Plains and revolves around such preserved foods as bread, beer, sausage, lard, and cheese (Arensberg 1963, 94). The wealthy metropolis benefits from access to fresh dairy products, fruits, and vegetables, but even today, many of these are highly seasonal. The practice of eating five meals a day probably developed in Vienna during the nineteenth century. Pezzl provides the earliest evidence for the mid-morning Gabelfrühstück, the fork-breakfast, in 1792. He describes people who work in the central district leaving their offices to eat in the *Kaffeehäuser* and *Beiseln* (pubs) around 9:30 A.M. Forty years later, Gross-Hoffinger notes that people of all classes leave work around 3:00 P.M. on some days, especially Thursday, to go drinking in the Beiseln or Heurigen, wine gardens (1833). The meals may have much earlier origins, but by the end of the nineteenth century Viennese from every social class expected to eat five meals a day, even if they could afford only one. For the rich, eating five meals was a way of preserving the older administrative and commercial organization of time while simultaneously demonstrating their autonomy from the more restrictive work schedule of the industrial workers in the suburbs. For the poor, eating a piece of bread at 10:00 A.M. or drinking a beer at 3:00 P.M. provided symbolic participation in the older organization of time and emulation of the autonomy of the rich.

In factories, such breaks were almost impossible to maintain on a regular basis. It was in the schools that most Viennese-born children learned the five-meal pattern. Only the Gabelfrühstück was recognized in the structure of the schoolday. Since school ended around noon, there was no need for the children to eat the Mittagessen or Jause meal. Dr. Leischner remembers this school experience as an uncomfortable one. Encouraged to bring their Gabelfrühstück from home to eat in class, students felt the tyranny of class concretely. One child ate stale bread spread with pork fat, while another ate a fresh roll with sliced ham and butter. It was what one ate, not when one ate it, that constituted the class content of the meal.

Before World War I, the first meal of the day, Frühstück (breakfast), took place within the household. Frau Riedl remembers that in lower-class homes it typically consisted of tea, bread, and lard. The middle class ate jam, cheese, or sliced ham on their bread. In the wealthy families, the English custom of eating eggs was a popular practice, especially soft-boiled eggs eaten directly from their shells with egg spoons. This meal was eaten after getting dressed but before going to work. Only those families with late starting times for work (managers and independent professions) could use Frühstück as a true coordinated meal. Werner Tuzzi, who began work at 7:00 A.M., drank his tea alone.

The Gabelfrühstück took place during working hours (9:30–10:00 A.M.) in the company of workmates. It typically consisted of a hearty soup or sausage and bread, accompanied by beer or coffee. The meal was taken in a Kaffeehaus or Beisel near work. Groups of workmates would sit at tables set for six to eight people or stand at counters eating, drinking, and talking loudly together. Oftentimes workers from nearby worksites would mix together at the same Beisel or Kaffeehaus. For workers who could not leave their shops, the practice was to take a piece of bread to work for the meal. Women at home would ignore the meal, or invite their neighbors, imitating the visiting pattern of the work world. This was a public meal, eaten in the company of non-household members. Werner ate his "real breakfast, coffee and something to eat," at a Kaffeehaus.

Mittagessen, the midday meal, was the major meal of the day. Pezzl shows how the starting time for Mittagessen was a class marker: The earlier the starting time the lower the class. Both Pezzl and Gross-Hoffinger indicate that the meal was eaten in the household. The midday meal lasted for at least an hour. Children were home from school. Most workers could easily walk to their residences. Those workers who could not return home for Mittagessen were forced either to forego the meal entirely, to eat food brought from home in the factory canteen, or to purchase food in a Beisel.

Frau Riedl remembers that soup was common to all midday meals. For lower-class families, the soup was often the only item in the meal. Better-off families would add a second course of potatoes, dumplings, or noodles accompanied by a savory or a sweet dish. The well-to-do were certain to have a meat course after their soup, and a sweet dessert. The famous pastries of Vienna are actually refinements of ceremonial foods from Moravian weddings that the provincial cooks of the Viennese rich served their employers as midday-meal desserts. The lower classes drank water or apple juice with the meal, the middle classes beer, and the upper classes wine. The meal was prepared by the oldest woman and her daughters in most households, or by paid cooks among the wealthy. After the meal, the adults would often take a nap. Werner had a schnitzel at a Beisel and took one and a half hours to eat it.

The origin of the Jause, the afternoon meal eaten at 3:00 P.M., is commonly attributed by contemporary Viennese to the snack eaten by wealthy people after their naps to refresh themselves before returning to work.[4] An alternative explanation is provided by the older guild tradition of ending work around three, with the entire workshop retiring to a nearby Beisel or Heurigen until supper (Kramer 1975, 14). The practice of taking this meal was most prevalent in the nineteenth century. Pezzl does not mention it in his scene of 1792, although he gives detailed descriptions of every other meal. By the turn of the twentieth century, 3:00 P.M. was the busiest time of the day for central district Kaffeehäuser. The meal became most closely associated with Kaffeehaus culture, the wellspring of middle-class activism in the last days of the empire.[5] Dr. Leischner remembers that the meal consisted of a coffee and, perhaps, a pastry. It was eaten in public with acquaintances of long standing, though not necessarily co-workers. The individual Kaffeehäuser became identified with different social networks, and people tended to frequent the same Kaffeehaus for their entire lives. Werner eats a Jause on those days when the work load is not very heavy. He goes to a Beisel instead of a Kaffeehaus and plays cards with his workmates.

Nachtmahl, the evening supper, traditionally consisted of a cold meal eaten at home. Frau Riedl remembers bread with sliced sausage (cold cuts) and cheese, accompanied by pickled vegetables or a mayonnaise salad. Her family drank a thin soup, beer, or apple juice with the meal. It was eaten after dark, rather than immediately upon returning home from work. In fact, it was often the last family activity before retiring for bed. The timing of the meal would vary with the seasons, occurring as early as 6:00 P.M. in winter, or as late as 9:00 P.M. in summer. Werner ate his Nacht-mahl alone when he came home from work, usually around 7:00 P.M.

In terms of preparation time, the household assembled meals on week-days as quickly as possible.[6] Preparation involved slicing bread and mak-ing soup.[7] The after-meal clean-up involved washing the soup pot, a few plates, cups, and knives. The kinds of foods that required longer cooking times were reserved for Sunday (if the household had a free Sunday). Provisioning a household for these evening meals involved buying a fresh loaf of bread every day, a scoop or two of lard, and a sausage to slice. The soup required only a bit of lard and flour to bind the water, and some caraway seed or vegetables for flavor. Noodles or dumplings could be made ahead of time. The shopper bought all of the supper things at the neighborhood vegetable stand or butcher in just a few minutes on the way home after work. Daily shopping for the evening Nachtmahl was the prevailing pattern until the work-time-reduction policies of the 1960s made it inconvenient. Those families in which all the adults worked managed their household meals by eating foods that were easy to buy and quick to prepare. Having a meat dish for Mittagessen, or a complex vegetable dish, like potato goulash, required the cooking services of a nonworking adult. In those households that could afford to hire a cook, the midday meals were masterpieces of Central European cuisine.

In the preindustrial public schedule, the mealtimes provided struc-tured breaks from work throughout the day. In fact, workers were never more than two hours from a meal break. This structure enhanced the workers' feeling of control over the pace of work. They could organize the various tasks according to the length of the work period between breaks. During these breaks, workers could socialize with each other, discussing the work and planning its future course. At midday, the workers returned to their households for a substantial length of time. This midday meal at home with spouse and children enabled working adults to exercise greater supervision over children immediately after school. The break enabled working people to attend to household tasks and responsibilities, as well as eating and socializing. According to both Dr. Leischner and Frau Riedl, this five-meal pattern reached its fullest expression and participation in the period immediately before World War I.

After the war, economic conditions in Vienna were terrible. There was so little food for such a long time that the modest, prewar level of consumption fell. This period coincided with the first Social Democratic government in the city. The legislation and ordinances passed in that political climate consolidated the workday to eight hours at the expense of the mid-morning and mid-afternoon breaks for non-factory workers and employees. The mid-afternoon break disappeared completely. The mid-morning break was reduced to a coffee break taken in the workplace. Before the war, even the poorest classes participated in the five-meal pattern if their workday structure permitted it. In the period between the wars, only the managers and well-to-do could maintain enough control over their work time to eat all five meals. The instability of the economic and political events of this twenty-year period kept people from returning to many of the preferred behavior patterns of the old imperial city. The mealtime conventions were poised for a change. It only remained for the reconstruction of Viennese society following World War II to determine the shape this new pattern would take.

THE THREE-MEAL PATTERN

With the exception of Werner Tuzzi, none of the people I knew in Vienna in the mid-1970s ate five meals a day. The ideal pattern was often identified by my informants as Frühstück, Mittagessen, and Nachtmahl, while the real pattern was actually closer to two meals, Mittagessen and Nachtmahl, or in the case of households without children, only one meal, Nachtmahl. Frühstück was more often a snack than a meal, unless there were school-age children in the household. In that case, Frühstück provided a convenient marker for getting the household dressed and prepared to meet their various work and school schedules. The actual eating behavior of a sample of Austrians, as reported in the 1981 time budget survey, is found in the Appendix.

Many work institutions permit a coffee break, and people continue to bring pastries or sandwiches with them for this meal. It is eaten with co-workers at the work site, and people take turns brewing coffee or tea. While it is technically a meal as I am defining the term here, the short duration

(commonly fifteen minutes) and lack of freedom to leave the worksite reduce its social importance for the Viennese, who refer to it now as a *Pause*,
a mere break of little social consequence, rather than a Mahlzeit.

In contrast to the late eighteenth century, almost everyone breaks for
Mittagessen at the same time, noon. When taken as a meal, Mittagessen is
eaten outside the home with coworkers or acquaintances in Beiseln and
restaurants. If the person has errands to run during the lunch hour, or is
dieting, the meal is often skipped, or taken as a snack. For others it remains
the major meal of the day. The site of the midday meal has changed from
household to Beisel. There are several reasons for this. The first is the
increasing distance between workplace and household. The increase in
commuting time has shortened the period workers have to eat Mittagessen.
The second reason is the reduction since 1970 of paid break time. Since
workers were not being paid for the full extent of their breaks, they min-
imized the unpaid portion. The shorter duration of the lunch break reduced
even further the opportunity to go home for Mittagessen. The third reason
was the increased availability of traditional Viennese Mittagessen menus at
low prices in factory canteens or subsidized cafeterias near the workplace.
For three or four dollars, the worker can enjoy a meal that only very
wealthy people could afford at the turn of the century. In the business
districts the number of restaurants that serve fixed menus on short order to
commercial workers has increased. For people who wish merely to snack,
the ubiquitous *Würstelstände* (sausage stands) provide the means. In
households with both adults working, eating Mittagessen at home is further
constrained by preparation time. When one adult stays home, having lunch
there is possible if the other adult has a short commuting time or is a
professional with independent control over work time. This is rare. Only
those mothers who prepare lunches for their children after school maintain
any remnant of the turn-of-the-century, household lunches.

For working households, Nachtmahl is the only daily meal that the
household can eat together. The Viennese say that one maintains one's
health by eating at least one hot meal a day. For those who ate cold
sandwiches for Mittagessen, Nachtmahl becomes the only opportunity to
fulfill this component of traditional nutrition. When both adults work, the
issue of who prepares the evening meal is only partially answered by
traditional gender roles. When a Viennese man cooks, it is his hobby.
When a woman cooks, it is her responsibility. If men do any household
chore, it is most likely to be meal preparation. Christoph Bettauer made
Frühstück for his wife and daughters. Since Viennese households tend to

be neolocal, with in-laws near enough to help, but far enough away to ensure privacy and independence, the two-income household must rely on its own adult cooks. Although Frau Riedl provided Jause for her great-grandchildren after school and Nachtmahl for her granddaughter and grandson-in-law after work, this was exceptional. A married couple divides the tasks of provisioning, food preparation, and clean-up early in their marriage. The division of chores tends to remain in place throughout the life of the household unless there is a dramatic change in the employment status of the adults.

To have a sense of the choreography involved in timing a household Nachtmahl, consider the following example of a household of two working adults and two children, ages twelve and nine, as typical of families in this particular circumstance.[8] The adults eat a two-course, warm Mittagessen at noon with their respective coworkers, which consists of soup and a plate of meat and vegetables. The children eat a lunch of soup and noodles with sweetened ground poppy seeds at their grandmother's house, where they stay after school until their mother fetches them. At home, they eat a traditional Nachtmahl of sliced sausage, cheese, bread, and fresh vegetables. The division of tasks in mounting this meal might be as follows: On the way home from work, the mother stops at her mother's apartment and picks up the children. Her mother also presents her with a bag of fresh tomatoes she bought that morning. In the meantime, the father has stopped off at the neighborhood *Feinkost* (delicatessen) on his walk from the streetcar to the apartment. Here he buys two different types of fresh sliced sausages and one type of ham in small amounts, 15 to 25 decagrams each (approximately 5 to 8 ounces), and two types of cheese, such as Emmentaler and Butterkäse, usually unsliced. Next door at the greengrocer's shop he buys a cucumber. At the next shop, a bakery, he buys half a rye bread weighing three-quarters of a kilogram (approximately one and a half pounds) and four rolls that he knows the children particularly enjoy. At the dairy store, next-door to the bakery, he buys a liter of milk for the children. The shopping has taken about twenty-five minutes, since the stores were crowded with other men and women buying their families' suppers. He arrives at the apartment only a few minutes after his wife and children. He puts the food in the half-sized refrigerator and changes his clothes.

In the meantime, the wife and children have changed and washed. Everyone assembles in the kitchen and the children discuss their schoolday. The parents discuss a variety of personal and household issues, as well as anything interesting they may have heard at work. After the family has been home for about half an hour, preparations for the meal begin. The youngest child sets the table. The wife puts the kettle on for tea. The father slices bread. The oldest child unwraps the sausage and cheeses and puts them on a large plate. Butter, a variety of mustards, horseradish, and occasionally anchovy paste or herbed cream cheeses are put on the table as well. The wife slices the cucumber and dresses it in vinegar and oil, salt, pepper, and a bit of sugar. The tomatoes are put on the table washed but uncut.

When the water is boiling, the tea is brewed. Then, the family sits down to table. Single slices of bread are buttered and either cheese slices or sausage and mustard are placed on top. The sandwiches are eaten, open-faced, with the hands. Cucumbers are eaten from individual bowls with a fork. Tomatoes are sliced in sixths and eaten with the fingers. The adults drink beer or tea. If all have their typical appetite, the sausage is finished, but enough bread and cheese are left over for Frühstück the next morning. This is one kind of Nachtmahl. The bread and sliced meats or cheese are always present, but there are over a hundred different kinds of sliced meats and cheeses. The particular combination varies from house-hold to household.

The children stack the dishes and clear the table while the adults finish their tea. Washing the dishes is traditionally a woman's responsibility, but not necessarily that of the oldest woman. Whoever unwrapped the sausage and cheese rewraps them after the meal. The condiments are put away. Clean-up time is roughly equal to preparation time. The entire meal last little more than an hour from start to finish. On those occasions when the family eats a warm meal, the preparation time is considerably longer. In recent years, microwave ovens and frozen forms of traditional meals have begun to show up in Viennese homes. These items help to relieve some of the time pressure on many families to produce a hot evening meal.

Public meal-taking has always been popular among the Viennese. The higher number of two- and three-salary households in the city supports the higher cost of public eating as a substitute for household cooking. Single-person households also support neighborhood eateries. In these restau-rants, *Hausmannskost* (home-style cooking), conviviality, and warmth combine to draw people out of their apartments for Nachtmahl.

Under the five-meal pattern, the Viennese ate two meals in public and three meals in private. With the loss of Frühstück, Gabelfrühstück, and Jause, they now eat one public (Mittagessen) and one private meal (Nacht-mahl). Many of the public eating establishments that developed to serve

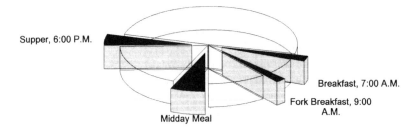

Supper, 6:00 P.M.

Breakfast, 7:00 A.M.

Fork Breakfast, 9:00 A.M.

Midday Meal

1792

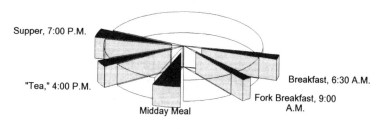

Supper, 7:00 P.M.

"Tea," 4:00 P.M.

Breakfast, 6:30 A.M.

Fork Breakfast, 9:00 A.M.

Midday Meal

1910

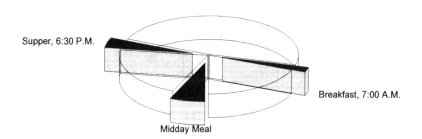

Supper, 6:30 P.M.

Breakfast, 7:00 A.M.

Midday Meal

1976

FIGURE 4: Mealtimes in Vienna, 1792–1976.

the older pattern, like Kaffeehäuser, now only survive in tourist districts. Others, such as Beiseln, expanded their Mittagessen menus. Since even lunch is often only a snack, fast-food establishments that serve individual eaters, including the traditional sausage stands and the new, North American hamburger and chicken franchises, are increasing. As urbanites cease to eat twice a day in groups of coworkers, the size, organization, and menu content of public eateries also changes.

When the constraints of the workweek are lifted on weekends, the older meal-time pattern returns. Children spend Saturday mornings in school. Their homecoming at noon is the opportunity for a coordinated, family Mittagessen. Sunday activities usually involve the whole family and provide another opportunity for a traditional midday meal. The following Nachtmahl is eaten later than it is on weekdays. Eating a Jause is most common on weekends. Without the rush to get to work, adults are more likely to eat Frühstück with their children. Only the Gabelfrühstück, the meal that typifies meal-taking among coworkers, is missing on these work-free days.

The persistence of the older pattern on weekends suggests that temporal patterning is redundantly embedded within urban cultures. Both the old and the new patterns are available. Family weekend activities sustain the opportunity to engage in the older pattern. Each generation nurtures joint family meal-taking on Saturday and Sunday. Although neolocal households have predominated in the postwar period, the weekend provides opportunities for meal-taking with parents and colaterals. These weekend meals imitate the era when joint families shared the same household schedule.

INDUSTRIALIZING MEALTIMES

Edmund Leach has suggested that activities like sleeping and eating act as boundaries between the more important activities of work and play. Commuting might also be added to this list of activities that we pay less attention to, as if somehow they did not count.

Each sees this boundary condition as special, imbuing sleeping and eating with a timeless quality that lends itself to the kind of symbolic production that often culminates in the development of stylized, controlled, and taboo behaviors (1976, 34–36). This explains the elaborate etiquette associated with these boundary activities.

The industrial reorganization of the older meal-time pattern suggests another way of understanding the role of meals in the schedules of urban dwellers. Mealtimes, travel times, and the sleep segment signal wholesale shifts in the orientations of people between the public and domestic orders of urban life. In the older pattern, work and meal-taking alternated between public and private. The individual was brought into contact with three sets of people: the household, the entire set of coworkers, and the narrower set of work-break companions. The alternation provided by the mealtimes juxtaposed the domestic order, the public order, and the particular set of network ties that overlapped and integrated the two, throughout the individual's day. Each grouping met at a different location: in the household, at the work site, or in an eatery. The mealtimes established a temporal structure that sustained the social and spatial separateness of these groups.

The three-meal pattern broke up the regularity in this alternation between the two orders of urban life. The individual still met with the three sets of people, but the opportunity to interact with family and friends was reduced. The industrial organization of time brings work activities to the forefront of the worker's consciousness by depreciating all competing social activities. As people live out their lives within this public schedule, figure and ground are reversed (Zerubavel 1981). It is the opportunity to interact with friends and family that really counts, not work. If social eating can take place only before or after work, the work itself loses additional social value. Reducing the opportunities to interact with others through fewer mealtimes makes the boundaries of the work segment feel even more rigid.

Meals lose their social character and become snacks because powerful institutional actors in the urban field establish the work segment as having a prior claim on an individual's commitments. These institutions easily overpower competing claims. It is primarily through the negotiation of temporal priorities and institutional dependence that the public schedule penetrates and intrudes upon the domestic one. As this short history of mealtimes shows, the process can operate effectively through seemingly irrelevant activities, like the duration of work breaks. As work time became increasingly rigid, social eating lost value. Meal-taking was postponed to a later time, or to the weekend. Social eating was a large part of what workers were asked to trade for a shorter work segment. They did this willingly, but not because meals in industrial cities do not count. Work and play simply count more.

CHAPTER 6

TIMING ACCESS TO MARKETS

Shopping in markets of various kinds is crucial to urban dwellers. Cities use their space to develop specializations other than food production. For the overwhelming majority of people in cities the market becomes the main mechanism for provisioning households. Even when redistribution centers or informal rural-urban supply relationships exist to distribute food, markets for other goods and services continue to fulfill household needs that are met by nonmarket mechanisms in nonurban communities. There are only so many different ways to create a distribution network between producers and consumers. Markets are perhaps the most efficient, though rarely the most equitable, of these distribution networks. Participation in a market requires three things: the availability of the desired goods and services; the availability of some chit, counter, or tender to exchange for the goods or services; and the availability of the market.[1] In other words, for an urban market to perform its function, the shelves must be stocked, the customer must have money, and the store must be open.

It is in this last requirement that merchants and populace interact with the public schedule. The timing of store hours is not often at the whim of the storekeeper. Store hours are coordinated with other public schedules. In the ideal urban marketplace, stores would be open whenever consumers desired to shop. Some cities have actually approached this ideal with twenty-four-hour supermarkets. Generally, shopping hours are more limited. Vienna has a very restrictive shopping schedule for an industrial city. This chapter explores the reasons why this restrictiveness is appropriate to the Viennese organization of time.

Both merchants' decisions and government policy determine the shopping-hour segment in the Viennese public schedule. Merchants open their shops at those times when they expect sales to exceed the costs of operation. Periods of high volume alternate with low periods. Merchants try to close their shops during these low periods. Since predictably low periods coincide with those times when people are working, the setting of shopping hours requires merchants to pay attention to the schedules of their customers.

Governments, too, have an interest in when shops are open. Because markets bring larger than normal aggregations of people together in relatively small areas, they create potential threats to public safety and therefore require greater supervision. Markets increase the level of street traffic and noise. Markets require labor that might otherwise be directed toward other work or household activities. Other urban institutions may see merchants as a threat, and will try to regulate markets as a display of power. Such policy concerns result in the regulation of market operations in the public schedule.

The market, theoretically, can exist anywhere that individuals engage in the exchange of goods and services. Merchants locate their shops in specific places to take advantage of a large supply of customers, a ready access to transportation routes, city services, and concentrations of specialized craftsworkers or laborers.[2] The interplay of these forces over time locates the most specialized, and therefore least frequently used, markets in the fewest places. Those shops that provide the most frequently needed goods and services appear in the greatest number of places. Grocery stores spring up close to residences, while the few stores for stamp and coin collectors are found only in the central business district of a large metropolis. Fewer people need the services of the stamp and coin merchants than need grocery stores.

Between these widely distributed, lowest-order places, like grocery stores and gas stations, and the clustered, narrowly distributed, highest-order places represented by the specialized shops, are a variety of intermediary central places. These intermediate places represent a mix of more specialized shops and generalized shops. In Vienna, as in all urbanized regions, marketplaces are arranged hierarchically, from small, generalized shopping strips in the residential districts, to intermediary shop clusters and shopping centers in district centers, and finally to specialized shops of the central business district. The defining feature of each level in this hierarchy of central places is how frequently large numbers of consumers are likely to need the goods and services provided there.

Merchants who occupy the lower-order places must rely on the shopping schedules of their local customers to a greater extent than merchants in higher-order places. The shops in lower-order locations have only local customers. The higher-order locations have local customers plus customers who travel to the location to take advantage of the more specialized shops. The greengrocers or bakers in a higher-order place have greater flexibility when trying to decide when to open. They can coordinate their store hours with the hours of the more specialized shops. The greengrocer or baker in a small neighborhood cluster can only coordinate the store hours with the schedules of customers from local households.

The tempo of shopping hours in a city represents the interaction of three schedules: the shoppers who, because of commitments to work and household, must shop at specific times; the government, which needs to secure the working conditions of clerks and maintain safety at a reasonable cost, and thus cannot allow markets to operate at every hour of the day and night; and the merchants who, because they must make a living, cannot remain open when their customers are elsewhere and cannot remain closed when their customers are available.

GOVERNMENT REGULATION OF SHOPPING HOURS

Ladenschlussgesetze (store-closing ordinances) are the oldest attempts by the city to create a public schedule. They originally closed markets on ceremonial days, such as the anniversary of the duke's reign or important church holidays. These were specific proclamations limited to a particular day. Guild organization allowed the master to determine holidays and workday duration. The commercial outlets of these guilds, the first shops to hire non-family members, followed the same rules. Government interest in store-hour regulation developed to control the frequent, impromptu farmers' markets that would spring up every morning on the city streets. These clogged traffic and created noise, conflict, and crime. Ordinances to regulate these markets date to the twelfth century (Petermann 1927, 46). As Pezzl describes in his scene of the city, by 1792 farmers' markets could operate only between 6:00 and 9:00 A.M. This freed the streets for morning traffic.[3] According to Pezzl, ordinary retail shops and commercial outlets opened at 9:00 P.M., closed at noon for at least two hours, and ended their business day before six o'clock. This schedule operated seven days a week. Sunday and holiday closings depended on the religious convictions of the shopowner.

Over the course of the nineteenth century, no additional efforts were made to control shop hours. In 1899, about fourteen years after the New Industrial Order attempted to close factories on Sundays and holidays, shop clerks still had no administrative protection from a seven-day work-week. Legislation in that year extended Sunday closing to all retail shops except food stores. This was the first store-closing ordinance enacted by the state to cover retail outlets other than farmers' markets (Ministerium für Soziale Verwaltung 1968, 48). The first protection against long work-days came in 1910 thanks to the agitation of the recently formed Union of Private Employees (Nekula-Benton 1967, 38–46). It required retail stores to close for at least a seven- hour period every twenty-four hours. This limited the length of a clerk's day to a maximum of seventeen hours. When the eight-hour- workday legislation passed in 1919, retail store employees remained outside the act's jurisdiction (Zeisel 1971, 52).

Retail store hours received very little attention in the waves of social-ist legislation after the two world wars. The first effort to limit storekeep-ers' control over the workdays of their clerks came only in 1958. This made retail clerks the last segment of the Viennese work force to enjoy the legislated work- time protection. This federal Ladenschlussgesetz required stores to close between 6:00 P.M. and 7:30 A.M., a total of thirteen and a half hours, or double the closing time required by the 1910 legislation. The ordinance recognized the importance of flexibility for food stores by af-fording them an extra hour in the morning and an extra half-hour in the evening.[4] In addition, the 1958 ordinance required all shops to close for an entire afternoon once a week, to compensate clerks for working Saturdays. The afternoon stipulated in the ordinance was Thursday afternoon, but the Bürgermeister, who is also a *Landeshauptmann* (governor) by virtue of Vienna's double status as city and province, and the *Landeshauptmänner* of the nine federal provinces can shift this to another day of the week if the commercial conditions warrant (Oesterreichischer Gewerkschaftbund 1958).[5]

This law remained in effect in Vienna from March 23, 1959, to November 15, 1965. When it expired, the Bürgermeister exercised his discretionary powers to make several changes. He moved the hour at which stores could open to a half-hour later in the morning (8:00 A.M. for general retail stores, 7:00 A.M. for food shops). He moved the free afternoon from Thursday to Saturday, requiring shops to close at 12:00 P.M. (12:30 for food shops). He created variances for retail operations whose customers needed to shop at odd times, such as stationery and office-supply shops in the business district, flower shops in residential districts, and Würstel-stände. Finally, he defined special closing times for the last workday before Christmas and New Year's Day, to better control the rush of traffic as workers hurried home (Kupka 1971, 94–100).

In contrast, the Landeshauptmann of Lower Austria, the state that encircles Vienna, allowed the ordinance to remain in effect as written until November 11, 1970, when it was finally coordinated with the Viennese schedule. This meant that Lower Austrian shops were closed Thursday afternoon and open Saturday afternoon a full five years longer than in Vienna. The Landeshauptmann provided a variance for all shops serving tourists during vacation periods, allowing them to open an hour earlier and close a half-hour later. He established specific variances that recognized the needs of specialized stores, or of towns with annual festivals or heavy seasonal tourism (Kupka 1971, 62–71). In each case, the Landeshaupt-mann recognized that centralized regulation of schedules destroyed commerce in lower-order or seasonal markets by reducing their flexibility.

The current federal ordinance gives merchants a substantial block of time in which to open or close their shops as they wish. If every moment were utilized, retail shops would be open seventy-five hours per week, and food shops seventy-seven and a half hours. This is just short of two full work shifts and almost half of the total hours in a week. In Vienna, a 1965 city-wide variance imposed a shorter shopping week of fifty-five hours for retail shops and sixty-three and a half hours for food shops. This restrictive variance was ratified by the 1970 ordinance. On the other hand, the Lower Austrian Landeshauptmann took the opportunity offered by the new federal ordinance to give shops in that province even greater latitude. From the last Sunday in March to the last Sunday in September, the shopping week increases to a potential eighty-seven and a half hours for retail stores and ninety hours for food shops. These shifts are summarized in figure 5. Within these limits, merchants are free to decide when they should open or close.

The ordinance closes these shops during the evening and nighttime hours when retail clerks should be free to enjoy the company of their families. If the shopping schedules of other households are squeezed as a result, it is up to those households, not the retail clerks, to adjust their schedules accordingly. Although work-time protection was late in coming for retail clerks, the trade unions and the Social Democratic party have shown exceptional good faith in stubbornly refusing to liberalize any part of this ordinance in the face of mounting public opinion that the shopping hours are too restrictive. This conflict, like those involving work breaks

1910 Ladenschlussgesetz
(based on 1885 Industrial Order, 11-hour day)

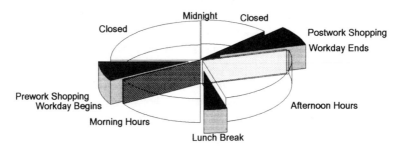

1959 Ladenschlussgesetz
(based on 1948 Federal Work Law, 8-hour day)

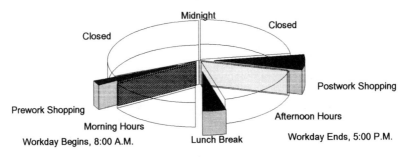

FIGURE 5: Shifts in Shopping Hours, 1910–1970. *Source: Kupka 1972.*

or the six-day schoolweek, caused households to adjust their activities to the demands of the public schedule.

SHOPPING HOURS AS A SOCIAL PROBLEM

On October 30, 1976, long-standing tension between shoppers and the store-closing restrictions broke into public debate. A newspaper article reported on the shopping schedules of the wives of federal and municipal administrators. Most of these women held jobs and admitted that they, like many of the women they knew, had no time to shop. They complained that the store-closing ordinance set unreasonable restrictions on shoppers, forcing them to rush around after work to buy fresh food for their families' suppers. As for general merchandise, the early store closings

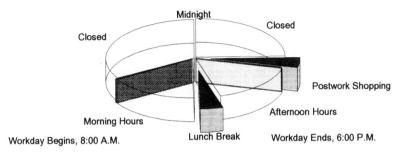

1965 Vienna Variances
(based on 1960 Federal Work Law, 9-hour day)

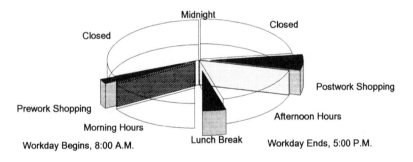

1970 Lower Austrian Variances
(based on 1969 Federal Work Law, 8.5-hour day)

made shopping for shoes or furniture a practical impossibility (Hammerl 1976, 3).

Of the eight people whose work and household schedules were discussed above, Johann Ulrich, Brigitta Hartinger, and Ernst Schönthal did no shopping at all. Christoph Bettauer bought milk for his family before going to work. His wife Johanna bought eggs on her way to pick up her daughter at school at 11:30 A.M. Erwin Walter sometimes shopped on his way home from work, but reserved Friday afternoon for what he terms *grosse Einkäufe*, the big shopping. Maria Tuzzi bought bread before eating breakfast. She did more food shopping later in the morning and clothes shopping in the afternoon. Margareta Koblischek bought bread and milk on her way from gym class in the morning. However she too does her most of her shopping weekly, instead of daily.

These accounts alone do not illustrate the conflict that Hammerl's article revealed. The issue was the subject of daily newspaper accounts, radio call-in shows, and television discussion programs. Public opinion polls showed clear support for a change in the store-closing ordinance to allow an extra half-hour in the evening. The ordinance empowered the Bürgermeister to make such adjustments; the Landeshauptmann of Lower Austria had already done so. Still, the government refused to bend to public pressure, arguing that the restrictive hours were necessary to protect the quality of life of all retail employees, but especially those working in numerous small shops. These were too difficult for the government to monitor effectively. History had shown that small shopkeepers exploited their employees in the absence of strict laws. The problem, as the government saw it, was not in the central district or with the big supermarkets, but rather in the small neighborhood shops employing fewer than five employees, almost all of whom were women. The Bürgermeister's political advisers felt that these employees needed to have their free time protected by leaving the closing times as they were.

The trade unions were militant in their refusal to support more liberal store closings. As Ernst Schönthal in his capacity as an official of the Union of Private Employees revealed in a candid interview:

> Once we start toying with the Ladenschlussgesetz we won't be able to extract ourselves. And others, such as the tourist industry, will begin to pressure for Sunday hours. And so on. . . . We fought very hard over the last hundred years for a forty- hour week for all workers. And all that energy would have been for naught over a small issue like this. . . . We had the same stringent closing hours while we had a forty-eight-hour week.[6] So that means we have actually increased shopping hours through our work-time reductions. There is no real reason to keep the stores open longer.

A large number of the households demanded exactly that. Two-thirds of the Viennese polled by a newspaper favored a liberalization of the shopping hours (Rabl 1976, 3). In spite of this, the city government remained firm. The households adjusted their shopping schedules.

Ernst understandably wondered why the eight hours won by workers between 1960 and 1975 had not made the shopping schedules of households easier. The answer lay in how the workweek was shortened, and not in how many hours had been gained. Workers decided how to structure the new workweek to best resolve their ambivalence toward work. In so doing, they did not consider coordinating the shopping schedule with their work schedule. When the shopping schedule of five and a half thirteen-hour days was established in 1959, people worked six eight-hour days. When it was adjusted in 1965 to five and a half ten-hour days, most people were working five and a half eight-hour days. Also in 1965, the Bürgermeister rotated the shopping segment to a position a half-hour later in the day. This allowed even those workers with long work segments two hours of shopping time after work. But in the 1970s, the shopping schedule remained unaltered even though the workday grew longer. It was the workers' decision to increase the length of the weekend at the expense of the short afternoon that brought more workers into conflict with the shopping schedule. Where had the eight hours gone? They became the two-and-a-half-day weekend. For those who wished to shop daily after work, the weekdays were uncomfortably tight. Shopping on the weekend was far more comfortable.

The readjustment in household schedules from daily shopping to weekly shopping was already under way in the early 1960s. The 1961 time budget survey reports that three-quarters of the employed women and one-fifth of the men interviewed shopped daily. People shopped every day of the week in almost equal proportions. Four-fifths of the respondents shopped at least as often as every other day (Grünwald, Krämer, and Weissel 1961, 39). By 1971, the total number of daily shoppers had dropped to less than a fifth of those surveyed. Shopping was clustered around the weekend: 30% shopped Monday, 8% Tuesday, 14% Wednesday, 4% Thursday, 28% Friday, and 66% Saturday morning. Sixteen percent reported that they shopped once a week, one-fifth shopped twice a week, one-fifth shopped three times a week, and one-third shopped four times a week or more (Mündel et al 1979, 272). Those who shopped three times a week made up four-fifths of the sample ten years earlier. This demonstrates a dramatic shift away from daily shopping and toward weekend shopping. Of the weekend shopping days, shoppers prefer Saturday to Friday or Monday.

The shift to weekend shopping schedules had a deadly impact on the retail market, especially the small food shops in the lower-order locations, with two to five employees. These shops provided a single type of foodstuff, such as meat, fruits and vegetables, dairy products, baked goods, or canned goods. They were located in clusters around the public transportation stops in narrow storefronts on the ground floor of apartment buildings. Customers could disembark from the trams or buses, do their shopping, and walk to the nearby homes. From 1964 to 1974, the number of these small retail food shops declined markedly. In the small inner districts, where the population was older, commercially employed, and declining in size and density, 30% of them went bankrupt in ten years. Ten percent disappeared in 1968 alone. The longer weekend, combined with the declining population, was responsible. In the mid-size districts, with their higher population density and more affluent population, 36% went bankrupt. The residents of these areas were the most responsive to the possibilities of the longer weekend. In the large outlying districts populated by the less affluent Arbeiter and Angestellte residents of the large municipal housing projects, 29% of the small shops were lost. There had been fewer of them at the start (Magistratsabteilung 66 1965; 1970; 1975).

These small shops were replaced by *Supermärkte* and shopping centers. Supermärkte are food shops in which a grocer handling canned goods and vegetables shares the same building space with a butcher, while keeping separate cashiers. Supermärkte originated in Vienna in the 1920s as part of the design of the earliest municipal housing projects. Throughout the 1960s, as smaller shops went bankrupt, Supermärkte moved into the empty storefronts, sometimes combining two or three storefronts to increase their floor area. Shopping centers began to be built in the 1970s. These comprise a number of small specialty shops and several large Supermärkte and department stores, all of which share the same enclosed pedestrian mall and parking facilities. By 1977, there were four such shopping centers in or around the city. The Supermärkte and shopping centers developed as a logical extension of the weekend shopping schedule. Because of their location, their development had a regional as well as a local impact.

Larger market complexes succeeded because they satisfied the scheduling needs of the new weekend shoppers. They were worth traveling to once a week. Having many concessions available in one place, as one shopped for an entire week's worth of provisions, saved time. But all Viennese saw the Supermärkte as an improvement. Werner Tuzzi describes the differences between the old and the new shops as follows:

> The *Greissler* [a small multipurpose food shop] is a place to go when
> you have forgotten something. You cannot do your big shopping there.
> They can't be as cheap as the big stores because they don't have as many
> things, and they don't buy them in quantity to make the price cheaper.

I don't know what will happen to the Kleingeschäfte [small shops]. I
hope they will always be there. They are so much more personal. You
know the butcher and how good his meat is. You know the best baker
in your neighborhood. I like to go to our farmers' market, to this
greengrocer, or that butcher, because I know they have good things. In
a supermarket it isn't so personal. There is only the cashier, and between you and her there is no relationship. She doesn't care if you buy
there or not. It's the same everywhere with these big shops. It's a mass
operation, insanely crowded and confusing. In a small shop, it's completely different. People thank you for coming and hope you'll come
back. They do more for you. In large shops, the only encouragement to
return is the price. In a small shop you are more likely to buy something
because it is beautiful, not because it is cheap.

The lower prices provided by the economies of scale and the loss-
leader specials of the Supermärkte were a strong inducement to shop there,
but cost was not the only consideration in the household's decision of when
and where to shop. Shopping in a Kleingeschäft takes longer than in a
Supermarkt. Although people know exactly what they want to buy in
Kleingeschäfte, they must wait for the clerk to serve them. I have observed
two clerks wait on ten people in twenty minutes. For workers who have
learned to value even twenty-minute breaks, the ten-minute wait feels like
a waste of time.[7] In Supermärkte, because one shops at one's own pace,
the time spent shopping appears to be shorter. However, as soon as there
is a line at the meat counter or a checkout line, discomfort increases. To
shop for a family's traditional cold supper requires waiting in at least three
shops: the butcher or delicatessen, the bakery, and the greengrocer. In a
Supermarkt, all the makings of the meal are in one place. One doesn't have
to carry some purchases while waiting to buy others. In a Kleingeschäft in
1976, shopping for supper for a household of four people averages twenty-
four minutes, and six dollars.[8] In a chain Supermarkt in the same neighborhood, purchasing the same market basket averaged twenty minutes, and
five dollars and seventy-five cents. The savings of four minutes and twenty-
five cents per day is offset by the loss of the social relationships, not to
mention tantalizing smells, sights, and sounds of the Kleingeschäft.

The time between the end of work and the store closings is tight. A
large proportion of daily shoppers are commercially employed women who
end their workdays at approximately the same time. This creates a rush in
the neighborhood shops between 4:30 and 5:30 P.M.[9] The crowds make

waiting in the Kleingeschäfte and in the longer lines in the Supermärkte equally unbearable. The result is a slow, steady shift to weekend shopping and the continued loss of large numbers of Kleingeschäfte.

Both Kleingeschäfte and Supermärkte are open on Saturday morning, but the Supermärkte tend to attract a greater proportion of the sales volume. Supermärkte provide greater savings in time and money. One can gather a week's worth of provisions in the amount it takes to visit three small shops, and enjoy discount pricing. Kleingeschäfte are inappropriate for weekly shopping because the purchases must be carried from place to place. Weekend shoppers can use an automobile to reach the Supermärkte with the lowest advertised prices and carry the groceries home.

The loss of the Kleingeschäfte in the neighborhoods was felt by the local community. These shops had provided an arena for social interaction, a place where one could meet and talk with neighbors. This was particularly important for older, retired people. For them, shopping for lunch and supper were the major social events in an otherwise lonely day. Even the younger working people shopping in the crowded stores after work met old friends and neighbors and passed the time in conversation while waiting their turn for the clerk's attention.

The loss of the Kleingeschäfte did not occur suddenly. As chronicled in the following account from Brigitta Hartinger, residents often watched storekeepers endure years of hardship before finally giving up:

> In the next apartment house there was a small food shop. The owners knew everyone and they would just write down the charges and you could pay every two weeks, or once a month. On Sunday, when all the other shops were closed, you could knock on the door and they would serve you because you were a neighbor. It was just like living in a village. They were Czech speakers who grew up in the district. Most of their customers could still only speak Czech. When the Yugoslav guest workers started to move into the district in the early 1970s, they could somehow understand each other. The shop became very popular with the Yugoslavs. But the owners made very little money. The whole shop was smaller than this room. The couple raised two children with that income, but could never spend a vacation together because they feared if they ever closed the shop for any length of time, their customers would go elsewhere. So they took separate vacations.
>
> When the Supermärkte began to open, people often went there because the prices were cheaper. Only the very poor, who could only pay

at the end of the month, continued to shop there. They had to buy more expensive food. The Supermärkte would only take cash.

Then came the value-added tax.[10] He had never employed a bookkeeper. He always did the books himself. So he began to get into trouble with the tax office. It was really terrible. In the end he had a nervous breakdown and had to go to the hospital. They closed the shop and moved away.

Changing patterns of shopping, changing demographic compositions of the neighborhoods, new regulations in tax reporting, and the tensions of managing a family-owned business are the villains in this story. The shopkeepers could handle any one of the problems by itself, but the combination in a short period of time was fatal to this business. Other small shopkeepers could tell similar tales.

Almost any strategy of timing work reductions other than the one that proved so popular would not have resulted in the shift to weekend buying and the decline of Kleingeschäfte. Instead, households might have added a full hour of potential shopping time daily. This is exactly what consumers were asking the government and trade unions to allow in 1976, but this time at the expense of the nonwork segments of retail clerks.

SHOPPING HOURS AS METROPOLITAN KNOWLEDGE

The conflicts within households between the Ladenschlussgesetz and work-time-reduction policies had different effects in the higher-order and lower-order locations of shops. The lower-order places were more vulnerable to bankruptcy than the higher-order ones. To understand why requires a more detailed look at how location creates variation in the hours of individual shops. Merchants have the option of closing and opening their shops as often as they like within the hours allowed. Shopkeepers set store hours in reaction to the shopping patterns of local households, which in turn plan their shopping activities in reaction to the work patterns of their adult members. As a feature of metropolitan knowledge, shopping hours represent the product of the interaction between shopkeepers and their customers. Unlike the work schedule, the variation in shopping hours arises from local, rather than regional, constraints.

To explore these local constraints, I surveyed the store hours of almost 300 shops in four different locations within the metropolitan region in

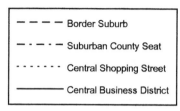

% Stores Open

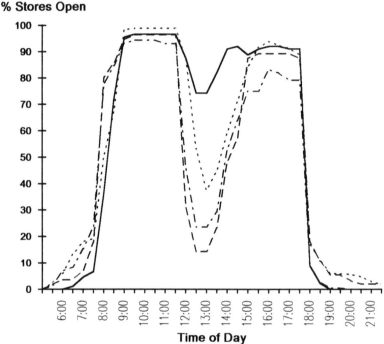

FIGURE 6: Shopping Hours per Week, 1981.

1981.[11] The locations reflect different levels of market complexity and differing characteristics in the schedules of the potential customers. Store hours are posted on the door or window of each shop. I recorded them by walking up the street. The mean average time the stores on the street were open was calculated (figure 6). Analysis then compared the pattern of shop openings and closings on two specific days (see figures 8 and 9).

The four locations include two shopping clusters within Vienna and two in suburban towns south of the city limits in the neighboring county of Mödling, Lower Austria. The following map shows the position of these locations in the metropolitan area. Each cluster represents the largest and most important local marketplace. Each includes shops catering to both frequent and infrequent customer needs.

Favoritenstrasse, a pedestrian mall almost a kilometer in length, is the major shopping district for the populous Tenth District, Favoriten. The cluster includes major department stores, a daily farmers' market (Viktor Adler Markt), banks, Kleingeschäfte, and various service outlets. Favoriten is one of the oldest working-class districts of the city; immigrant laborers from Bohemia and Moravia originally settled there. If it were an independent city, it would be the second largest in Austria. This large population supports a higher-order market along Favoritenstrasse. Many suburban residents also travel to shop on this street because it is near the southern rim of the city.

Across the city from Favoritenstrasse is Josefstädter Strasse. It is the

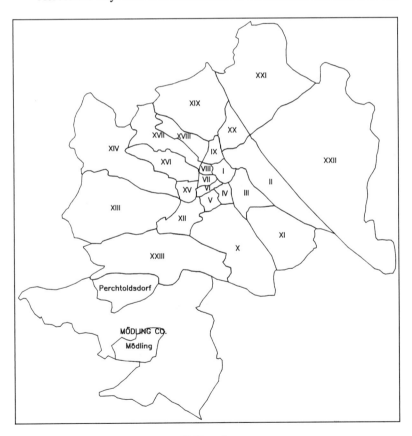

FIGURE 7: Map of Vienna with Mödling County.

main street of a small, centrally located, eighteenth-century district developed under the patronage of Emperor Joseph II, and named in his honor. The street is a major traffic artery with automobile, bus, and tram traffic throughout the day. Kleingeschäfte fill the first floors of late eighteenth- to mid-nineteenth-century apartment buildings. The resident population features a higher proportion of retired people and dependent housewives than is found in Favoriten. The street has many restaurants and Kaffeehäuser, and one of the city's most important theaters. Among the Kleingeschäfte are numerous specialty and luxury-item stores. With their window displays, these hope to attract theatergoers to return during business hours. The street represents a mixture of a residential market and a specialized luxury market.

The two other locations lie outside the political boundaries of Vienna. They were included to test the hypothesis that the difference in the store-closing ordinances between Vienna and Lower Austria would have little effect on the actual duration of the shopping week.[12] A second reason for including these locations is that they are excellent examples of the suburban residential areas that are growing in population every year. The Vienna metropolitan region extends far beyond its political boundaries as people commute from these suburbs to work in the city, and commute from the city to work in the industrial parks in the suburbs.

Mödling is the seat of the county that bears its name. It is a medium-sized town of 18,000 inhabitants. Its shopping cluster is a long main street that ends in a traffic-free, pedestrian zone featuring many Kleingeschäfte. This central business district includes many administrative and governmental service offices that are not found in the other three locations. Numerous service agencies, including insurance, health, real estate, and banking, occupy storefronts alongside food shops and clothing stores. A large industrial park neighbors the town. The central business district includes hardware stores and engineering companies to service the needs of the industrial park. The town is far enough from Vienna to exhibit some independence. It employs its own residents in locally owned shops and banks. Since the early 1970s, the entire area has undergone significant suburbanization. An increasing proportion of its population every year are Viennese who commute to the city on the commuter trains or the Autobahn. In spite of its historic autonomy, Mödling is increasingly drawn into the Viennese public schedule as that schedule integrates more of its resident population.

Perchtoldsdorf is an older, upper-middle-class suburb of Vienna; it is also situated in Mödling county. It is a wine-growing district with several Heurigen that attract visitors throughout the year. Officially classified as a *Marktgemeinde* (market community), it is a town of over 11,000 people. The market center includes three intersecting streets. The shops serve local residential customers. Because of the relative affluence of the suburb, these include several luxury shops that otherwise would rarely be found in such a small market. Perchtoldsdorf borders on the city boundary. Many of its residents shop in the neighboring Viennese district of Liesing and use Mödling for its government services.[13]

During the week, the average number of shopping hours in these four locations ranges from a low of forty-two hours to a high of fifty hours. For the two Viennese locations, the hours represent over four-fifths of the total hours allowed by the ordinance. In the two Lower Austrian locations, the hours represent just under three-fifths.[14] Viennese merchants are approaching their legal limit of open hours, while Mödling county merchants leave a substantial amount of potential hours unused. From store to store, the Lower Austrian clusters exhibit a smaller standard deviation around the mean, while the Viennese marketplaces have a larger standard deviation. The Lower Austrian merchants tend to open and close their shops with little regard for other shops. In Vienna, merchants open and close their shops at the same times.

The emerging picture of merchants' decisions concerning store hours in these four places is consistent with the model of merchant decision-making developed at the beginning of this chapter. Merchants located in lower-order places must rely on the buying patterns of their local populations to such an extent that it costs them to open when local shopping activity is low. Thus, the Perchtoldsdorf and Mödling locations reflect greater variety in the responses of merchants as they cater to the specific shopping schedules of their customers. Merchants located in higher-order places must depend on the shopping patterns of customers who are not local residents. These include those who work in and around the market cluster, visiting customers attracted to more specialized stores, and other shopkeepers. Ground rents in such higher-order places are high, requiring a higher sales volume per day to cover the increased overhead. The result is a lower variation in the number of open hours.

Monday and Saturday are among the two busiest shopping days of the week. Saturday hours include the concentrated four-and-a-half-hour morning shopping segment created when the Landeshauptmänner of both Lower Austria and Vienna decided to use Saturday afternoon to satisfy the required free afternoon of the Ladenschlussgesetz. Figures 8 and 9 graph the percentages of shops open at a given hour in the four locations as revealed by the shopping hour survey.

Starting with Monday, the greatest variation occurs around midday. The *Mittagssperre* (midday closings) occur in all four locations but vary considerably in starting time and duration. The Viennese explain the Mittagssperre as the persistence of an older schedule of public life. They point to the importance of the midday meal and the desire of shopkeepers to emulate the wealthy by closing their shops at lunch and spending those few hours with their families. Heinz Ritter was the first of many informants who suggested that the custom was in imitation of Mediterranean societies, especially Spain, which close their shops in the afternoon to avoid the hot sun. Copying the Spanish style in dress and manners was common in Vienna in the years after the election of the Emperor Charles V (1526) and the ascendence of the Spanish branch of the Habsburg family.

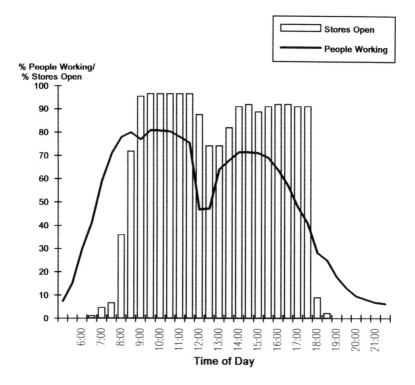

FIGURE 8: Shopping Hours on Monday, 1981.

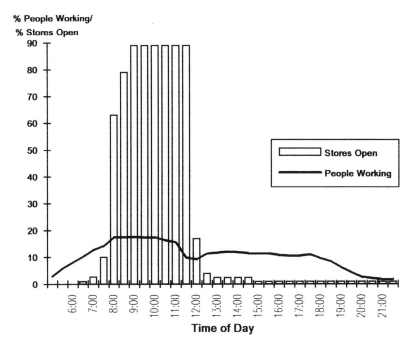

FIGURE 9: Shopping Hours on Saturday, 1981.

While this may account for the practice in Pezzl's time, it does not explain the persistence of the custom. Clearly, the practice of closing one's shop at midday for one or two hours appears archaic in relation to the industrialized workday. One hundred years ago, the first Ladenschlussgesetz mandated that stores close between 11:00 P.M. and 6:00 A.M. That meant that merchants could keep their stores open for seventeen hours. In practice, retail stores opened around 8:00 A.M. and closed around 9:00 P.M. Only food stores opened for the full lawful period. Most of these stores were Kleingeschäfte employing four to seven clerks. The owner of the store was often present throughout the busiest times of the day, which were most likely to be the morning and the evening. The Mittagssperre allowed the merchant to close the shop for three hours in the middle of the day as a practical work break. When the stores reopened at 3:00 P.M. the merchant and the clerks still faced a six-hour work shift before finally closing the store for the night. The reduction of store hours has made this strategy obsolete; still, many Kleingeschäfte hold to the practice of closing for at least part of the old three-hour Mittagssperre.

Most of the shops on Favoritenstrasse have no Mittagssperre. Only one-fifth of the stores close for lunch. On Josefstädter Strasse, half of the stores are closed between noon and twelve-thirty, reopening slowly over a two-hour period. By 3:00 P.M., over 90% of the stores are open. The stores that are most likely to participate in this closing pattern are the food stores, which are closely linked to the shopping schedules of local residents. Eighty percent of the stores of Mödling and Perchtoldsdorf have Mittagssperre of varying durations. Merchants appear to set their schedules independently from their neighbors.

On Saturday, stores on Favoritenstrasse open quickly between 7:30 A.M. to 9:00 A.M. Eighty-eight percent are still open at noon, but by 12:30, 98% are closed. The 2% that stay open through the afternoon are flower shops and Kaffeehäuser, both exempt from the Saturday afternoon Ladenschluss. The Josefstädter Strasse shops open slowly on Saturday, reaching 84% at 10:00 A.M. This is lower than the 98% open at 10:00 A.M. Monday. Some merchants do not bother to open on Saturday at all. The merchants in the Lower Austrian towns differ as to when the shops should open Saturday. In Mödling, the shopkeepers take advantage of the increased number of potential customers by opening early. Here, too, fewer stores are open on Saturday than on Monday. The 75% of the shops that open in Perchtoldsdorf on Saturday open later than in Mödling, and almost immediately begin to close again. After 12:00 P.M., Perchtoldsdorf has the greatest number of shops open of any of the locations. This reflects Perchtoldsdorf's special status as a Heurigen village, a position that carries with it automatic variances in the Ladenschluss. It is traditional for Heurigen visitors to bring food to the wine gardens. Shops that sell take-out food must be available locally to serve these needs on weekends and evenings. They represent 9% of the shops in the market.

The larger the pool of residents available to shop during the day, the greater the potential sales volume. A large potential volume puts greater pressure on merchants to increase store hours. Available shoppers include household members who do not work, or who work near the market. In Perchtoldsdorf and Favoritenstrasse, a large number of the residents commute to work elsewhere (figure 10). The shopkeepers lose this portion of the potential pool of shoppers during the day. Of people employed in service occupations, five times the number arrive to work on Josefstädter Strasse each weekday than leave residences on the street for jobs elsewhere. The influx of population represents a higher potential buying volume during the week than is available on weekends. Mödling has a very

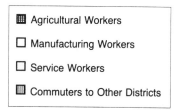

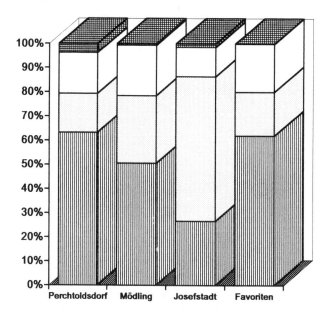

FIGURE 10: Commuting Patterns and Noncommuting Work Force in Four Locations in 1981. *Source: Österreichisches Statistisches Zentralamt 1972.*

small net difference in the shopping pool during the week. The number of potential shoppers also remains at the same level during the day as it does before and after work. These are the kinds of local conditions that produce different store hours.

HOPPING HOURS AND INTRAREGIONAL COMPETITION

The power of some markets to draw customers away from neighboring markets of similar complexity also can influence decisions about store hours. This is the kind of competition that takes place within large metropolitan regions, that is, between the central city and its suburban communities. The distribution of shoppers in a region develops as the shoppers decide when and where to shop based on their needs and on the availability of stores. If a location tries to ensure a consistent pool of customers for itself by changing the rules, it prevents other locations from making enough money to survive. When this strategy is successful, substantial portions of a region are left poorly serviced and market-starved. This uneven development produces the top-heavy urban system (Smith 1976, 261), which exhibits uneven concentrations of productive growth, capital, and market diversity. These top-heavy urban systems draw more than their share of producers and suppliers because they inhibit potentially competing centers from forming (Smith 1976, 30). This happens when a variety of administrative, and sometimes even military, operations aim to minimize competition and centralize economic power in the central city. Smith has argued, *contra* Berry (1971), that uneven regional development is not a stage in the economic maturation that disappears as market centers develop to fill in positions between the metropolis and the village. She sees uneven development as the product of the political administration of a regional economy. Competitive forces that would otherwise result in a more orderly, stepwise hierarchy of markets, are thwarted by political intervention. The top-heavy system disappears only when its central city is no longer powerful enough to defeat the regional competition (Smith 1976, 32).

Vienna is a central city with a powerful concentration of wholesale and retail markets. The large towns surrounding it are in competition with the city to wrestle sales volume from it. Vienna keeps its monopoly by resisting its neighbors' efforts to gain a favorable market position. The political manipulation of shopping hours is a tactic in this competition. The following case illustrates both the nature of the threats and the political force Vienna has applied to meet them.

On September 22, 1976, Lower Austria opened its first shopping mall, Shopping City Süd, in the village of Vösendorf, five kilometers from the southern boundary of the city, just south of the district of Favoriten. The planners of this cluster wanted to make it the most important market in Mödling county and southern Vienna. It was located within easy reach of eight Viennese municipal districts and the Lower Austria counties of Mödling and Schwechat. Its potential customer pool was in the millions. The projected sales volume permitted record levels of discounting. The site was near an electric rail line that originated in the center of Vienna. An

Autobahn ran nearby. However, no direct exit to the shopping center was built until 1989, exactly because the city of Vienna did not want to make shopping there too easy. To use the Autobahn to reach the shopping center before the exit was built one literally had to drive in circles. In addition to Favoritenstrasse, there are large district marketplaces in nearby Meidling, Liesing, and Simmering. Nor was Vösendorf considered out of the way for more distant Viennese residents. The factory where Johann Ulrich and Erwin Walter worked was located in an industrial park a few kilometers south of Shopping City Süd. Over 50% of the industrial workers in Mödling county commute from Vienna every day and would drive past the mall (Nieuwalt 1957, 254; Indrak 1978, 8).

Although shopping centers were not new to the metropolitan region, the size of this mall was extraordinary. The enclosed mall would connect a Supermarkt, a major department store, two major furniture stores, eight restaurants, representatives of almost every major Austrian shoe, clothing and textile manufacturer, and fifteen specialty shops. The majority of leaseholders were merchants who already had established outlets in Vienna itself. The use of the English name Shopping City connoted an American scale and efficiency. The existing shopping malls at the time were all on the north side of the city. The central business district's pedestrian malls, such as Favoritenstrasse or Kärntner Strasse, were just opening as Shopping City Süd was in its construction phase. This was the first shopping center built in Lower Austria that was close enough to Vienna to compete directly for Viennese shoppers.

Since Shopping City Süd was in Lower Austria, its planners tried to manipulate the political boundary to their advantage. They requested a Ladenschluss variance from the Lower Austrian Landeshauptmann to use Thursday as the stipulated free afternoon for Vösendorf. This would allow the mall to remain open for the entire day Saturday. The change from Thursday to Saturday afternoon closings in Lower Austria had occurred only six years earlier, in 1970. This earlier change brought Lower Austrian shops into the same weekly schedule as that of the Viennese shops, and afforded Lower Austrian retail workers a longer weekend. In requesting the variance, the Shopping City Süd planners intended to add five more hours of shopping time to the busiest shopping day of the week, while the mall's nearest Viennese competitors were closed. Intrigued by the revenues this added sales volume would bring his state, the Landeshauptmann gave tentative approval to the variance, with the final approval scheduled to come just before the complex was to open. As a member of the People's

Party, he also saw the possibility of embarrassing the Viennese Social Democrats. For employing this tactic, the Austrian minister of commerce, a Social Democrat, dubbed Shopping City Süd "The Shark" (Rauscher 1976, 3).

The tentative approval of the variance by the Lower Austrian Landeshauptmann mobilized Viennese merchants. Both the municipal and federal chambers of commerce stated their disapproval. The Union of Private Employees saw the move as another effort to erode the progress of shopclerks. All three groups recognized the loss of jobs and profit in those extra five hours. The Ministry of Commerce computed that the variance would mean a loss of 176 million dollars (in 1976 schillings) in the first year alone (Leitner 1976, 3). With the chamber of commerce applying pressure to its members who had invested in the project, and the union applying pressure on the Lower Austrian Landeshauptmann through its representatives in the Paritätische Kommission, including the threat to take the decision out of his hands with a new federal Ladenschlussgesetz, the request for the Vösendorf variance was ultimately rejected. The complex opened with the same shopping hours as its Viennese competition and was still successful. Without the competitive edge the extra hours would have afforded the complex, the foreign investors sold their shares to Austrians at the earliest opportunity. This tied the future policies of the complex even more closely to the Viennese public schedule.

This case shows how the Viennese organization of time is dictated to the larger metropolitan region through the political process. The strength of this public schedule lies not in its support from politicians but in its support from merchants. Even those who had invested money in Shopping City Süd saw the threat to their long-term market position behind the short-term gains of the shopping complex. The variance was rejected when these merchants began to withdraw their support for it. Having become successful in a market where shopkeepers paid attention to coordinating their hours with others to share the same pool of customers, they were not ready to compete against themselves and their Viennese outlets by suddenly changing the rules.

Merchants behave toward the Ladenschluss as workers behave toward the standard workweek. The stipulated boundaries become rigidly defined activity segments. Merchants keep a high degree of uniformity in their shopping hours in spite of changes in the shopping behavior of customers. Predictable busy periods in the late afternoon and weekends are preferable to no predictability at all. A clearly defined shopping segment solves a particularly thorny problem for merchants. It creates the same hours for everyone, regardless of the size of their payroll or the number of their outlets. Because no one can predict what the outcome of unrestrained competition in shopping hours would be, all merchants, the powerful and the powerless alike, cling to the fixity of the Ladenschlussgesetz. From the merchant's point of view, eliminating the Ladenschlussgesetz and its uniform restrictions would be an invitation to disaster. The shopping-hour segment thus transcends local constraints and becomes a domain of metropolitan knowledge.

In 1988, ordinances that required different kinds of stores to close at different times were declared unconstitutional. In their place, Parliament passed new laws that required all stores to close at 6:30 P.M. Stores may choose to remain open until 8:00 P.M. one night per week, or until 6:00 P.M. one Saturday afternoon per month. Clearly, the relief provided by the new law does not substantially change the constraint on shopping times. It merely provides an additional periodic alternation for shopkeepers and patrons. An informal survey of the cashiers at the supermarket where I shopped in 1988 indicated that very few people were taking advantage of the longer shopping hours once a week. Another informal conversation with these cashiers eighteen months later revealed that the trend had held and that not enough people were taking advantage of the extra hours to pay the overhead. I did not systematically test these observations across the city, but I was not surprised by the cashiers' observations. In the decade between my initial interviews and the changing of the laws, people had adjusted their behavior. They had found times to shop that were appropriate to their altered household organization of time. There was no longer any reason for the laws to change.

CHAPTER 7

TIMING PLAY

The industrialization of time is a process of defining segments of time as separate, specialized periods of activity. Previous chapters have illustrated this process with work, meal-taking, and shopping. In the case of work and shopping, institutional prerogative constrained individual choice. There remains one domain of activities in which the public schedule performs a different role: play.

In his meditation on human play, Huizinga gives the most comprehensive description of it. Play can be an element in almost every other activity, including work. Like all other human actions, play involves the manipulation of images in the mind and the acting out of these images in behavior. What sets play apart from other domains of action is that these playful images are voluntary, superfluous, and disinterested. Play is voluntary in the sense that one must be a willing participant throughout the activity. As soon as it is forced, the activity ceases to be play. Play is superfluous because play activities can be postponed indefinitely and need not occur at all. When they do occur, they are highly satisfying. Play activities are disinterested because they serve no other function than to fulfill their objectives. Play cannot be manufactured and sold, although the opportunity to play can be marketed. Above all, play is one domain of activity over which individuals exercise complete control. Play is the antithesis of industrial work.

Play activities are more self-contained than other kinds of actions. Huizinga notes that play usually creates its own boundaries in time and space, suspending those boundaries that may have existed before play begins. When play begins and ends, and how often the activities are repeated, are intrinsic parts of the meaning of play. For example, the four-year period of the Olympics, the best of three or five sets in a tennis match, or the number of betting opportunities in a poker hand are different kinds of tempi inherent to the play itself. Play occurs in specially defined spaces, such as a playground, a living room, or a stadium, and is governed by rules that limit the range of behaviors. These rules create an order within the limits of the play activities but need not bear any relation to the ordinary social order. Indeed, play activities often invert, negate, and otherwise treat the rules of social life as the object of play. They create an extraordinary social order that is less tolerant of deviance than society as a whole. Winning by the rules is a great part of the delight realized from play. The rules inevitably provide an important role for chance to determine the outcome of the play. The triumph comes from overcoming these obstacles imposed by chance (Huizinga 1950, 4–13).

Play is separate from other kinds of activities because it juxtaposes the certainty of order with the ambiguity of chance. Yet players are never completely isolated from the ordinary social order. Habermas, among others, sees the organization of work in a society as consistently mirrored in the organization of play in three ways.[1] First, play has physically restorative qualities that go beyond sleep and meal-taking. The restoration of physical strength also depends on adequate relaxation and exercise. If workers were in more complete control over the pace of their work tasks, restorative play would take place immediately after exertion. Under industrial schedules, restorative play must be postponed until the work segment is finished.

Second, play suspends the control exerted over the tools and skills used during work by managers and the owners of enterprises, enabling these to be used in such self-directed pursuits as "do-it-yourself" projects, busman's holidays, gardening, and home and automobile maintenance. The industrial organization of work channels workers into participation in a process of production but provides no immediate stake in the products themselves. The social value of work is reduced to wages. Suspenditory play occurs because individuals seek recognition and prestige for their skills, which are more readily acknowledged in play than in work.

Finally, Habermas sees a compensatory function of play. In compensatory play, people acquire skills, and seek recognition, in areas unconnected to their work activities. Specialized markets afford individuals the opportunity to display what they can do. Those opportunities may range in complexity from the ticket to the sporting event in which one might test one's knowledge of the players' abilities and game strategy, to the Kaffeehaus with its international collection of newspapers in which knowledge of a second language is displayed to peer into a different society. At higher levels of skill, the player rejects ready-made play opportunities in favor of self-directed ones. For example, one learns to play a musical instrument or tennis, even though professional music and tennis are available through public telecommunications media. Even among those who are content to listen to the radio, compensatory play affords them the opportunity to know musical groups, the history of a particular musical style, and gossip about the lives of musicians. Compensatory play makes up for the diminished role of reflections of self-worth on the job in the same way that suspenditory play fulfills the lack of social acknowledgement of skill and restorative play provides balance for the lack of control over the pace of work.

Habermas constructs his typology dialectically by imbuing play activities with images of control that work activities deny. All Viennese play, but only two-fifths work. Habermas's formulation, though insightful, is not sufficient to account for all the patterns of Viennese play. There are restorative, suspensitory, and compensatory activities that appeal to all urban residents regardless of their employment status. Thus, work may account for the proportions of the different functions in the choice of play activity, but not the form of those activities. The form of play, unlike the form of work, is the product of metropolitan knowledge.

Like English speakers, the Viennese use the word *spielen* (to play) most often when referring to children's activities. The voluntary, disinterested, and superfluous activities of adults are *Freizeitgestaltung* (free-time activities). These are divided into two categories: *Erholungen* (recreations)[2] and *Vergnügungen* (entertainments or amusements). The primary distinction is one of control over the timing of the activity. With Erholungen, the participants determine scheduling and duration of the activities. Vergnügungen are scheduled by others, such as sports organizers or nightclub operators. The duration of the activity is in the control of the organizer, not the participants or spectators. To participate in an amusement means to participate in another segment of the public schedule. With recreation, the self-determination of the household reasserts itself.

Since the 1970s, the historical drift in Viennese play has been toward greater involvement in Vergnügungen. In another scene, entitled *The Seasons*, Pezzl observes that only church services and theatrical performances were scheduled. The overwhelming number of play activities he observed were self-directed recreations. The recreations changed seasonally, with each season having its distinctive social event and appropriate food. In the spring the favorite recreation was strolling along the ramparts of the city between 11:00 A.M. and 1:00 P.M. and eating sweet herb soup for breakfast. In summer the wealthy Bürgers held private garden parties in the suburbs, complete with fireworks. Fresh fruit, crabs from Hungary, ice cream, and wild mushrooms were the appropriate foods. In autumn the nobility returned to the city from their estates, rekindling the round of social events and the spectacle of the baroque parade that held the interest of the common people so completely. The preferred foods were game animals and fresh wines from the nearby villages. In winter the play activities centered on *Fasching*, the ball season that commenced on New Year's Day and ended on Ash Wednesday. There were many other ways of overcoming the boredom of winter, including parties, picnics, games, concerts, and sleigh rides. The favorite foods to serve guests were frozen saltwater fish, pheasants, and oysters (1923, 217–20).

Pezzl also provides a scene of "weekend" life in preindustrial Vienna. In 1792, Sunday was the only nonwork day in the week. Only members of guilds or employees of highly religious or enlightened masters could take advantage of it. Relatives and friends came together in the afternoon for a stroll in the parks or the suburbs. The parks contained *Lusthäuser*, playhouses that served food and drink. People could sit at tables in a garden, playing cards or listening to music. In the suburbs, families hiked through the nearby forests, stopping at a Heurigen on the way home to share a picnic and drink the vintner's wine. At sunset, they returned to the city (220–23).

In the 1820s, during the transition to industrialism, the pattern of play had changed very little in the intervening thirty years. The seasonal recreations of balls and trips to parks or suburban garden parties, and the year-round visiting in private homes remained popular. These visits would involve only relatives and close friends. A social evening consisted of dinner followed by card playing and conversation. Children often accompanied adults to these parties and would play among themselves. Gross-Hoffinger describes people swimming in the Danube, fireworks on clear June evenings, the continuous parade of carriages and beautifully dressed people moving back and forth along the Grand Allee in the Prater, folk festivals that could draw half the population to the Prater on the first of May or to the week-long Brigittenauerfest (Gross-Hoffinger 1832, 124–35).

Beginning in the later nineteenth century, the kinds of amusements available to the city dweller, especially the theaters, began to increase. The more central the theater the more prestigious, and the more expensive the ticket. While the central theaters played Shakespeare and German tragic drama, the outlying ones played the satires of Raimund and farces of Nestroy. Confined to one performance each evening, the theater performances became the model for scheduling all limited-engagement amusements in the future.

Currently, there are two sets of schedules for entertainments. The first is the medieval calendar of saint's days and feasts commemorating important events in the Bible. The most important feature of this schedule is the offering of public mass in the churches. Whether people attend these services or not, the ritual schedule continues to structure the governmental and economic institutions of the city. Sunday mornings are free of competing public activities. The public calendar incorporated the Christian feast days in the ritual calendar as well. The Christmas and Easter holidays are the most important of these, but additional feasts are celebrated around Christmas and throughout the late spring. Because they tend to cluster in specific seasons, these have a great impact on the cycles of play activities throughout the year.

The second influence on the entertainment calendar is the administrative schedule. It regulates people's movements during the day, political holidays, special markets, festivals and fairs, and the activities of the national theaters, museums, and libraries. One administrative feature that has survived since Pezzl's day is the apartment house lock law. All apartment houses in the city must have their front doors locked at 9:00 P.M. Guests must arrive before nine and leave as a group to spare the hosts having to run repeatedly up and down the stairs to unlock and relock the front door.

Timetables for mounting exhibitions and planning subscription concerts govern the schedule of the federally owned theaters, libraries, and museums. Concert and performance schedules are announced only a month ahead, even though new performances and exhibitions are planned years in advance. Large placards glued to the hundreds of kiosks that dot the street corners, especially in the Innere Stadt, announce the schedule for the year each autumn. The rigidity of this schedule, the enormous sums spent to maintain these institutions, and their central, Innere Stadt location have contributed to growing resentment by many, especially younger, Viennese toward these amusements. A popular protest, known as the Arena Occupation, occurred in 1976. The hundreds of young people who took part declared in their manifesto that the "culture palaces" of the Innere Stadt were too far away from people's residences, too expensive, and scheduled for days and times that made it impossible for ordinary wage earners to attend. They resented the huge portion of the federal budget for support of the arts that these institutions absorbed and demanded the establishment of cultural centers in the districts where ordinary people lived, so that they too could enjoy excellent theater and musical performances. Although the protest ultimately resulted in very little substantive change, it revealed the constraints that centrally administered amusement schedules create for households in large metropolitan regions.

The scheduling of arts festivals, special markets, and trade expositions is also centrally administered. The Wiener Festwochen, an annual festival of the arts, film, and theater, takes place in June. Trade fairs and expositions are mounted at the *Messegelände*, fair grounds in the Prater, and at the *Messepalast,* near the Ringstrasse. The Vienna Fair, held in mid-March at the Messegelände, emphasizes Austrian industrial and agricultural products. A second fair comes in the fall. It is reminiscent of a state fair of the midwestern United States. Special markets are held on the name days of patron saints in those districts and suburbs that still retain aspects of their preindustrial schedules. In Vienna itself, a special market is held throughout Advent. Called *Christkindlmarkt*, it offers Christmas-tree decorations, traditional presents, and items for celebrating New Year's Day. Composed of temporary kiosks assembled in the small park in front of the city hall on the Ringstrasse, the Christkindlmarkt is extremely popular with adults and children. The smells of the roasted chestnuts and cotton candy evoke strong memories of childhood Christmas celebrations that attract people to the market throughout their entire lives. Those are some of the play activities observed by Pezzl and Gross-Hoffinger that can still be found in the city, even if they are now augmented by automobiles, public address systems, and outside lighting.

THE STRUCTURE OF THE YEAR

We usually think of agricultural societies as preoccupied with seasonal cycles of economic and social activities. Industrial cities have a yearly cycle of activities, too. Periods of intensified production, with greater opportunities for overtime, alternate with periods of lower intensity. During these low periods, residents tend to take time off from work for vacations and holidays. This seasonal cycle produces opportunities for play that don't fit within the free periods of the ordinary weekly schedule. The three- and four-day weekends generated by the public holiday calendar and the guaranteed vacation time stipulated by the federal work laws break up the pattern of alternating workdays and weekends into extended work-free periods at various times of the year.

The production cycle of Vienna's industrial manufacturing is not constant. Two periods of intensification of four and six months each are followed by two month-long lulls. The first busy period runs from February to June; July and August are a time of low productivity. The second period extends from September to December, followed by another lull in January.

The slow times favor vacation-taking. Viennese workers receive increasing amounts of paid vacation time depending on the number of years of service to the same employer. The first law to deal with paid vacation time (1946) guaranteed a minimum of twelve days a year, rising to eighteen after five years and to a maximum of twenty-four days after fifteen years. In 1964, the minimum increased to eighteen days, rising to twenty-four days after ten years and thirty days after twenty-five years (Zeisel 1971, 78–81). In 1972, the minimum vacation time rose to twenty days; in 1986, to twenty-five days. In addition to vacation time, all workers get two months' additional salary, or two months' average wages if paid hourly. The first of the extra month's wages are paid at the time the worker takes a summer vacation. The second arrive before Christmas. While much of the Christmas pay goes to buying presents, in many households enough remains for a small vacation.

Austrians enjoy more paid public holidays than any other European work force except the Spanish and Italians. The thirteen holidays in the calendar include two national holidays: *Nationalfeiertag* on October 26, which commemorates the return of state sovereignty in 1955, and *Staatsfeiertag*, also known as *Tag der Arbeit*, on May 1. This was originally a folk festival celebrating the beginning of spring (Gross-Hoffinger 1832, 129). In 1890 Viktor Adler took advantage of the large crowds to lead the first march in support of trade-union solidarity. The march was a peaceful one, in spite of fears to the contrary, and the tradition of public demonstrations and marches remains a part of the international workers' movement to this day (Rotenberg 1984). But politics have not appropriated every folk festival. Other fests include *Fasching* (Mardi Gras) with its masked balls, and the celebration of the *Heilige Drei Könige* (Three Kings) on January 3 when chimney sweeps go door to door collecting tips to bring good luck in the coming year. The latter is one of eleven feast days carried over from the medieval Roman Catholic calendar. The Austrian state has observed these ceremonial days continuously since 1590 (Wolff et al 1969, 13). The holiday calendar shuts down factories and stores in another state effort to control work time. The current holiday calendar has been in effect since 1967 (Haubeneder 1971, 63), and workers are guaranteed a fourteenth day for a religious observance of their choice.

Some of these ritual feasts, like Christmas, are immovable; each year they fall on the same day of the month but a different day of the week. Others, like Easter, are moveable feasts, which fall on the same day of the week, but a different day of the month. The following table shows the distribution of the twelve paid, ceremonial holidays.[3] Three holidays occur on Sunday: Easter, Whitsuntide, and the Ascension of Mary. Holidays tend to cluster at the end of the two periods of industrial intensity, late spring and early winter. The Viennese celebrate the name day of Saint Leopold, the patron saint of Vienna, as a city holiday on November 15. Other provinces may have other holidays particular to them.

TABLE 1

PUBLIC HOLIDAYS

January 1	Neujahr (New Year's Day)
January 6	Heilige Drei Könige (Epiphany)
April *	Ostermontag (Monday following Easter)
May 1	Staatsfeiertag (International Labor Day)
May*	Christi Himmelfahrt (Ascension)
June*	Pfingstmontag (Pentecost Monday)
June*	Fronleichnam (Corpus Christi Thursday)
August 15	Maria Himmelfahrt (Ascension of Mary)
October 26	Nationalfeiertag (National Holiday)
November 1	Allerheiligen (All Saints' Day)
November 15	St. Leopoldstag (Saint Leopold's Day)
December 8	Maria Empfängnis (Advent)
December 25	Weihnachten (Christmas)
December 26	Stephanitag (Saint Stephan's Day)

Note: An asterisk indicates a moveable feast.

The late spring group begins with Easter Sunday and Easter Monday. Because of the possibility for at least a three-day weekend, many residents leave the city and go to their weekend cottages or to the Mediterranean to enjoy the first bloom of spring. Ascension and Corpus Christi occur one month apart on Thursdays in May and June, providing two four-day weekends. In-between these feasts is Pentecost, a Monday holiday and a three-day weekend. Schools let out on the last Friday of June. Throughout the summer, the Viennese take longer vacations until the beginning of school on the first Monday in September. The month of August is so popular for vacations that the city appears deserted of traffic during the day.

The early winter group begins at Advent and continues through Epiphany. December 8, 24 (half-day), 25, 26, 31 (half-day), January 1 and 6 are fixed calendar dates that often occur on workdays. It is possible to take an extra paid vacation day the Friday or Monday intervening between the holiday and the weekend if the holiday happens to fall on Thursday or Tuesday. It is too expensive in many manufacturing concerns to start up production for a single isolated day. When the factory does remain open, workers can use one of their twenty-one minimum vacation days, creating a four-day weekend out of a Tuesday or Thursday holiday. Schools let out from December 24 to January 7. Many people take winter vacations during this time.

Adding all these work-free days during the year yields surprising results. A Viennese worker with eighteen vacation days in a year with an average number of extra days off during the Christmas week and during the spring holiday season works only 120 days a year. This is the most impressive effect of the work-time-reduction policies of the Social Democratic program. In 1959, when more people worked Saturdays, workers needed two vacation days to link a Thursday to a weekend. Now they need only one. For the workers who moved from a six-day to a five-day workweek, the result was a net loss of sixty-four workdays per person per year between 1960 and 1971. In effect, a sixth of the year was returned to workers as Freizeit.

The yearly cycle includes the same alternation between work and play found in the weekly cycle. The year is essentially divided into two halves with a period of vacation-taking at each end. The marker for this division is the Catholic calendar; however, any relationship between the contemporary Viennese experience of this calendar and that of the medieval Church on which it is based is purely coincidental. As Habermas notes (1958, 712), "The cessation of work, which in certain peasant or handicraft societies was organized through the natural rhythm of the year and the corresponding traditional festivals, comes under the pattern of the mechanical partitioning of work time. Where these natural rhythms continue to exist, the unity between work and play falls apart." The clusters of winter and spring holidays signal the beginning of the play season, but do not determine its duration, its activity content, or its meaning in the lives of the Viennese. The yearly cycle, like the weekly cycle, creates homogeneous work and nonwork segments and separates them in time in a reliable and predictable fashion.

THE ENTERTAINMENT INDUSTRY

The Viennese use the term *Kultur* to refer to scheduled play opportunities involving *Unterhaltungen*, the offerings of the "entertainment industry." Entertainments were all but nonexistent before the industrialization of urban life. This industry now includes the interdependent production, distribution, and marketing organizations designed to make programs available to Viennese consumers at appropriate and accessible times. In this sense, Vergnügung and Unterhaltung are closely related. Vergnügung refers to the pleasure-taking goal of the activity, while Unterhaltung refers to the scheduled, often elaborate setting in which the amusement takes place. Some Unterhaltungen depend on the technical innovations that industry made possible, such as radio and television. Others, such as organized sports, developed as a consequence of the changes in social organization brought about by industrialization.[4] Still others, such as cabarets, Kaffeehäusern, restaurants, music halls, theaters, and later, cinemas, developed from older forms that already existed. Over the last 200 years, these increased in number and diffused from the Innere Stadt to the suburbs.

Entertainments in Vienna run on an evening schedule. This avoids conflicts with the established work segment. It also requires people to participate after the work segment has ended. Attending entertainments during the work segment is deviant. A group of workers gathered around a television set to watch a ski competition during the workday may be tolerated, but leaving work to attend that competition is sanctioned with lost wages and even suspension. Among cinemas, only those Innere Stadt locations showing erotic films schedule afternoon screenings. Altogether, the Viennese spend over three hours a week on entertainments. Four activities in particular account for almost all of this time: radio, television, cinema, and sports.

Radio is the most accessible of entertainments. People listen to it most often at home, with smaller audiences listening on car radios and at work. Half the audience listens on weekdays and slightly less than half listen every day of the week. People often listen alone, but group listening, especially by young people, is also common. The duration of radio listening is highly variable. Selected portions of listeners listen only at specific times or to specific programs, while others play the radio constantly. Radio listening frees the hands and eyes, making it an entertainment that can be enjoyed simultaneously with housework, driving, or work activities (Mündel et al 1979, 272, 311).

The Austrian radio service dates to the 1930s. There are currently four broadcast channels in the state radio and television monopoly, the Österreichischer Rundfunk (ORF). Three of these were first introduced in 1967. The so-called first channel, Österreich 1, features classical music, current-events discussions, hourly news and weather summaries, detailed news magazines, and religious programming. It attracts about 10% of the audience. The second channel, Österreich Regional, is the most popular. Some of its programming of light music is distributed nationally, but most of the broadcasts originate in regional studios, providing family-oriented programs, music requests, farm reports, local events reportage, and sports programming. Its midday journal, *Autofahrer Unterwegs,* is the most popular radio program in the nation. The third channel (Österreich 3) is the one young people listen to most often. The first two channels end their programming around midnight; Österreich 3 is a twenty-three-hour service, going off the air only between four and five A.M. Brief news reports are broadcast hourly. News and cultural affairs are offered between noon and six o'clock. Österreich Regional and Österreich 3 are commercial channels, while Österreich 1 is commercial-free (Sandford 1976, 148). A fourth channel, Radio Blue Danube, is an English-language broadcast with news and features in Spanish and French as well. It was introduced in 1979.

Radios are located throughout the household, in bedrooms, living rooms, and kitchens. These locations reveal at least three different times when radio listening is likely to occur: during meals, while preparing for work or for bed, and during the evening hours. Programming on all three channels takes these activity patterns into account. In-depth news discussions are aired during the Viennese mealtimes. Evening programming features popular music and concerts. Early morning transmissions give short reports on news, weather, and traffic, and feature peppy musical selections.

As a play activity, radio has few rules. Its orderliness derives from the quality of the programming and the regularity of its schedule. It can become a companion, broadcasting familiar formats with the same announcers each day of the week. Its chanciness arises in the unpredictability of the music played. This is more striking in the youth-oriented channel than it is in the other two, which announce their music schedule weekly. Most important, radio listening provides stimulation and imagery during the most routine of chores: dressing, food preparation, and commuting. In the workplace, where play activities are stigmatized, radio listening is rare. On visits to the countryside, where so many other possibilities for play exist, the radio is almost nonexistent.

Television is also a predominantly household entertainment. The only place where people watch television outside the home is in certain Kaffeehäuser. This is a holdover from the 1950s, when owning televisions was expensive and Kaffeehäuser bought them to attract patrons. In 1980, five out of seven households had television sets. To use a set, the household must purchase a receiver license from the ORF every year (Magistratsabteilung 66 1981, 370). The license fees pay for program development and equipment maintenance. Half of those who own receivers watch programming on weekdays and three-quarters watch on weekends. With such a large audience, television is the most powerful disseminator of information in Austria.

The duration of television watching on weekdays shows a strong central tendency, while the extent of weekend watching is more variable. That is, people view programs for similar lengths of time each weekday, but on weekends they watch for different lengths of time. Television watching is more of a social activity that radio listening. Groups of family and friends watch television together, often commenting to each other about the action on the screen. It is preeminently a household-based entertainment for which there is no public equivalent (Mündel et al 1979, 272; 299; 311).

The ORF broadcasts two channels of television programming, Fernsehen 1 (FS1) and Fernsehen 2 (FS2). In addition, a cable service enables households to receive six German-speaking channels from the Federal Republic of Germany and Switzerland and four English-speaking satellite channels. The two Austrian channels compete with each other with programming. The competitive atmosphere in the ORF generates more challenging fare, while German television tends to resemble the commercial programming of the United States. Of the two, FS2 is the more highbrow channel, even though each deliberately repeats the other's programs over the course of a season (Sandford 1976, 148–9). Both channels are commercial, although commercial messages are broadcast between programs. Sponsors do not exercise control over particular programs, and programs are not interrupted for commercial messages.

The programming schedule seems to take the activity patterns of households into account. The entertainment segment is concentrated in the evening hours. Daytime shows include educational programs, the occasional morning transmission from a ski event or auto race, and a late-morning movie. For most of the afternoon, when children ought to be doing their homework, there is no broadcast. The first of the evening programs, beginning about 4:00 P.M., are educational, including language courses, cooking lessons, or travelogues. These are followed by children's programming and syndicated series, which are often American imports dubbed into German. The news hour begins at seven with separate programs for local and international coverage. The main entertainment programming of the evening begins at 8:15 P.M. It may include variety shows, films and teledramas, political and current affairs discussions, documentaries, or sports programs. These programs last for forty-five to sixty minutes. Around 10:00 P.M., a news summary is broadcast. The end of programming varies from day to day. On FS2, for example, it is customary to repeat the major program from FS1 after the news. On most weekdays, programming ends around 11:50 P.M. Brigitta Hartinger described staying up until 11:30 to watch a political discussion on television. With such a short program schedule and such uniformity between the two channels, the similarity in day-to-day weekday television viewing becomes understandable. There simply is very little choice.

In terms of total television viewing, the Viennese averaged one hour and twenty minutes a day in 1974. Even before the advent of cable, different audiences viewed different programs. Women watched the main program of the evening almost twice as often as men. Men watched sports eight times more often than women. The popularity of news programs increases with the age of the viewer. Viennese sociologists found that the most often cited motive for watching television is to "escape" the problems of the day. The second most frequently cited reason was to dispel loneliness, especially among retired people, who spend 43% of their waking day watching television. The group that spends the least amount of time watching television is young people between the ages of fifteen and thirty (I.F.E.S. 1974, 9–10).

Television sets are found in living rooms. They are the focus of attention whenever they are turned on. As Ernst Schönthal remarked when explaining why he did not have a television set:

> In the 1950s, when they first came out, we were invited to friends' houses to view the program. It was so silly! Here you were in the home of a friend that you liked and cared about, and no one was talking. Everyone was focused on the Glotzophon (boobtube). When it was over you said good-bye. There was absolutely no interaction.

Such television visiting still goes on, but television watching is either a substitute for socializing or an amusement carried on within the home. Its orderliness lies in the certainty of its programming. Its chanciness lies in the content of specific news, sporting events, or entertainment programs. Because it engages both the eyes and ears, television's images crowd out social interaction, movement, and interruptions.

Cinema and spectator sports are examples of entertainments outside the home. In both, the duration and timing of the activity are beyond the control of the spectator. The schedules are published in newspapers. Professional sports leagues in Austria are essentially private corporations but are subject to special sets of laws and public oversight. Professional events are the least frequently scheduled Unterhaltungen and command large audiences when they are broadcast. Sports are scheduled during nonworking hours, primarily on weekends. The most popular spectator sport is soccer, followed by hockey and skiing. Soccer attracts a great deal of interest from men. Numerous betting pools purport to reward people who are familiar with the strengths and weaknesses of the teams. The schedules reflect the seasonal qualities of the sports, with soccer matches scheduled for spring and fall, hockey and skiing for winter and spring.

Privately owned cinemas are in every district. They tend to show mostly foreign films because Austria's film industry is small. It produced approximately ten films a year during the period of this research. People view important foreign films in the cinemas in the Innere Stadt, sometimes with subtitles, but more often with overdubbing. After a few weeks, these films move out toward the more successful neighborhood theaters and eventually to the smaller outlying houses in the larger districts and suburbs.

The number of cinema visits had declined dramatically since 1960. In that year, three out of every ten people reported that they had never been to a cinema, while four in ten went once or twice a month and three in ten went three or more times a month (Arbeiterkammer 1963, 52). A decade later, in the 1974 survey of participation in entertainments by the Institut für empirische Sozialforschung, six in ten people never went to the movies, while 15% went once or twice a month and 22% three or more times (I.F.E.S. 1974, 35). This decrease in cinema visits has led to a 32% decline in the number of cinemas in the city. Those primarily affected include small, neighborhood theaters (Magistratsabteilung 66 1961, 1975). Even among frequent theatergoers, people visit cinemas in the Innere Stadt much more often than the neighborhood movie houses.

Within the entertainment market, the role of theaters has changed. In 1960, they were physically closer to the household and served as the primary source of out-of-the-home entertainments for most wage-earning families. Today, with television playing that role, the cinema has moved away from the household both spatially and temporally. It now attracts groups of friends at least as often as it does family groups (Mündel et al 1979, 299). The appeal of the Innere Stadt cinemas is the chance to see a first-run film with a famous producer or actor. Film actors can become cult objects in Vienna as they do in other societies. In the home, women are more likely (42%) to watch films on television than men (22%). Women appear to instigate cinema visits outside the home. As a play activity, moviegoing combines well with recreational eating either before or after the performance. It is a common weekend evening activity for groups of friends.

The entertainment industry supplies play activities to the Viennese in two forms. The public-sector entertainments of television and radio are spatially and temporally integrated within household life. The private-sector entertainments are like ordinary markets that must adapt their locations and schedules to maximize customer access. Theater, music concerts, cinema, and sports events are scheduled to ensure the largest possible audiences. They are located to draw audiences from the widest possible area.

BEING SOCIAL

Socializing for the Viennese means being in contact with people who are not members of the household. This may include visiting, talking on the telephone, writing a letter, or attending a party. The nature of the relationship determines where, how often, and with whom this socializing takes place. The Viennese understand three grades of relationship among people who are not *Verwandten* (relatives). *Fremden* (strangers) are people who may not know each other's names or, even if they do, know very little about each other. Fremde do not socialize, except through unplanned, chance meetings. *Bekannten* (acquaintances) include a much broader range of people than the English usage of the word connotes. Bekannten are workmates, neighbors, shopkeepers, friends of friends, and people met on vacation. Only a very small number of people one knows ever leave the category of Bekannten to become *Freunde* (friends). This category is reserved essentially for people with whom one grew up. Sometimes acquaintances one has known for many years acquire the same level of intimacy as Freunde, but this is rare. The reason for such an exclusive category for friendship is that friends in Vienna provide more than emotional support and favors. Acquaintances are expected to offer such support under most circumstances. Friends provide moral models for each other, reflecting each other's values and serving as the primary sources of social meaning outside the family. Friends keep no secrets from each other. The judgments of friends are taken very seriously. This degree of emotional involvement is usually reserved for family, and even then only close relatives. The emotional line between Freunde and Verwandte is a narrow one. Freunde ought to be so well known to the entire family that they are treated as collateral relatives. For these reasons, Viennese do not extend the bounds of friendship easily.[5]

The mark of friendship is the restricted use of the informal second person singular pronoun *du* in direct speech. Normally Austrians, like most other German speakers, use *Sie*, the third person plural pronoun, in direct speech with strangers and acquaintances to acknowledge respect and distance. Children who grow up together address each other as du, as do members of the same family. The first time two adults agree to be *per du* with each other they perform a ritual of drinking a glass of wine, beer, or brandy with their arms locked together. Today this informal pronoun is extended even to people whom one has known for a significant time without necessarily creating bonds of friendship. Students automatically use du with each other, regardless of age. Only among the older generation is one likely to encounter people who have known each other for years and still use the formal pronoun with each other. Adults and small children use du with each other.[6] In spite of these rules of extended usage, the use of du still marks the network of Verwandte and Freunde from the sea of Fremde.

Most *Bekanntenkreise* (circles of acquaintances) include people with whom one is both *per du* and *per Sie.*[7]

Acquaintances are entertained in a *Lokal* (public house) such as a restaurant, a Beisel, or a Heurigen. In 1971, four out of ten visits with nonrelatives took place in Lokale, while only slightly more than one in ten visits took place in the household. The Lokale are perfect arenas for socializing. They serve food and drink, they are easily accessible, and they create a very specific atmosphere of conviviality, which is often called *Gemütlichkeit* but is actually a more intense, urban coziness than that usually implied by Gemütlichkeit. Thus, while Viennese Lokale share some superficial features with the rural Austrian *Gasthaus* described by Honigmann (1963) in their clientele, spatial design, hours of access, and symbolic actions, they are metropolitan places.

One Lokal, the Kaffeehaus, has such a distinctive style that visitors often identify it with the city itself. The Kaffeehaus was the meeting place for artists, philosophers, revolutionaries, and the literati of the *fin de siècle.* The tradition of service, the total absence of the feeling of being rushed, the assortment of foreign newspapers, and the waiters' use of fictional honorific titles for all clients reflect this bygone era. These Kaffeehäuser are large halls filled with small booths and tables. A party of six has a hard time finding a table large enough to accommodate all of them. Kaffeehäuser cater to interaction among small groups of friends. White linen, crystal, and gold-leaf-rimmed china contrast with the red or green velvet upholstery and dark wood paneling to give the room a much cozier feeling. For the price of a cup of coffee, a patron can sit at a table until the Kaffeehaus closes. At regular intervals, the waiter will bring a fresh glass of water on a silver tray. The purpose of the glass of water is not to rush the patron to pay the bill, but to make the visit more comfortable. The appeal of the Kaffeehaus for socializing is the feeling of timelessness that sets in after the waiter brings the first order of coffee.

The colloquial expressions *Stammgast* (regular guest), *Stammtisch* (regular table), and *Stammlokal* (regular establishment) refer to the eternal ties that bind a set of clients to a Lokal.[8] Long association with a public place is rewarded by linking the patron to the Lokal through the extension of fictive bonds of descent. In this case, the establishment is "genitor" to a band of "collateral" acquaintances. In his autobiography, the Viennese-born film director Otto Preminger (1977, 175) tells of returning, after thirty years, to the Kaffeehaus he used to frequent. Soon after he sat down, an old waiter brought him the cup of coffee with milk and the sweet roll that he always ordered and greeted him with, "We haven't seen you in some time, Herr Professor." Preminger's anecdote shows how permanent the Lokal considers the *Stamm* relation with a frequent client.

Another Lokal, the Beisel, is usually located at the street corner in a neighborhood. Particularly old and venerable Beiseln are found in the Innere Stadt, but the ones in the neighborhoods are used more frequently. Each one serves a specific brand of beer or a specific region's wine, bistro-type food, and homemade pastry. Just as the Kaffeehäuser are the graceful reflections of highbrow tastes, the Beisel is the unadorned reflection of the taste of people. It, too, has glass and porcelain, but these are functional and durable. The tables are bare wood, polished smooth by years of wiping. The hall is small and crowded with tables. The walls are yellowed with cigarette smoke and kitchen grease. Beiseln are noisy places where men and women play cards, share a few drinks, and gossip.

Beisel food is *Hausmannskost* (home cooking). It is prepared by the owner's family on the same kind of stove the patrons use. The food is tasty, warm, and inexpensive. It is also a welcome change from the cold cuts of a traditional Viennese supper table. The main consumption activity in Beiseln is beer drinking. Although the Viennese drink whiskey and brandy on special occasions, the drinks of choice are beer and wine, which are consumed in large amounts. Beiseln provide a congenial place in the neighborhood for friends and acquaintances to spend an evening drinking together. Entertaining in one saves the host the trouble of lugging bottles back and forth from the market, and it is almost as comfortable as the living room. Most Beiseln have a large number of Stammgäste, who form a tight circle of acquaintances. This makes Beiseln the center of social activity in the residential neighborhoods.

Restaurants and *Weinkeller* (wine cellars) are also Lokale where socializing takes place around food. Formal Viennese cuisine is very elaborate and refined. When properly executed, it is among the most engaging in Europe. The rules governing the construction of dishes represent an amalgam of the peasant traditions of the Austro-Hungarian Empire, spanning the multiple ecologies of the Alps, the Central Plain, and the Mediterranean, Black, and Baltic littorals. The Habsburg emperors brought French and Spanish chefs to their kitchens who added their knowledge of sauces and flavors to the peasant dishes. The complexity of this cuisine makes food an important focus of conversation. The city abounds with food hobbyists who know the best restaurants to go to for this or that dish.

While all food is celebrated, the Viennese have a special affection for uncultivated foods. The popularity of forest mushrooms, compotes of wild berries, poached brook trout, and roasts of venison and boar require careful forest management and scores of professional hunters. These products are seasonal and restaurants that provide special game menus during the autumn are usually full. Because restaurants are expensive, people visit them less frequently than they do Beiseln. Restaurants are reserved for weekend socializing. They vary considerably in style or atmosphere. Meals are never rushed; spending two and a half to three hours at a restaurant is common. As arenas for socializing, restaurants appeal mostly to friends and relatives rather than acquaintances.

Regardless of the type of Lokal visited, Viennese are always clear about who is inviting whom. The role of the host retains certain obligations. The host must initiate the date of the meeting, choose the site, make any necessary reservations, set the time, arrange transportation for non-driving guests, and pay for the food and drink. In other words, the host is responsible for entertaining the guests even though the interaction is taking place outside the home. Because of this effort by the host, the guests incur a gift debt that leads to a reciprocated invitation. Once the debt has been repaid, the relationship is free of obligation and can peacefully attenuate. For this reason, socializing in Beiseln is more likely among acquaintances than among friends and relatives. Among the latter, socializing outside the home involves joint hosting, in which one household assumes responsibility for the food bill while another pays for the wine. When an invitation is reciprocated among acquaintances, the host does not try to do the guest "one better." Instead, the reciprocating acquaintance will try to match the quality and style of the Lokal that was the site of the original invitation.

Viennese seem to prefer to emphasize the atmosphere and ambience, instead of the expense, when hosting a social evening. The feeling one gets when sitting in the Beisel, the restaurant, or the Kaffeehaus is a quintessentially urban one. The dress of the patrons, the theatrics of the servers, the conversation topics, and even the decor, all refer to a shared sense of historical location deeply embedded in metropolitan knowledge. Such arenas enable the patron to reinterpret the relative degrees of solidarity and separation in social standing with the other patrons. These evenings are opportunities for status advertisements, both to the immediate group of friends and to the Lokal as a whole. What makes these activities play is that they are voluntary, disinterested, and superfluous displays; the more serious presentation occurs during work activities. What makes them quintessentially urban is only really seen fully when one crosses the boundary between the city and the country. Here, at the frontier of their metropolis, the Viennese manipulate the images of the urban order more freely. On the edge of the city, surrounded by the open countryside, they confront their metropolitan lives directly.

THE RURAL NEXUS IN VIENNESE PLAY

Unlike entertainments, recreational activities are self-scheduled. Because of the crowded schedules of the weekday, recreations take place primarily on weekends. Thousands of Viennese flock to the Wienerwald, summer cottages in neighboring regions, garden plots in special settlements, and sports centers. The Viennese perceive these recreation areas as outside the city. Part of what constitutes being *auf dem Lande* (in rural settings) is the memory of periods in the city's history that a particular piece of forest or farm country can engender. In Pezzl's time, agricultural villages were less than a kilometer from the city walls. Walking there to purchase fresh produce and wine was a common household activity, especially on Sunday. The frontier of the city moved farther up the slopes of the Wienerwald as agricultural villages became industrial suburbs and finally large municipal districts, but the frontier zone itself still exists. One can find it by taking any streetcar to its end-station and walking up any street with a rising grade. Within minutes, one finds oneself in vineyards, fields, and forests. Turning around, one can see the grey rooftops of the city extended below. Thus, *das Land* (the rural) is directly contiguous with *die Stadt* (the metropolis).

Another way of defining das Land is through the dimension of social time. Das Land begins at the point where one becomes aware of living a different rhythm. The existence of agricultural or forest work is prima facie evidence of this shift in social tempo. Here, finally, the constraints of the public schedule loosen. The pace of life is dictated by the life cycles of plants and animals, a rhythm that seems to precede the devices of the metropolis. Combining fresh air, rigorous exercise, and the freshest possible foods with the tempo of nature, the Viennese believe, will restore the body's balance. It is not only the body human that finds its equilibrium in the crisp air of the Wienerwald; the body social renews itself as well. In the countryside one can establish a critical distance from metropolitan life, symbolically juxtaposing the ideal of the egalitarian, closed, corporate, peasant community with the hierarchical, open, industrial alliance. It is when one can suspend the metropolitan pace that the urban order comes into focus.

Weekend activities that take the resident out of the city are very popular. In the 1971 time budget survey, a third of the respondents had hiked in the woods and a quarter had taken a recreational drive during the previous weekend. Over the last three decades, the number of Viennese who have purchased summer cottages has risen sharply. These cottages tend to be located no farther than a four-hour drive away from the city. The federal government encouraged buying a vacation home by making subsidized mortgages available to people with moderate incomes. These weekend cottages are often farmhouses whose former owners have moved into nonagricultural jobs and built themselves larger, more centrally located homes. Housing developers created weekend-cottage condominium estates, with a common swimming pool and sauna. While actual figures on the number of Viennese households that own these cottages are not available, on long weekends the density of traffic in all the municipal districts falls off sharply. Interview partners attribute this to the large number of people leaving for their weekend cottages. These cottages let families walk or drive in rural settings, eat healthy food, and breathe fresh air while being away from the city in time and space.

For those who choose not to travel so far for their rural recreations, a favorite place to hike is the Wienerwald. The crescent shape of the Wienerwald itself determines the direction of the walk. It is an all-day activity. One hike I participated in began around 9:00 A.M. on an exposed southern slope so that the sun's warmth could beat back the morning chill. We arrived by streetcar to a former wine village that was now comfortably embedded in the wealthy, residential district of Hietzing. We walked along established, well-marked trails, arriving at a Gasthaus around noon. After a lunch break that could have included picnic foods but on this occasion took advantage of the Hausmannskost of the Gasthaus, we resumed the trail, crossing over to the northern slope to avoid the midday sun. Eventually we found ourselves walking through the vineyards that grow on the exposed eastern slopes. We had walked almost halfway around the crescent of the Wienerwald from its southern foothills to midway between the center of its arc and its eastern terminus at the Danube, a distance of thirty kilometers. By then it was 4:00 P.M. and we looked for a Heurigen in which to refresh ourselves. Two hours later, stuffed with picnic food and dizzy from a bit too much wine, we lurched down a steep street to another streetcar that brought us back to our downtown apartments. In terms of juridical boundaries, we had never left the city. But in our play, we had walked as far from the urban life as our feet could carry us.

The Heurigen that vintners establish for patrons to sit in and sample their wine are a traditional and popular social arena in rural play. The intention of the vintners in establishing the gardens was to sell wine directly to the public. Over the last hundred years, Heurigen have become an institution for drinking, socializing, and symbolizing the distance between Stadt and Land. Viennese visit them during the week and on weekends. For those who live in wine-growing suburbs, Heurigen are the local Beiseln. Heurigen also serve as the rest stops for another weekend recreation: the long automobile drive in the countryside that includes visiting a "drive-to" Gasthaus for lunch and a Heurigen for supper.

The Viennese wander through the countryside with family and friends. Wandering alone occurs less than 10% of the time. Households hike together, but joint hiking by related households is rare. Hiking with friends is as common as hiking with one's household (Mündel et al 1979, 299). The duration of the hike can last twenty minutes or the entire day. Younger people take longer hikes. Older people cover less distance, but choose trails that include historically interesting sites or scenic views. The trails are well marked and graded. Some are considered quite strenuous. Most hikers have special shoes and hiking costumes that reflect traditional rural *Trachten* (folk costumes). People converse as they hike, greeting strangers they pass on the trail with a smile and a "Grüss Gott." Along the trails of the Wienerwald, the community of wanderers become fictive members of the same circle of acquaintances.

People who live in mountainous areas are likely to develop hiking and skiing skills. Now that the automobile and the telephone have taken over the transportation and communication functions between Alpine village clusters, Austrians hike and ski as forms of play. Those Austrians whose geography is relatively flat, like the Viennese, embrace hiking and skiing with even greater enthusiasm. The Wienerwald is topographically complex terrain, but well suited to horseback riding, even in winter. There is no ecological basis for boosting hiking to its preeminence as "life-skill-turned-recreation." Instead, hiking is an imitative re-creation of the life-skills of other, more Alpine Austrian life-styles: it is peasant envy—city dwellers playing at being Alpine farmers. It is part of a complex of symbolic involvements that include romanticizing the life-styles of farmers and foresters, imitating their dress, idealizing their social and work lives, prizing their foods, extolling the idyll of their communities, and wishing to incorporate these qualities into metropolitan life. In Western constructions of metropolitan knowledge reinterpreting the rural as the pastoral is commonplace.[9]

In Vienna, this search for the pastoral community is at the base of those forms of play in which households participate. Raymond Williams has charted the changing image of the pastoral in English literature over the past 400 years. He finds in the English experience a quality that I recognized in Austria as well: a mystification of the actual conditions of rural life to simplify the critique of the inequities of the urban order (1973, 36–40). Real villages in the Vienna Basin are very close to the city, both spatially and in terms of historical experience. For many city dwellers, villagers were neighbors and sometimes relatives. A continuity of social networks and a shared sense of locale exists between the Viennese and the wheat farmers and vintners. In the late nineteenth century, the city annexed ten whole villages into new municipal districts. These villages had long since transformed their agricultural work into industrial employment. Evidence of preindustrial agriculture is hard to find anywhere in the Vienna Basin. Only in the Alpine villages far to the west do ecology and distance conspire to preserve the farming community of the Viennese pastoral ideal.

As previous chapters have described, the urban order is one of hierarchy, ambivalence, bureaucratic constraint, and isolation. In his extensive intellectual history of industrializing Austria, William Johnston has suggested that the increasing perception of severed connections with neighboring communities within the metropolis may underlie the emergence of xenophobia in general and anti-Semitism in particular. In his view, the close-knit emigré communities of nineteenth-century industrial workers were a constant reminder to the Viennese urbanites of their lost *Gemeinschaft,* their lost community (1972, 27). Their longing for that sense of identity, social connection, and rootedness in a locality generated intense resentment toward Jews, Czechs, and Poles. These groups had managed to preserve these social forms through *Landsmannschaften* (ethnic clubs) and similar associations based on shared provenance. Whether or not this explanation of Viennese xenophobia during the period of intensive industrialization (1870–1945) is sufficient, it does help explain why the most ardent supporters of romantic nationalism, the self-love that is the reverse of xenophobia, dress in rural folk costumes and playfully imitate the necessities of rural communities.[10]

The wine-growing villages are situated in the low hills on the rim of the city, betwixt and between the urban and the forest. It is here that the Heurigen are located. The word Heurigen is derived from the adjective *heurige*, meaning current harvest, or latest vintage, because the vintner offered visitors tastes of the latest vintage in the hopes of selling them a few bottles to take home. Grapevines are known to have grown in the area since the Bronze Age. The name of the city itself, *Wien*, is probably a reference to Wein (wine).[11] Official recognition of Heurigen is as old as the city itself. A ninth-century Markgraf, the Babenberger duke Leopold I, issued a market ordinance allowing wine growers to sell individual glasses of their wine to potential customers (Sinhuber 1980, 11). A 1784 proclamation by Joseph II created a special license for these vintners' outlets. The proclamation required that the vintner sell only those products actually produced by him and his family. He could open his garden only a certain number of weeks each year, originally restricted to the warm-weather months. Now Heurigen licenses permit a maximum of 300 days, or until the wine runs out, whichever comes first. Joseph II's definition of the Heurigen was an effort to preserve its special character as an operating vineyard and prevent it from becoming another kind of Gasthaus. The proclamation made investment in such enterprises by nonfamily members unprofitable, unless the investor was also willing to produce the wine. By Gross-Hoffinger's time, visiting Heurigen had become an important part of Viennese recreations (1832, 113). It was an inexpensive activity because the wine was cheap and people brought their own picnic foods. Members of all urban estates mixed easily in these gardens; only the aristocracy and their imitators avoided them. As the industrial workers moved to Vienna from the provinces, they too began to visit the Heurigen.

There are many reasons to visit a Heurigen: to refresh the group after a hike, to socialize with friends or acquaintances, to eat supper, to relax after work, to sample the wines of the town, or to celebrate a birthday, name day, or anniversary. The gardens are open throughout the day and evening. They attract entire families, including small children; groups of single people; dating couples; and retired people. In 1971, family groups amounted to 42% of Heurigen patrons. Visits by groups of friends and acquaintances made up 30% percent of the total. Single patrons, the most common visitors to neighborhood Beiseln, accounted for only 5% of visitors (Mündel et al 1979, 299). Entire families, spanning many households and generations, often visit Heurigen together.[12]

The gardens are first and foremost places to drink wine. The amount consumed and the tolerable level of inebriation are closely circumscribed.

Since the wine is strong, especially when young, strategies for avoiding drunkenness abound and constitute a significant portion of Heurigen knowledge. The gardens usually provide a buffet of homecooked foods for those who have not brought a picnic. Patrons drink and eat outside at long wooden bench tables in good weather. Waitresses take the wine orders. Individuals collect their meal at the food counter. Strings of lightbulbs and candles provide illumination after sunset. In cold or wet weather, the visitors move indoors to a small heated hall. Visiting is less frequent when the weather is inclement.

Although Heurigen are a kind of Erholung, which the household can schedule freely, the requirements of a Heurigen license do determine which particular Heurigen the household will visit on a given night. The operation of a Heurigen is limited to 300 days. Since the vintner is only allowed to sell wine and foods that he or his family produces, the amount of wine made that year further constrains the number of open days. The life cycle of the grape vines, the balance of rain and sun during the summer months, and the amount of land under cultivation, all affect the quantity of wine available. When the wine runs out, the vintner cannot buy more from another producer to keep the garden open. The vintner must notify the licensing agency three weeks before he intends to open the garden, stating the exact dates the garden will remain open. If he overestimates the demand for his wine, he must close without having sold the quantity he had planned. If he underestimates the demand, he must close the garden early and cannot use the remaining days at another time. One way of hedging against these risks is to own more than one garden. The actual number of vintner families in the Wienerwald towns is small. Any member of the family actually engaged in the wine-growing corporation can hold title to a garden in his or her own name. These can even be situated in different towns. The wine supplies can then move from garden to garden, each with its own 300-day limit.

In comparison with the work schedules of people in the city, the Heurigen schedule forms an irregular pattern of opening and closing. Not knowing whether a favorite garden will be open is an element of chanciness that makes Heurigen visiting a form of play. Since the 1700s, a tradition has evolved of hanging a *Buschen* (bunch of evergreen boughs) from a pole over the entrance to announce that it is open to dispense wine. The official name for a Heurigen, *Buschenschank*, is a compound of Buschen and *Ausschank* (tap).[13] When a Heurigen is open, it is *ausg' steckt* ("hung-out"). To make it easier for visitors to find the gardens that are ausg'steckt, the village vintners' association places a large tablet on the main roads entering the village. On this tablet, each vintner hangs a small metal plate with the name and address of the Heurigen.

The Heurigen sits between the city and the countryside in the spatial imaginings of the metropolitans. Temporally, it is separate from both the tempo generated by the institutions of the city and the tempo of the green cycles of the forest. Within this margin, a highly elaborate repertoire of symbols is available for visitors to manipulate. When they leave the topics of the city and their daily lives behind, four Heurigen topics dominate the conversations of visitors: the Biedermeier wine cult, the wine trance, the rural romance, and the wine therapy. Each of these categories of images playfully applies wine drinking to different aspects of the urban experience. The manipulation of symbols in the Heurigen is an effort to resolve persistent contradictions within the urban order. In other circumstances, discussion of these contradictions could incite resentment and disorder. The Heurigen's distance from the public square and the public schedule makes it possible to open these issues and symbolically resolve them.

The Biedermeier refers to the period of Viennese social history that commenced with the Congress of Vienna (1813) and ended with the Revolution of 1848. The name was coined in the 1850s. It connotes a parody of the *kleinbürgerlich* (petit bourgeois) values of modesty, privacy, comfort, and public reserve that came to dominate the city during the first half of the nineteenth century. The retrenchment from Bonapartism and the continuing fear of liberal republicanism made political activism, artistic achievement, and other forms of middle-class accomplishment suspect. The period coincided with the adaptation to new work institutions, new citizens, and new social priorities.

To escape these pressures, the best-known artists, musicians, and poets, among them Franz Grillparzer and Franz Schubert, retreated to the Heurigen. There, they could discuss politics and art in the gay and carefree gardens, safe from the secret police and the informers that Metternich's government had recruited from the lower classes. Then, remembering the poverty of spirit and the repression that infected their city, these middle-class burghers would break into spontaneous weeping. Many ultimately took their own lives in defiance of a metropolitan order that undervalued individual achievement. Today, visitors share this image of the Heurigen as a repository of those ancient liberal values of the then young middle classes, flourishing above the distant city. As one Viennese has described it:

The green bunches hung over the great portal of the low French-style house, the bottles with their pearl-breath wine, the lantern over the red-clothed picnic table under the trees, zither and accordion music, gentle singing, tender winks in the direction of both the wine and the girl, and then, a wink in return . . . and in the background, the blinking lights of the distant radiant city. This is the real Heurigen as it was in the Biedermeier. Only today, it is harder to find (Leitich 1941, cited in Sinhuber 1980, 34; translation mine).

That is how the Viennese I met understand the relationship between Heurigen and Biedermeier. Heurigen represent an expressly *bürgerlich* (middle-class) nostalgia, in much the same way that the Fourth of July in the United States enshrines a late-nineteenth-century, small-town nostalgia.

As play, the Biedermeier wine cult involves the search for the authentic Heurigen experience. The criteria for authenticity include the qualities of the wine, the location of the garden, and its accessibility. The wine must be an unadulterated, local product. The garden must be located in a true peasant village, i.e., one in which people make their living from agricultural instead of urban employments. Those that are too easy to get to, or that are always open, are less desirable. Many Heurigen visitors keep lists of those gardens that were satisfactory on earlier visits. The erratic schedules of the gardens ensure that many visitors will study the tablet of metal signs at the entrance to the village, or walk around the village until they find one that is ausg'steckt, familiar, and not too crowded. This search is for spiritual authenticity as well, and it fills the visitors with a special excitement and anticipation. If at the end of the search the visitor finds a garden that resonates with the Biedermeier, the effort was worthwhile.

In the gardens, the process of imbibing the wine also has symbolic import. I refer to conversational themes that center on these symbols as the wine trance. In effect, one plays at getting drunk without ever losing control. The goal is to achieve an altered state of consciousness that is gay and carefree. This is accomplished by labeling and talking about various stages of inebriation as one experiences the effects of the wine. There are four such stages. The first stage is unnamed and begins with the warming, relaxing effects of the first glass of wine, while the last stage appears as a loss of control, slurred speech, exaggerated movements, and nausea. It is the two middle stages that are important in this biosocial balancing act.

The second stage is called *Schwipserl*, or being *beschwipst*, the smallest degree of drunkenness. While people are beschwipst they are happy and laughing, and conversation is animated. The ideal is to maintain this state for the entire evening, while continuing to drink more wine. One does so by preparing the stomach ahead of time by eating foods that are high in fat, such as *Schmalzbrot* (pork lard and pan drippings spread on rye bread) and *Speckbrot* (raw bacon on rye bread). Imbibers believe that such foods coat the stomach and reduce the absorption of alcohol. One can also reduce the rate of absorption by adding mineral water to the wine, to create a *Spritzer*. In this fashion, the glass always appears full, although the portion of wine is constantly being diluted.

The second stage is evaluated positively. The third stage is viewed negatively. It is called *blau* (blue), and begins when the gaiety begins to fade and the conversation turns maudlin and angry. At this point, the drinker has lost the balance. But this condition carries neither sanction nor stigma; visitors know that it is very hard to maintain the beschwipst stage. Only experienced wine drinkers can avoid misjudging the power of the wine and getting the blues. Continued drinking leads to the final stage of drunkenness, referred to as *besoffen*. Drinkers who allow themselves such excess consumption display a lack of good sense. When this happens to inexperienced wine drinkers or tourists, it is merely funny. When a native behaves in this manner, it is a violation of the norms of public drinking. Such people are viewed as *primitiv* (low class), and Heurigen that encourage these drunks quickly lose their Biedermeier mystique and their more moderate patrons.

The play element in drinking, then, is to become beschwipst and hold that state for the entire evening. The trance is desirable because through it, the emotional modalities of the Biedermeier and the rural pastoral become accessible. The orderliness comes from one's wine-drinking experience and technique. The chanciness arises from the different strengths and the unpredictable power of the wines. Anyone can become drunk. Only through the modulation of food, wine, and mineral water can the visitor successfully achieve the desired trance.

The community of wine growers is another storehouse of pastoral values. Heurigen meditations on its qualities result in another cluster of images I call the rural romance. The Heurigen enable the city resident to experience vicariously membership in the *Banntaiding*, the closed, corporate, rural community whose roots extend back to the manorial economy of the Middle Ages. This is available to the modern metropolitan through fictive friendship with a vintner. Fictive friendship is a variety of acquaintanceship in which the two people affect greater than usual intimacy in one narrowly defined area of common interest. What sets it apart from true friendship is that it is narrowly defined. What makes it different from acquaintanceship is that within its narrow limits lies the assumption that the relationship is lifelong and reciprocity is generalized. Since fictive friendships in Austria are often as difficult to achieve as true friendship, establishing fictive friendship requires years of patronizing the same Heurigen. One must learn a vintner's schedule, become a Stammgast, sit at a Stammtisch, bring guests to the garden often, eat at the buffet, compliment the vintner's wife on the quality of the food, always take at least one bottle of wine home, put one's name on the mailing list for special tastings, and most important, knowledgeably engage the vintner in conversation. The vintner responds to these demonstrations by learning the patron's name and bringing him special bottles to taste as an *echter Weinkenner* (a true oenophile). Eventually, the two men drink a glass together, begin to address each other with du, and thereby extend fictive friendship to each other. Through this relationship, the guest gains fictive membership in the rural commune. For the city dweller this is a moral rebirth, an opportunity to consider oneself part of the purer, more honorable life of the countryside while still living the social and economic compromises of the city.

As the rural romance serves to refresh the spiritual balance of city folk, ethnomedical ideas about wine and the salubrity of the outdoors serve to restore the physical balance of the body. The final cluster of images refers to the therapeutic value of Heurigen visiting. The idea that moderate wine drinking is beneficial to the body is widespread in both rural and urban Austria (Honigmann 1963, 426). The Austrian wine industry quotes endorsements in its promotional literature from well-placed physicians attesting to the curative efficacy of wine. They claim that taking antibiotics with wine increases the rate of absorption into the body. They offer wine as an effective treatment for infections of the bowel. It can be used both as a disinfectant and as a prophylactic against traveler's diarrhea. The doctors who testify to these benefits are quick to point out that wine is harmful when abused (Traxler 1981, 6–7). Moderate wine drinking is part of the prescription for good health.

The locations of the Heurigen also figure in the maintenance of health. Viennese ethnomedicine is a variant of the Southern European humoral complex. It classifies body states, disease, food, and environments as dry or wet, in addition to hot and cold (Ackerknecht 1958, 64; Ragucci 1981, 226, 233–34). Different types of winds combine with different conditions of bodily openness and closure to produce both beneficial and detrimental influences. The most beneficial of winds is *frische Luft*, literally, fresh air, but more specifically, a cool breeze of moderate humidity. This contrasts with the air of enclosed spaces, which is cool but too moist, and the *Föhn* (Alpine wind), which is both too warm and too dry. The formula for good health is a warm meal, fresh air, and exercise every day. The Heurigen provide all three elements: a warm meal of wholesome farm foods from the vintner's buffet, the fresh breezes of the Wienerwald, and the exercise of finding a satisfactory Heurigen amid the twisting, rising lanes of the wine villages. The Viennese can sit in their Heurigen for hours, confident in the belief that they are doing so for their health.

Taken as a set, rural recreations represent an alternate tempo in an alternate space. They provide the Viennese with images of meaningful choices and of a satisfying community life that the prevailing urban order denies them. Rural recreation is restorative because it combines physical exercise and health-giving foods and air. It is suspenditory because it enables the household members to use their organizational skills to further their own ends, instead of to promote the efficient daily reproduction of labor power. It is compensatory because it allows the household to reject the available opportunities for public entertainments in favor of self-directed activity. This is especially true in the case of regular Heurigen visiting, since that activity includes vicarious participation in an idealized community that pays greater attention to individual self-worth. The Viennese value rural play precisely because it provides such effective contrasts with the hierarchy, ambivalence, bureaucratic constraint, and isolation of the urban order.

PLAYING WITH TIME

The primary effect of limiting the opportunity for play in the household schedules of Viennese has been steady growth in the importance of amusements over recreations, especially the scheduled activities of the entertainment industry. Because these are more easily coordinated with the work schedule, it is easier for households to choose them than to actively seek alternatives. These entertainments are quintessentially urban. Television, radio, cinema, sport, and the more expensive, less frequently attended activities of theater and concerts, provide the audience with sets of images that reflect the most refined experiences of urban life.

Leaving the city, and engaging the tempo and landscape of the rural life, are characteristics of the recreational activities households schedule for themselves. The actual life of small towns is not what they strive to embrace. The urban households select from their fantasy of rural life images that provide the sharpest contrast with the Viennese urban order. A weekend cottage, a Heurigen visit, or an occasional walk in the Wiener-wald can evoke such images. Only in such distant settings can the house-hold regain control over its play. But households did not always have to go so far or work so hard to play at recreations they could freely select and control. Both Pezzl and Gross-Hoffinger attest to a wide range of house-hold recreations in the city before the transformation of work. Over the course of industrialization, either the location of these recreations, such as the esplanade that lay before the ramparts of the walled city, or the cus-tomary segments of recreation in the early morning and during the long lunch break, have disappeared.

Viennese wage earners depend on their work institutions for their households' livelihood. This commitment brings with it a variety of con-straints on activities in time. The desire to join one's household in free play must be channeled into those segments of the day or week in which the public schedule deems play activities appropriate. This has led to a rou-tinization of the scheduling for play. That is, the nonwork segments of the household schedule occur in approximately the same position each work-day and each week throughout the wage earner's work life. When it is time to play, one had better do so. What ought to be a voluntary, disinterested, and superfluous activity becomes a necessary, market-oriented, scheduled requirement. This routinization in itself is neither good nor bad. It is merely another way of organizing activities. Nor is the evolution of this industrial variety of play necessarily less satisfying than the older, ideal-ized variety to which Huizinga addressed himself. It is decidedly different from the pattern of play that existed in the city in 1792, when play fre-quently interrupted the work segment itself. It is also different from the play patterns of the turn of the century, when workers toiled eleven hours a day and there were few affordable or accessible scheduled entertain-ments. In its own terms, the pattern of play created by the shapers of the public schedule conciliates and humanizes the industrial urban order at the cost of asking people to live an oxymoron: scheduled spontaneity.

CHAPTER 8

TOWARD AN ETHNOLOGY OF URBAN TIME

Urban time is a highly varied cultural artifact. It is a feature of every urban experience, but has different characteristics in each city. Whether these particular experiences are reflexes of a set of common urban processes or unique historical artifacts that defeat any effort at generalization remains to be seen. The evidence points to the existence of a common set of processes. Some of these transcend the metropolitan experience. Regional differences in mode of production tend to privilege certain ways of dimensioning time over other possibilities. The resulting symbol system links the temporal to the political, legitimizing both institutions. Temporal systems direct people's attention to some aspects of time and away from other aspects. These modal orientations within temporal systems limit behavior (Rotenberg 1991).

In addition to the political-economic, ecological factors also contribute to the formation of temporal systems of all societies. These include the ways in which the physical topography limits movement, the distribution of resources in space, the restrictions on behavior caused by the alternation of day and night, and the impact of seasonal climatic changes on people's behavior. These ecological factors broadly constrain everyone's behavior within the geographical limits of a region. They are not exclusively urban factors, though they may have different effects in cities than they have in villages. This is because cities may attribute different meanings to the scope of activities during the day and during the night, for example, and not because day and night alternate differently in cities than in the countryside.[1]

The primary function of all social time institutions is to establish a routine for purposeful action. In capitalist cities, as we have seen, this routine is shaped by at least three forces: the population, the technical order, and the activism of political factions. But these forces include self-limiting structural contradictions. The natural growth of the population in these cities requires people to live over an increasingly large area. The large number of people and the use of automobiles on streets built for horse-drawn carriages make movement slow and congested. Travel time increases. Industry becomes decentralized. New competitive urban clusters arise. These attack the constraints of the existing routine to gain a market advantage. The natural growth of the population also produces retired people, dependent family members, or others who are disengaged from the pace of industrial work. They move through the city at a different rhythm. This sometimes complements and sometimes conflicts with the rhythm established by the work, school, and market institutions. Thus, adherence to a common routine coexists with nonadherence in the metropolis as a whole and in its households. Temporal deviance is at least as common as temporal conformity. Nevertheless, the routine is visibly normative, while the counter-routines represent an invisible deviation. To draw attention to them involves drawing attention to the structural contradictions that produce them.

The routine of the capitalist public schedule gains its normative power from its connection to the regulation of work time and the state's role in enforcing work-time standards. Although there are important variations among occupations, all wage earners are subject to standard work-shift durations and standard positioning of the work shift in the daily cycle. This regulation of work time is itself an artifact of the industrial technical order, which sees all factors of production as necessary objects of control. The locus of this control is the manager. Being at work means being under the authority of another person, whose power comes not from the society of workers but from the investors and owners of the enterprise. Managers define and supervise every aspect of the workers' life on the job. The work segment stands in sharp contrast to the nonwork segments in the routine of wage earners. Industrialism separates work from life, even as it separates the workplace from the living place, and work time from living time (Habermas 1958, 92). The Viennese feel a profound alternation in the meaning of their work and nonwork activities. This alternation of meaning then spills over into the organization of their household lives and the activities of non-wage-earning household members. The organization of time under authoritarian control in the workplace eventually permeates the most intimate spheres of social life, even as the household struggles to retain some degree of self-direction.

This alternation of self-directed household life with slavish work life is not experienced in Vienna in as raw a fashion as it is described here. Instead, the legislative actions informed by a political program mediate the experience. This program both supports the authoritarian structure of the work life and seeks to create opportunities for choice within the household. It is the contemporary version of Austro-Marxism as practiced by the Social Democratic party in Parliament, and by the Austrian Trade Union Council in the Paritätische Kommission. These federal actions included systematic reductions in the duration of work between 1961 and 1975, increases in vacation time, store-closing ordinances, and a liberalization of the school week. The contrast of work with nonwork creates an ambivalence toward work, which many workers resolve by overvaluing their nonwork activities on weekends. This reaction led to decisions to reallocate newly won time to the weekend. Since only portions of the population adhere to these regulated routines, different residents of the metropolitan region experience the public control of work time, shopping time, and school time differently. Schoolchildren, for example, continued to go to school six days a week long after some of their parents had carved a four-and-a-half-day workweek for themselves.

The public schedule has evolved under conditions that guarantee conflict between public institutions and households. These conflicts force either the household or the institutions to change their schedules. The Viennese day contains only an average of sixteen waking hours. When one institution demands a larger share of that day, other commitments must give way. On a daily basis, the allocation of time is a zero-sum game. This conflict between households and institutions is so common for most Viennese that unconsciously they have given up one hour of sleep over the last thirty years.

URBAN TIME

Modern, urban settlement provides a special opportunity to observe the development of routine patterning. Freed from all ecological restrictions by technology, the temporal patterns must be accounted for through social relationships. Nature merely provides convenient points of reference for activity shifts that are primarily social in nature. According to Moore

(1963, 5) the necessity for simultaneous actions generates a different kind of relation (synchronization) from the necessity for a specific ordering of relations (sequence) or the necessity for an event to recur at a specific frequency (rate). The descriptive dimensions of activities in time, including duration, sequence, timing, and tempo (Lewis and Weigert 1981, 433) are "social periodicities [that] do not appear when time is measured by merely physical succession."[2] Unlike physical time, social time is uneven and irregular. Unlike physical time, the perception of what are the important periods of time will change with history. As these perceptions change, the temporal dimensions of activities change.

Each dimension originates independently of the other three. The decision of how long to engage in an activity, or in what order activities occur, lies within the scope of individuals and households. Tempo involves the coordination of simultaneously occurring activities and timing concerns the frequency of recurrence of activities. These are interhousehold actions and thus beyond the control of individuals and households to regulate. The observable organization of time in urban society is the historical product of the interaction of two different orders of control over activities: a lower order of control, involving the decisions of individuals and households and primarily concerned with issues of duration and sequence, and a higher order of control, involving the association of individuals with institutions and a concern with timing and tempo. The higher-order controls of tempo and timing constrain the latitude with which the lower-order dimensions can develop. The choice available to individuals and households of what can be done, when it can be done, and for how long one can do it becomes narrower as the patterns of timing and tempo become more specific. Temporally, as in so many other aspects of urban life, institutions dominate households. The ethnology of urban time is an effort to analyze these macrosocial and microsocial linkages through the temporal patterning of city life.

THE LOWER-ORDER DIMENSIONS OF URBAN TIME

The length of time over which an activity lasts is a direct result of will and desire. People can change their attention rapidly between activities or sustain attention for days. Even when they are specifically enjoined to remain at a task, people vary the direction of their attention periodically and seek distractions. People can do two things at once, such as ironing clothes and watching television (DeGrazia 1962). Some activities have highly routinized and predictable durations, such as commuting to work. Others, like housework, can vary from day to day. It is in the desire to remain involved with an activity that the true measure of duration lies.

Why people choose to remain at an activity can be interpreted from two different perspectives: the utilitarian and the normative. The utilitarian perspective sees duration as the product of some problem-solving behavior. In this view, an activity lasts as long as it does because people choose to do it instead of another activity. The normative perspective sees duration as the product of role commitments. In this view, the duration of an activity lasts as long as it does because people's social commitments constrain them to attend to the activity for a customary period of time. In the actual lives of individuals, no such simple and orderly division of motives is possible.

Living in an industrialized society that symbolically equates time with money makes it difficult to understand that not all time can be exchanged for currency. People need to sleep, eat, and have a family life, none of which have purchasable substitutes. The belief that time is money is interesting in itself, especially since it gives increased explanatory legitimacy to utilitarian perspectives on duration. This is what Godelier (1977, 169) has called the "process of fetishization." The fetish is the monetary value of time. It takes on increased power to explain social life through a mysterious, or at least indirect, relationship to wages, the only real economic empowerment available to most people. Becker's application of neoclassic economic models, such as the theory of the firm, to household time allocations is an extreme case of this fetishization (1965). One researcher (Carlstein 1982, 26) has labeled the use of neoclassic models in time budget studies "academic sophistry." At best, these models naively gloss the "value" of social constraints on economic behavior (Plattner 1989, x; Rotenberg 1988, 149). Undoubtedly, the popularity of this perspective among economists has a political-economic component, namely, that data explained in this way is directly comparable to other factors of production in operating accounts and therefore familiar to the bureaucratic agencies that support economic research.

In the normative view, the emphasis is on the repertoire of roles to which people commit themselves. Each of these role commitments carries with it a set of activities. Each activity has a customary duration. This duration is not always consistent in each recurrence of the activity. Instead, it is "measured" by the satisfaction of role obligations, as these are understood by the people involved. In some of these role commitments, the recurrence of the activities is regular and consistent. I have taken to calling these continuous role commitments. They include jobs and the meetings of voluntary associations, school classes, and similar public institutions.

In other role commitments, the recurrence of activities is irregular and discontinuous. Often the people involved in the relationship commit time to each other when one or the other expresses a need. I call these on-demand role commitments. They include parenting responsibilities, maintaining contact with friends and relatives, and similar activities. As people make commitments to institutions and other people, the continuous and discontinuous demands for their attention mount. Eventually, the remaining time affords them just enough hours for food and sleep. The total time available to households or any other grouping in society is equal to the role time commitments of its members.

Two questions that derive from this normative perspective provide an effective framework for interpreting durational data. What are the understandings people have of how to satisfy customary role commitments to others? These are part of the ideal behaviors expected of members of a society. Laws, regulations, and ordinances are good sources for discovering these expectations in urban societies. More informal expectations, such as how long a social evening ought to last, or how long a hike in the woods should take, can be discovered through participation. What is important here is not the customary duration itself, but the amount of flexibility people have. Even though some salaried employees leave work early, a stern manager could fire them for doing so. On the other hand, some mothers remain at home with young children for years, while others return to work within months after giving birth. This study looked at the flexibility built into the store-closing ordinance and at the increasing lack of flexibility in play activities. Many other behaviors that could reveal more about the temporal norms of a metropolis could not be included in a single study.

The second question is, what degree of uniformity exists in the customary durations from relationship to relationship? Which salaried employees are likely to leave early and which managers are likely to fire them? Which mothers are more likely to remain at home and which will return to work early? This question focuses attention on the variety that can exist within the normative framework in the daily life of urban society. Consider how differently the factory worker, gas installer, secretary, and executive interview partners experienced the norm of the forty-hour workweek. That analysis of normative variation revealed how differently individuals experience work if they have some control over the rate of their activities. The analysis of other patterns of variation might reveal additional keys to the variety of metropolitan experience in general. This is important because, on the surface at least, metropolitan culture appears fragmented and discontinuous. Normative evaluations of variation, like this study of work time, can show the uniformities in meaning that lie beneath the surface behaviors of urbanites.

Neither the utilitarian nor the normative perspective can encompass the entire problem of urban time organization. In the utilitarian perspective, free choice does not determine the duration of activity. In the normative perspective, normative constraint does not completely decide duration. Roles do constrain choice. Yet, individuals also reserve a certain portion of their time for themselves and protect it from the encroachment of role demands. Zerubavel has called this private time (1981). People also waste time. That is, they ignore the demands of a current commitment without transferring their attention to other role commitments. In the midst of this complexity, only close observation can uncover the variety of meanings underlying the activity organization of households.

Because time budget studies express durational data in numbers, there is a temptation to assume that these numbers are high-quality measurements from which statistical inferences can be made. Time budget studies come from the tradition of studying the household monetary budgets.[3] Unlike money, time does not come in discrete units. A minute is not the same class of phenomenon as a dollar. Dollar scales have a true zero point. That is, it is possible for a budget account to have no dollars at all. It is not possible for an activity to have no minutes. Minutes do not have a true zero point. If one activity does not occur, another fills the allotted time. Secondly, the interval between dollars is always the same. Even if a dollar has a corner missing, it is still a dollar. The interval between minutes is constant only in the theoretical sense. No measurement device is precise enough to guarantee two minutes of equal length.[4] More important, we experience minutes as if they are of unequal length. Some feel endless, while others fly by.[5] Lewis and Weigert (1981, 452–53) attribute this sensation of time "shortening," the feeling that time is passing too quickly, to an increase in the number of identifiable events embedded within a temporally defined experience: "Because older persons have longer temporal 'horizons' or memories, a year appears as a temporally shorter distance to someone 80 years old than to someone 8 years old." Similarly, because we are likely to be more active, a vacation feels as if it is flying by too quickly. The measurement of duration that does not take these issues into account reflects a false precision that has no validity beyond the conventions of the community of scholars devoted to the techniques of measurement.

If we can recognize and deal with these problems, durational data can yield important profiles of the variability in life-style within a population. Durational data provide behavioral evidence of the shifts in the public schedule. The three Viennese time budget surveys that I rely on to describe work schedules in this study are separated from each other by ten years. The changes in the categories of time did not change significantly in the course of the thirty years. What did change were the public regulations concerning work time. The differences in duration measured by these studies become a means of examining the changing preferences for action under the new constraints.

Individuals also exercise some control over the order in which they perform activities. The dimension of sequence superficially resembles that of the higher-order dimension of timing. Both generate a schedule as their principal artifact. The difference between timing and sequence is really one of scope. Timing refers to the coordination of simultaneously occurring activities within a population, while sequence refers to the ordering of activities within the life of an individual or household. Sequence is a lower-order level of control in the temporal organization of cities because individuals establish sequences to make their activities predictable to others. Sequences are a way of knowing where household members are at a given time. The predictability itself is important because people's activities and their responsibilities are not likely to share the same space throughout the day. If individuals can be counted on to follow the sequence they establish, they can be located in the complexity of urban space more easily.

Within these sequences, not every activity carries equal weight. Some activities involve no interactions with others and thus lack social significance (Sorokin and Merton 1937, 619). Leach suggests that all schedules have elements that could be considered as "time out" activities, which serve as boundary markers between other, more socially important activities (1976, 34–35). These include work breaks, seasonal markers in the annual cycle, holidays, mealtimes, travel times, and sleep.[6] These markers divide the day, week, and year into segments. Within these segments, the more important activities take place. These include the obligatory activities imposed by role commitments and the discretionary activities, reflecting the available choices. Within the obligatory activities, the commitment types can be continuing or on demand. The continuing commitments tend to fill the schedule. The on-demand commitments spill over and distort it, such as a sick child preventing a parent from arriving at work on time. The normal requirements of on-demand commitments still enable people to subscribe to predictable sequences of activity.

Schedule patterns reflect the temporal conventions of society. Such conventions are normative, constraining the actions of the population through widely shared notions of how schedules ought to be arranged. Zerubavel has described this aspect of schedules as providing a temporal map of society. He suggests that our temporal norms grow out of the rigid and repetitive qualities of the schedule. Against this solid temporal ground, figures, such as events and persons, pass as normal and noticeable. When events or persons appear out of schedule, violating the ''anchor of normalcy,'' people become startled and upset (1981, 21). The degree of discomfort is in direct proportion to the stake people have in maintaining the convention. People might interpret an anomalous event differently. Are adults who attend midweek afternoon sporting events unemployed, self-employed, or malingerers? Is the neighborhood bar that schedules two ''happy hours,'' one at four o'clock in the afternoon and one at seven in the morning, trying to accommodate an early-morning alcoholic community, or one with a large number of night-shift workers?

In the real world, there is a significant amount of slippage between the norm and actual activity schedules. This discrepancy can grow so large that those who are out of phase with the workaday world, such as the unemployed, the homemaker, the pensioner, the tourist, the artist, the self-employed, the odd-shift worker, the presocialized child, and the stranger to the city, find themselves living in what is literally a different urban world— one that presents them with a set of opportunities that is simultaneously more limiting and more liberating. Werner Tuzzi's work schedule afforded him more possibilities for shopping, eating, socializing, and playing. It was liberating precisely because his activities slipped between and among the more highly regulated and more carefully overseen work activities of the majority of the wage-earning residents. Tuzzi's schedule is temporally deviant.

What is important about these conventions is not that they exist but that they persist. Time conventions can channel the flow of activities and limit choice, but when they do so, it is always as the result of concerted political or economic policy, especially the influence of higher-order controls of timing and tempo. The midday meal in Vienna is a good example. In Pezzl's time, this mealtime was a period of household interaction, social meal-taking, and recreation. It represented a flexible activity segment, and people of different ages and dispositions used it to different purposes. It remained a flexible schedule segment, until it became the pawn in the negotiations between trade unions and industrial managers over the definition of the workday. The flexible hour or two in the middle of the day became a break from work. Schedule conflicts defined its boundaries precisely. Portions of it were paid. Then not paid. Then paid again. People stayed in the factory or office building because they had no time to travel home for lunch. Eventually, the most important social moment in the day lost its meaning to the rigidity of the industrially defined midday break. A simple convention of individual sequences becomes an artifact of the exercise of institutional power when viewed historically.

THE HIGHER-ORDER DIMENSIONS AND THE PUBLIC SCHEDULE

At its core, urban life demands temporal interdependency and the relinquishing of individual control over some portions of the day and week. Administrative decisions create, maintain, and reproduce the higher-order dimensions of social time: timing and tempo. Each decision attempts to make the best use of the committed time of individuals. Organizational time planning creates a reference system that can be widely broadcast and understood. Telling time becomes a domain of metropolitan knowledge that a child must learn. This includes the recognized time units, such as the clock, the calendar, the day, the hour, the minute, and the degree of precision (punctuality) required in different settings. Although individuals also employ clock time for lower-order time planning, it is the product of higher-level operations. It is used most consistently in time planning efforts.

The units that compose the reference system may have natural referents, such as the astronomical cycles, or be totally artificial. The existence of weeks, hours, and minutes points to the needs of urbanites to increase their time reckoning to include units for which no immediate natural referent exists.[7] In this way, urban centers can exhibit widely divergent time units, such as the method of dividing the day and night into the two sets of twelve temporal hours. As the seasons change, the number of hours remains the same, but their durations increase and decrease. Such a system did develop in early modern Europe (Bilfinger 1892, 8–58). The widespread ratification in the 1890s of a single global time-reckoning system based on the Greenwich meridian is an example of the diffusion of a single reference system within the world market. The precision in time reckoning also can vary considerably. Urbanites need to reckon time in smaller, more precise units than agriculturalists do. This has led to elaborate ethnoastronomies capable of extremely fine precision. As technological capabilities catch up with the social need, people begin to wear their own watches and chronographs (Landes 1983).

The time reference system is the common denominator for the higher-level dimensions of timing and tempo. In this respect, it plays a role similar to that of household role commitments in the origins of duration and sequence. This system is passed from generation to generation in a manner that is strikingly impervious to change. When change is necessary, many of the older elements are redefined. The reference system of a living city has a stratigraphy from which earlier patterns of timing and tempo can be read. The echoes of the older reference system are heard behind the newer rhythm. Here is another source of variation in the tempi of cities.

Timing is the dimension through which the public activities are coordinated and sequenced. The public schedule assigns each organization specific units of time in which to operate and prevents competing organizations from operating simultaneously. In cities with strong social antagonisms, the public schedule also may keep people apart. In its barest form, the public schedule is a necessary series of interactional boundaries. Goodenough (1963, 94) has described how the competing institutions and interest groups lend stability to this schedule as follows, "Because they solve so many problems so well, schedules often represent a delicate balance that allows for little alteration without serious dislocation effects. So many different wants are likely to be involved in the several activities within the schedule as to make it difficult for people to see how they could alter it radically." Community organizers, development agents, reform governments, and administrators of new institutions all face the problem of overcoming the inertia of the public schedule. Finding room to insert new activities in such schedules is like trying to persuade people on a crowded bench to squeeze together to create room for one more person; the potential for a seat may physically exist, but to create it requires the cooperation of people who will only be made more uncomfortable if the change is successful.

Institutions compete with each other to command the attention of city residents. The more powerful institution dominates the less powerful one. Those of roughly equivalent social power accommodate each other in a reciprocal fashion. More often than not, accommodation is not possible. Factories, offices, markets, and schools, for example, cannot always keep the needs of the others in view while working out their own schedules. Municipal governments often must exert pressure to bring order to a traffic pattern, reduce noise at night, shield workers from disruptive split-shift practices, or protect children from being left alone. When schedules between institutions do not conflict, Bock calls them *coordinated*. When conflicts do arise, he calls the schedules *correlated* (Bock 1966, 97). Households are likely to find their schedules correlated with the public schedule more often than not. Since household roles require meeting unpredictable demands, formal accommodation by institutions would require much decentralization of authority. As Bock has noted, the temporal power of institutions means being able to say, "Do it now, or else!" Giving households veto power over such demands negates the authority of the institutions.

Such was the case with the correlated shopping hours proposed for Shopping City Süd. By having the shops open longer than was possible within Vienna, the planners hoped to attract more Viennese shoppers. The longer hours would reduce the conflicts between shopping activities and other Saturday household activities, such as housework and child care. The expanded shopping hours never took effect, over the objections of ordinary householders, because of the power of commercial and trade-union interest groups within the city. The metropolis maintained its authority to channelize behavior through the public schedule.

Moore suggests that the competition between institutions could become so intense that it could eventually add up to more hours than individuals actually have at their disposal (1963, 10). These periods of competition are not likely to be evenly distributed throughout the schedule. This gives rise to an alternation between diffuse and compact activity phases first observed by Nelkin among migrant farm workers (1970). This alternation in the intensity of activities within segments is also applicable to urban public schedules. Compact activity phases occur when competition among institutions for individuals' time is strongest. Activities during this phase have a clear focus. A single institution commands the activity segment. It sanctions deviations and interruptions. Adherence to the schedule segment boundaries is closely monitored. Diffuse activity phases occur when institutional competition begins to slacken. Activities during this phase have multiple foci and reflect the greatest responsiveness to the needs of individuals. Individual control over time is at its height. There is no specific tempo. Activities recur irregularly.

In Vienna, industrial work time enhances the alternation between the phases of compact and diffuse activity. By squeezing many of the social interactions out of the work segment, disciplining the work force to concentrate on work tasks only for the length of the shift, and reducing the length of break time, managerial and trade-union interests have created a compact, almost homogeneous work segment. When wage earners leave the temporal authority of their workplaces, their activities become diffuse. In the nonwork segment, the individual may set a routine: a visit to a pub on the way home to supper, television, and bed; or a stop in a Kleingeschäft for cold cuts, supper with the family, homework with the children, household chores, and bed. This self-directed, after-work routine is flexible. Opportunities shape the pace of activities. This alternation of compact and diffuse phases is evident in the weekday routine, but not on weekends.

To maintain public order, authorities cannot allow the competition among institutions to exclude the diffuse phase entirely. Only during the diffuse phase can households reproduce the population, shop for goods and services in the marketplace, and take time for rest and play. When the reallocations of work time during the 1970s began to develop unforeseen consequences for shopping time, planners were powerless to save the Kleingeschäfte from being replaced by Supermärkte. The city cannot allow the compact phase to disappear entirely either. In Pezzl's day, even the guilds expected workers to pay undivided attention to their work. The public schedule provides a measure of certainty that both phases will recur at regular intervals.

Tempo is the repetition of activities at a specific rate in a specific location. Changes in the balance of power among institutions in a city will result in the recognition of differing claims on the time of members, and a different public schedule will develop. Institutional power in cities lies in the control of access to strategic resources, or wealth. Every city includes institutions that generate wealth, administer the wealth of the surrounding hinterland, or provide opportunities for consuming wealth. Each depends upon the repetition of activities at regular intervals to maintain itself. Each has different requirements for repeating its activities, and this yields different tempi. The tempo of a city is a composite of the tempi of its institutions.

The question of whether a single tempo reflects a large population with complex, multifunction institutions concerned some theorists in the early 1950s. Hawley (1950, 290) spoke of a single "functional routine of an urban community." This routine is established when the most important institutions contribute disproportionately to the overall experience of tempo, creating a characteristic rhythm. Halbwachs, on the other hand, sees tempo as built up from the social relations between individuals and institutions. This yields as many tempi as there are possible social relations (1947). Tempo, as used here, incorporates elements of both perspectives. It recognizes Halbwachs's multiple origins of social time, but sees some of these social relations, specifically those of the market and workplace, as involving domination. It takes Hawley's notion of a functional routine as a model for those specific historical periods when a single technical order dominates the workplaces.[8] The last 200 years of Viennese history reveal two such periods. The first is the period of the centralizing reforms of Maria Theresa and Joseph II, when a technical order based on bureaucratic administration dominated. The second is the period of industrialism (1848–present), when the appropriate use of labor and technology focuses on generating highly efficient production rates. In-between, the two technical orders competed for control of the public schedule.

Because the number of dominating institutions in cities is limited, they offer a convenient set of labels with which to compare tempi in different urban regions. Fox has developed a set of categories for talking about the dominating roles of cities in their regions. For him, cities combine both ideological and urban organizational density in their separation from the larger society. This separation underlies the urban cultural roles linking the city with state society (1977, 31). This is similar to Hawley's notion of functional routine. Like Hawley, Fox emphasizes the organizational density of the urban region and the functional linkages between urban and state authority. The categories of cultural roles for cities that Fox discusses are ceremonial, administrative, commercial, colonial, and industrial (1977, 32–36).[9] These represent aggregates of political and economic organizations through which cities order the economy of the surrounding region. Vienna has at one time or another played all five of these roles.

This framework has the virtue of sorting out certain strategic relationships between city and countryside that are useful for discovering the organizational priorities of the urban center. Of course, more refined typologies and modeling of relationships would result in more subtle and nuanced understandings, but I am interested in blocking out a general framework for understanding the relations of power and temporality on the same level as Eric Wolf's attempt to find strategic relationships among technology, economy, and politics in world history (1982). Like Wolf, I am less interested in the precision of the typologizing than I am in the insights that the typologies can expose. I do not presume pure types in history or society, nor am I arguing for a unilineal pattern of development in economic, political, or temporal institutions. We should expect that the societies we encounter will be mongrel historical hybrids of these various types. My interest here is in unpacking the various contributions of these different urban arrangements to the political and temporal whole.

The ceremonial city subordinates resources and technology to the maintenance of religious and political authority. Ceremonial cities are perhaps the earliest urban experiences in human history. The tempo in ceremonial cities grows out of the calendrical round of rituals, feasts, war preparations, sacrifices, and political ceremonies. Outside Europe, many cities have played this role. The best studied included the classic Mayan cities (Coe 1971; Tedlock 1982), Rajput India (Fox 1971), and the Balinese Negara (Geertz 1980). These ceremonial cities have certain organizational characteristics in common. The permanent urban population is small, except during important ceremonies. The settlement is completely dependent on the immediate hinterland for provisions. These cities accumulate wealth through a redistributive economy in which peasant cultivators exchange their produce for ceremonial services. The ceremonies connect the prestige and power of the city to that of the state religious ideology. What sets this kind of city apart from the ceremonial role in all cities is that its very existence depends on these functions (Fox 1977, 41).

In addition to specific symbolic content, these centers distribute a particulate variety of time, that is, a language of time that divides experience into "discrete self-subsistent particles (Geertz 1973, 393)." The astrological calendar and the method for casting a horoscope are remnants of a European particulate language of time. Gurvitch (1964, 112) notes in his analysis of the tempi of "charismatic theocracies" that "awareness of these social times and a real effort to master them is made only by the organizations of the state-churches." The knowledge of which times are auspicious and which inauspicious resides with the religious authorities in the city. Whatever systems of time reckoning the peasants of the hinterland may have had, the particulate time of the ceremonial centers usurps control over the timing of local, kin-ordered social commitments. The impact of this calendar on the hinterland is to break down and reorganize the economy by controlling the frequency with which tribute must be brought to the ceremonial center (Fox and Zagarell 1982, 16). Serving the ceremonies of the calendar is the only legitimate reason for urban residence. The permanent populations of ceremonial cities are necessarily small. All activities are directly or indirectly involved with the ceremonies.

Even in this earliest of urban experiences, tempo is a direct expression of the pattern of domination. The tributary states that formed in Mesoamerica made use of a pervasive understanding of calendrics and horometry to undermine local authority and legitimate central authority, as well as for scheduling the payment of tribute. All segments of society from the centers of power to the marginal peasant producers were involved in this temporal structure and accepted its reality. The timekeepers themselves rivaled local authority in the villages, and the kings and nobles in the capital. The powerful were legitimated through the interpretations of a temporal structure in which the present political meaning of space, person, and occasion is conjoined with the mythological past, as well as the apocalyptic future. Power holders themselves were not timekeepers, but timekeepers exercised their power sometimes for and sometimes against specific persons in authority. Power holders were planners in the sense that they plotted and carried out conquests aimed at increasing the tribute-paying regions of the state. They did so in consultation with the timekeepers and courted disaster if they took action without prior consultation.

Many temporal categories in Vienna derive from that period in the city's history when it was under Roman control, first as a fortress and later as a Roman Catholic ceremonial center. The so-called *ordinatio horae* (practice of the hours) of the armies of the Roman tributary state first stripped peasant recruits of individual choice, substituting a repetitive sequence of drills, exercises, marches, and rest periods. The Roman military divided the day into eight watches of three hours each, four during the night and four during the day. Troops had a specific activity to perform during each watch. The militarized state created by the Augustan caesars incorporated the hours into administrative practice. From these government offices, the timekeeping system diffused into the temporal classifications of work activities of slaves and citizens alike. The canonical hours that regulated monastic life among the tributary states of the European Middle Ages stemmed directly from the Roman *ordinatio horae,* but with some modifications. The monastic day was divided into seven periods of prayer, or offices, each announced with the ringing of bells and each assigned to a different part of the day. The bells further marked off the periods of the day for all who could hear them, carrying the Roman rhythm far into the hinterland.

The oldest church in the city, Ruprechtskirche, was erected in the eighth century. The ceremonial role expanded in 1137 when Saint Stephan's Cathedral was chartered. The cathedral became the center for Catholic ceremonial rites in the Ostmark. The center was elevated to a bishopric in 1469 and to an archbishopric in 1723. With each elevation, more of the countryside was brought under Vienna's ceremonial control. Through the church ceremonials, the division of the day into hours, first into two sets of twelve and later into twenty-four hours, and the division of the year into weeks of seven days each became part of the temporal consciousness of the region. Sunday, the day of Christ's resurrection, was established as the Sabbath. The tempo of the city rested in the recurrence of the hours from day to day through the chanting of the office in the cathedral and other churches, and in the cycle of masses during the week, which culminated in high mass on Sunday. Competing ceremonial organizations of time, such as the Saturday Sabbath of the Jewish community, which coexisted in the city almost continuously throughout the medieval period, were stigmatized and confined to ghetto practice.

Another artifact from the period of Catholic ceremonial hegemony over the public schedule is the cycle of feast days throughout the year. Some of these days recur on the same calendar day each year, such as Advent, Christmas, and the feasts of the saints. Others refer to cultic events that are analogous to, though specifically segregated from, events in the Hebrew lunar calendar. They occur on different calendar days each year. These fixed and moveable feasts combine with the industrial weekend today to create two seasons of extended weekends that initiate the more popular periods of vacation-taking in the yearly round.

The administrative cultural role organizes the public schedule through political oversight of public activities. Administrative cities differ from ceremonial centers in two respects. First, an administrative city is the political, economic, and communication nexus for all neighboring regions. This organizational role swells both the size of the center and the importance of its institutions. Second, the population is likely to be a large, densely settled, stable, and multiethnic one that is drawn to the center because of patronage, the complexity of the market, and the ease of communication. The size and complexity of administrative cities attract other functions. Thus, purely administrative cities are the exception rather than the rule. They can be seen in the capital districts of empires and other large states. Even then, their boundaries are contiguous with those of civilian districts which include other cultural functions.

The large disparities in wealth, power, and privilege within the administrative city engender conflicts over access to strategic resources, the institutions to manage these conflicts, and elaborate, status-defining deferential behaviors. These developments sever the urban population from the egalitarian hinterland. Still, the break is not a complete one. Fox observes that administrative centers adopt stylistic elements from the surrounding countryside to foster identification across the social gap (1977, 61–62). Cities with public schedules that reflect administrative hegemony include Rome and Constantinople at the height of their powers, the castle towns of the Tokugowa Shogunate (Yazaki 1968), and the cities of Cairo, Damascus, and Aleppo under the Mamluks (Lapidius 1967).

The urban life of Chinese cities has been dominated by administrative functions for 1,200 years. Lien-Sheng Yang's study of the history of "official hours," market times, and work times provides a clear picture of the administrative tempo (1955). The primary feature is a well-defined regularity. Unlike the particulate individuality of ritual tempi, administrative time produces predictable sequences. Once in place, these sequences are slow to change. Those changes that do occur are usually the result of either increased market activity and the growth of commercial functions, or the loss of administrative power.

In any competition between the demands of efficient administration and sacralizing ceremony, the administrative wins. Mikalson provides a telling example from Athens where ceremonial feast days would often conflict with the scheduled meetings of the Ekklesia. If the matter was sufficiently urgent, the calendar provided that the archon could intercalculate one or more days at a time, to push the feast out of the way (1975, 3). This would be unthinkable in a city whose regional authority depends on maintaining the sanctity of the round of ceremonials.

Decentralization reinforces control. In Vienna during the eighteenth and early nineteenth centuries, semiautonomous units, such as guilds and neighborhood councils, determined the tempo of the activities under their control. These included the closing of the district gate at night, or limits on the work time of member workshops. The result was a series of nested sequences, of wheels of repetitions of activities within other wheels. At the appropriate times of the day, month, and season, civic events would arise that were common to all the administrative sequences, creating the sense of unity and shared experience. These included folk fests and annual markets, or the anniversaries and birthdays of the royal family. At other times, the cycles would swing people away from each other, emphasizing the particular and local character of life. Pezzl's scene of the different classes of people taking their midday meals at different hours illustrates how these sequences can overlap at some points and diverge at others. Each unit followed its appointed sequence, which is the quintessential characteristic of the tempi of administrative cities.

The tempo of the commercial routine develops in those cities whose wealth comes primarily from long-distance trade and commerce. Commercial cities depend on their hinterlands for only modest supplies of labor and resources. The wealth and power of the region is disproportionately concentrated within the city. Such cities dominate their regions, choking off the development of competitors within their range. Commercial towns initially developed throughout the world as trade centers along river trade routes, caravan stops along the Silk Road, or as port cities in the trading communities of the Christian-organized Atlantic Ocean or Muslim-organized Indian Ocean. To see these towns merely as nodes in a commercial trade network obscures the role of trade in shaping the organization of production. This connection is documented in the history of capitalism in Europe. Something akin to this historic movement underlies the development of commercial towns globally.

European capitalism replaced a tributary mode of production over a 500-year period between the thirteenth and eighteenth centuries. It did so by organizing productive activities into market relations that were far more powerful than the organizations available to tribute takers. The overwhelming volume of medieval production for tribute was mixed agricultural in type and manorial in scope. Manufacturing was limited to the technological needs of the farmers and the military needs of the baron. There was little production for the market and little market consumption outside of the few urban centers. Production was not timed. The farmers simply went about their chores according to the traditional, orally transmitted almanac for the region, and performed manufacturing activities during the winter months. Local tribute takers extracted surpluses from captive producers and protected their hold over the serfs from other tribute takers through extensive military alliances.

In the late-medieval period, protoindustrialists organized textile factories in some urban centers using unskilled and semiskilled labor. The workday was initially structured by the bells of the nearby monastery. It was in the small manufacturing centers in Italy and France that transition from the medieval repetitive sequence of meaningful days to the modern repetitive sequence of meaningful activities took place. The distinction between these ways of thinking about hours is easier to make in German than it is in English. The term *Horen* refers to the medieval concept of hours in which not every moment is contained with the hours named. Rather, the time it takes to chant the office of that particular service is the duration of the hour. The period of time that follows does not count, until the next named hour and its service is encountered. What is being emphasized in this system is the exactness in the recurrence of the rituals and the relative unimportance of any competing activities. The term *Stunden* refers to the modern concept of hours in which every moment of the day is located within one of the twenty-four units of equal duration. What is being emphasized is the openness of the system and its capacity to accommodate any number of activities, ritual or secular, that need to be located within the day.

In these early factories, time had already become money, workers had already become factors of production, and the structure of the work had already become a matter of contention between the first large concentrations of wage laborers and their employers by the end of thirteenth century (Le Goff 1980, 43–57). For example, by medieval convention, it was at the canonical hour of around 3:00 P.M., rather than at midday, when both monks and workers were permitted to pause from their labors, eat a snack, and begin to put away tools for the next day. Employers were believed to be unscrupulous in their timekeeping, moving the hour of None, which was more difficult to identify externally, later and later in the afternoon, to extend the morning's work activities. By the mid-fourteenth century, frustrated workers became more demanding that this pause be linked to something objective, such as midday, instead of some two hours later. This led to the recognition of the first important subdivision of the workday, the half-day. The factory owners agreed to recognize midday as the point when workers could take a break, but insisted that they return after the break for more work. The break would last from the bells at Sext to those of Nones. The actual end of work was signaled by the bells for Vespers. The name the workers used for the break remained Nones. In this way, the canonical hour of Sext disappeared and midday came to be known as *nona* in Italy, *nonne* in France, *Nonzeit* in German, and noon in English. (Bilfinger 1892, 59–90).

During the Renaissance in Europe, the particulate system lost its power to dominate the language of time in urban life. For a period of 400 years multiple temporal structures coexisted before one of them became the pervasive capitalist mode. In all there were nine different regional systems, each distinguished by its own method for counting the hour. By the fifteenth century, the canonical hours had been reduced to Matins, Prime, Terce, Sext, Nones, Vespers, and Complins. Vigils, a service around 2:00 A.M., was delayed until daybreak and combined with Matins. The old Roman system of watches became the basis for the system of temporal hours. These divided day and night into two equal divisions of twelve hours, which varied in length from season to season.[10] The planetary hours were computed in the same fashion as the temporal hours, but were applied to charting the movements of the planets. This gave planetary hours cosmic significance. Finally, there were five systems of dividing the day into twenty-four equal hours: the Italian hours, which started counting the hours at the onset of darkness, about half an hour after sunset,[11] the Babylonian hours, which began counting the hours at sunrise; the Nuremberg hours, in which the number of hours attributed to day and night changed from mid-summer to mid-winter;[12] whole clock hours, in which the twenty-four began at midnight and the hands of the clock took an entire day to revolve; and the small clock hours, also known as the French hours, which began at midnight and divided the day into two equal periods of midnight to midday and midday to midnight, with the clock's hands revolving through the numbers twice. This last system was adopted throughout Europe in the seventeenth century and remains the standard method for dividing the day (Doggett 1986, 105–6).

The slow but certain development from multiple systems to a single temporal system coincided with the gradual victory of capitalist organizations over the administered economies of fourteenth- and fifteenth-century mercantilism. This development was not merely the diffusion of a single way of painting clock faces. It was the acceptance of the idea that a single method for naming time in all localities made the market principle itself more legitimate. The market is a universal mechanism capable of distributing goods and services effectively through the dual principles of supply and demand pricing mechanisms, and profit rationality. Initially, each major market location would select its own time structure from the nine available. The one selected may or may not have been the same one used by the administration of the town or the surrounding countryside. The commercial clock tied the market center to other market centers with which it carried on trade relations. In so doing it regularized the departure and arrival times of postal carriers with their pricing newsletters, bills of exchange, and bills of lading.

These so-called courier hours had been in existence in one form or another since the eighth century and provided an important degree of certainty that these all-important, hand-carried instruments of commerce were moving across the land at a regular rate (Maurice and Maurice 1980, 156). Thus, under the 1555 Augsburg Courier Ordinance, a marketeer could be certain that a letter delivered to the post by 8:00 A.M. on Saturday would arrive in Venice at 8:00 P.M. on Tuesday, giving the Venice correspondent the entire night to reply and deliver the response by 8:00 A.M. Wednesday to the post for delivery in Augsburg by 8:00 P.M. on Saturday. The standardization of the names for clock time in both cities reduced the chance for errors and lost opportunity between correspondents. It guaranteed that a bill of exchange posted on Saturday would not actually be presented for payment until three days later.

The standardization of time structures across regions was made possible by improvements in the technology of mechanical clocks. Landes (1983) has provided a history of this technology and there is no need for me to repeat the sequence of innovations he describes. The investment in innovation over the several centuries that he documents speaks to the importance of ever greater precision in time measurement under the capitalist mode. Courier ordinances, the organization of factory and office routine, and the increasing interest by states in regulating market activity all required a broadly accepted standard for temporal precision. This was provided by the mechanical clock.

Those aspects of time about which the merchant could be certain were the length of a journey, the period of a debt, or the number of months until the next harvest. But not work time. Work time comprised periods of relative inactivity alternating with frantic speed-ups. The inactive periods were caused by delays in the delivery of raw materials, the lack of a work contract, seasonal alternations in the availability of nonguild labor, and the preexisting tributary calendar of the medieval Catholic church, which marked a sequence of feasts on saints' days. Immediately before, during, and after these feasts, no work was performed. They occurred often enough to reduce by half the number of workdays in the year. As part of the reforms undertaken by the Church during the Counter-Reformation, these feasts were replaced by Sabbath observances during which smaller cash tithes could be collected. Sunday was a workday and was not observed as a day of rest by most of the Christian population of Europe before the seventeenth century (Hill 1964).[13] Instead of Sunday, workers throughout capitalist Europe observed Monday as a day free from labor. Known as Saint Monday, or sometimes Blue Monday, this day was devoted to sleeping late, getting drunk, shopping, or attending to official errands. Oftentimes, the lethargy of Monday would spill over into Tuesday and Wednesday, leaving Thursday and Friday as days for intensive work efforts, before work slowed again on Saturday and Sunday in anticipation of the coming Monday. Even within the workday itself there was an uneven distribution of labor effort. Workers slept late, ate after rising, slowly attended to work in the afternoon, and worked most intensely in the early evening as the light began to fail. Thus, preindustrial work activities were consistently irregular within the day, week, and year. Work sped up as the delivery date for contracted products approached. At that point, it was necessary to compensate for the collective impact of the inactive periods.

In each of a city's roles, the relationship of the city to the hinterland is different. The ceremonial city is the most closely tied, economically and culturally, to the surrounding villages. The administrative city cultivates a cultural gulf but remains dependent on the hinterland for its wealth. The commercial city completes the break, relying on its hinterland for little of its wealth or values. In the colonial city, the patterns of dependence run both ways. Like the administrative city, the colonial capital is dependent on the hinterland for labor, provisions, and trade resources. Like the commercial city, it dominates the region, forcing the hinterland communities to depend on its markets for employment and nonsubsistence resources. Temporally, the colonial city is a mixture of the administrative, the commercial, and the ritual-based patterns of the peasant villages. In their temporal as well as political organization, colonial societies refract, as in a prism (Riggs 1964), the traditional world with the imperialist's world into a new social experience.

The colonial city attempts to impose an administrative tempo of rigid sequences on the bureaucratic, military, transport, and commercial services. Yet it must rely on the local organization of the hinterland for the labor, transport, and food. Cooperation has its price and resistance its rewards in such situations. The hinterland finds it easy to evade and dismiss the temporal rationalism of the urban administration. The colonialists find the indigenous tempi inadequate for their needs and dismiss the locals as lazy.[14] Colonial cities generate a disjunctive tempo that defeats precise sequences of administration with the punctuated rhythms of the agricultural village.

As the capital city of an empire and, more explicitly, as the object of distrust by the reaction to centralized authority, Vienna underwent the colonial experience of time in the period before 1848. Administrative control of sequence prevented the feared political aspirations of the middle class from surfacing in Viennese society. Entertainments were curtailed. Curfews were imposed. Military patrols and secret police surveillance increased. In the fashion of a colonial city, a disjunctive public schedule evolved with both formal and informal rhythms. The formal rhythm required people to submit to the overbureaucratized sequences of the suspicious administration if they wanted to use any of the government's services. This lengthened the amount of time it took to open a business, receive an import or export license for products, secure a loan, or travel to other regions. The informal rhythm enabled people to circumvent the formal sequences by relying on network ties between commercial operators and administrators. These networks required constant cultivation. Opportunities for public interaction during the workday between entrepreneurs and administrators evolved, such as the specialized meals Gabelfrühstück and Jause, and the Beiseln and Kaffeehäuser in which to eat them. Through these informal networks, the commercial operators obtained expedited government services. Those with the right connections pursued their commercial tempi, while those without suffered under the inertia of a hostile administration. As in all colonial cities, local administrators undermined the control of the imperialists. In Vienna, the role of these local administrators was played by the proguild forces. The inefficiency of government services available to the antiguild, industrial forces set in motion the events leading up to the Revolution of 1848 and the emergence of the liberal state.

The industrial transformation reorganized work around more consistent periods of activity. Known as "the establishment of work discipline" in the literature, this was a change in the power of the work-giver to include the power to time activities. The primary reason for the change was the increasing complexity in the division of tasks brought about by the factory system, the costs of new technology, and the increasing use of unskilled labor which the new division of tasks made possible. E.P. Thompson has written on how this work discipline was created and enforced in England during the eighteenth and twentieth centuries. I have found that many of the same mechanisms existed in Central Europe as well.[15] Work discipline was the great "social problem" of these centuries. Most of the voices that controlled the official media of the day, including politicians, clerics, authors, factory owners, and newspaper publishers, decried the sloth and idleness they saw around them. They berated workers for their inattentiveness to diligence. A Confucian-like equation evolved in Europe in which work discipline, productivity, and efficiency became officially aligned with moral virtue. At the same time, work discipline became associated with wage incentives. The more disciplined the worker, the better the pay (Thompson 1967, 79–81).

The process of socialization to work discipline began with the un-skilled and slowly moved up the skill ladder. Throughout the period of early industrial transformation and, in many cases, still today, the most skilled and sought-after workers set their own pace of work. The powerless at the bottom of the skill ladder were dismissed for not arriving on time at the beginning of the shift or end of the break, leaving too early at the end of the shift, or not paying complete attention to their work during the shift. By the beginning of the nineteenth century, the demand for work discipline had spread to the semiskilled positions. In England, the reaction among workers brought the first trade unions into existence and contributed to the first working-class consciousness of their sudden and swift separation from the control of their work activities (Thompson 1963).

Industrial production in Europe originated in the small towns and minor regional centers. Not until the organization of work was fully de-veloped did industrial entrepreneurs move into the cities. They did so to benefit from the established communication networks for access to raw materials and specialized financial markets. The modern industrialists found the technological time sense that had developed under commercial treatments of time adequate in most respects. The commercial work pat-terns of urban craftsworkers were too diffuse for the industrial managers.

The shift in the domination of the public schedule by first the com-mercial, then the administrative, and finally the industrial technical orders, altered the tempo of urban life for all Viennese. Because of it, workers lost control over the sequence of work tasks. Managers were imposed over craftsworkers to ensure time discipline and adherence to the rate. The older time patterns of the commercial guild work organization, such as the Sunday to Monday weekend, disappeared. The seven-day workweek trans-formed time free from work into a new resource to be controlled. The structure of the workday was compacted; socializing on the job and breaks were reduced to the barest minimum. Adult males who might object to the imposition of work orders by a manager lost jobs to more pliant women and children. This changed the social composition of work organizations. Only the job stripped workers of control over where to turn their attention next, the nonworking life had no such regimentation. This separation of functions is the hallmark of the industrial technical order.

The timing and tempo of a city reflect the power of some institutions to dominate the durations and sequences of households. These institutions compete with each other and generate a public schedule that dominates the activities of individuals, and through them, their households. Individual experiences of urban time result from being at the point where these differing dimensions of time converge. The organization of time in cities is not merely a collection of conventions that accumulate over time. It is a mirror of the power relations inherent in the social order of the metropolis. It comprises the full complexity of formal and informal groupings of people in precisely the relations of solidarity and dominance that link them to resources. The unwrapping of these activity patterns makes this complexity intelligible.

APPENDIX

his study takes the *Wohnung* (the dwelling unit or household) as its unit of analysis for purely practical reasons. It is possible to define, bound, and compare households, albeit with some difficulty. The more theoretically appropriate unit of analysis in Vienna is the *Bekanntenkreis*, the network of persons who share the greater part of their lives and their understandings about life with each other. It is unwieldy to define and work with networks as units of analysis within the urban field. The very size and complexity of urban regions bring about continuous shifts in the composition and activation of social networks throughout the lives of individuals. While the boundaries of a network unit could be expressed statistically, my feeling is that the methodological benefits do not outweigh the effort involved. Nor is it entirely clear that the Viennese understand their Bekanntenkreise as operating units apart from their participation in the dyads which comprise those networks. The dwelling unit offers a more workable unit of analysis. The household segment of the network remains intact for substantial portions of time. It also operates as a unit in a number of important activity areas.

Familie (the family) also is a potentially effective unit of analysis. The family assembles on a regular basis to engage in important activities. On closer examination, the family as a unit turns out to be quite problematic. First, families are spread out among a number of households, some of which may be quite distant from each other. Contemporary Viennese practice is neolocal postmarital residence, although ideally the young couple would like to stay within walking distance of at least one parental household if they intend to have children and need assistance with child care. However, the cost and availability of apartments often dictate a greater distance. Second, statistical summaries that allow me to generalize across the metropolitan region take the household, rather than the family, as the

207

basic unit. Third, old friends are likely to play as important a role in the activities of the household as nonresident family members. This is why the network would be a far more useful unit than the household, if it were more workable. Thus, the household remains the most effective second choice.

The data-gathering strategy of the study was to explore the households comprising a number of networks, collect information from these households, and then fit the data against the structure of households in the city. The demographic structure of the city is less complex when viewed as a distribution of household types than it is for any other independent variable. When households are linked to employment class, the number of categories in a scheduled sample begins to approach a workable number for a single researcher to interview in depth. To appreciate this requires some background in the demographics of the city.

The population on March 31, 1981, according to the national census, was 1,531,346.[1] Austrians, unlike Germans, tend to comply with the census process. A large number of Yugoslav and Turkish guest workers became citizens, while others remained in the city illegally after their contracts had expired. They are likely to be underrepresented in the census figures. As of June 1982, 9% of this population were under ten years of age. Twelve percent were between ten and twenty. Nine percent were between twenty and thirty. Fifteen percent were between thirty and forty. Seventeen percent were between forty and fifty. Thirteen percent were between fifty and sixty. Eleven percent were between sixty and seventy. Six percent were over seventy. Although these percentages reflect an aging population, the average age in the city has been dropping steadily from a high of 41.6 years in the 1971 census to the current 37.2 years. The top-heavy character of the population pyramid is the product of the high population losses and low birth and infant survival rates associated with World War II and its aftermath.

The total number of employed people constitutes 44% of the population. Of these, 43% are women. The vast majority of employed people (92.4%) work for another individual, organization, or institution. Of the remaining employed people, 7½% are self-employed, and 2½% are employed within their family. Of those who work in the private sector, 34% are paid hourly and 53% are paid a monthly salary. Thirteen percent of all employees work in the public sector. This includes the various state-owned energy, commercial, manufacturing, and artistic enterprises, as well as the agencies and bureaus of a modern industrial state. A quarter of the population are retired and receiving pensions. Another 30% of the population are dependent household members. Homemakers are nearly 30% of this group of dependents, while children under the age of fifteen represent 50%. The remaining 20% of dependent household members include children over fifteen who are still in school (13%), unemployed adults (5%), and older adults who are not receiving pensions (6%).

There are 710,100 households in Vienna. The head of household is a wage earner in 55% of these households. Of these, 10% are self-employed, 16% work in

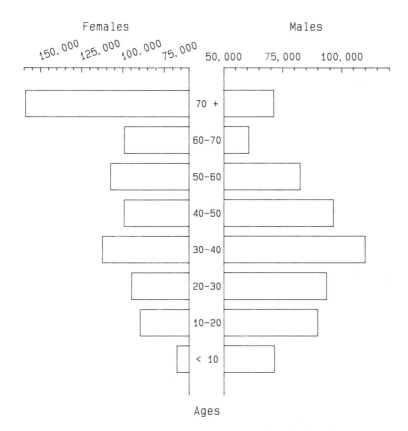

FIGURE 11: Age/Sex Structure of the Viennese Population. *Source: Magistratsabteilung 66, 1983.*

the public sector, one-third earn hourly wages, and one-half earn monthly wages. Among those 45% of households where the head of household is not working, 91% are pensioned. This study focuses on households with at least one wage earner.

Sixty percent of the households with unemployed heads are single persons, and 31% are two-person households. Because of the large number of small households, the average household size is 1.2 people. Households with employed heads of household are larger. Only one-fifth are single-person households, 28% are two-person households, 26% are three-person households, 18% are four-person households, and 7% are households with five persons or more. This yields an average size of 2.06 persons for households in which the head of household is employed.

The following table lists the personal and household characteristics for the Viennese who befriended me and helped me to understand their lives. Their names

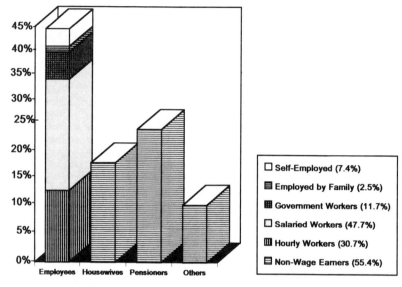

FIGURE 12: Structure of the Viennese Work Force, 1982. *Source: Magistratsabteilung 66, 1983.*

have been changed to protect their privacy. The information refers to their occupations, ages, and years in residence as of 1976.

THE VIENNESE TIME BUDGET STUDIES

Viennese sociologists have compiled three large sample time budget studies. The first of these was conducted in 1961 by researchers at the Bildungsabteilung of the Kammer für Arbeiter und Angestellte in Wien. The published report gives the mean responses of a sample of 2,073. The sample was compiled from the address list of the Viennese members of the Arbeiterkammer. This would include all trade-union members, employed or unemployed. Respondents were interviewed and the answers to a scheduled questionnaire were recorded. These questions asked people to specify both durations and frequencies of various activities. Both of these sets of responses were averaged for subgroup differences. The subgroups that were considered salient in 1961 were gender, employment status, education, and age. Chi-square tests for significance were performed on the subgroup differences (Kammer für Arbeiter und Angestellte 1961). The emphasis of the study is on *Arbeitszeit,* work time (35% of questions), and *Freizeitgestaltung,* leisure time (60% of questions). Because the data represent respondents' estimates, rather than the record of the sequence of activities over a day, the data cannot be used to observe the effect of public schedule constraints.

TABLE 2

CHARACTERISTICS OF INTERVIEW PARTNERS

Family Name	Gender	Age/Yrs. in Vienna	Birthplace	Occupation	House-hold Size	Chil-dren
Eichl, J.	F	55/30	Vienna	Journalist(E)	2	0
Eichl, H.	M	57/10	Bohemia	Chemical Engineer(E)	2	0
Ritter, H.	M	32/32	Vienna	Electrical Engineer(E)	1	0
Neubacher, I.*	F	21/3	Lower Austria	Office Clerk(E)	1	0
Lihotsky, M.	M	33/15	Graz	Pol. Scientist(E)	1	0
Hartinger, B.*	F	59/44	Vienna	Secretary(E)	2	0
Hartinger, K.*	M	67/30	Berlin	Chemical Worker(W)	2	0
Matouschek, J.*	F	23/23	Vienna	Teacher(E)	1	0
Pindt, B.	F	24/24	Vienna	Secretary(E)	1	0
Schraube, H.	M	32/25	Vienna	Restauranteur(I)	2	0
Tuzzi, W.*	M	27/10	Lower Austria	Gas Installer(E)	3	1
Tuzzi, M.*	F	23/9	Lower Austria	Teacher(E)	3	1
Schönthal, E.*	M	65/60	Vienna	Executive(X)	2	0
Koblischek, M.*	F	33/30	Bratislava	Housewife(H)	4	2
Koblischek, H.	M	35/35	Vienna	Journalist(E)	4	2
Weihsmann, L.	F	25/25	Vienna	Teacher(E)	1	1
Weihsman, M.	M	26/4	Prague	Teacher(E)	3	1
Gütl, G.	F	32/32	Lower Austria	Interpreter(E)	1	0
Ulrich, J.*	M	55/55	Vienna	Chemical Worker(W)	2	0
Walter, E.*	M	54/52	Vienna	Chemical Worker(W)	2	0
Meindl, P.	M	30/30	Vienna	Watchmaker(I)	5	3
Mayreder, H.	F	78/64	Kiev	Medical Technologist(R)	1	0
Bettauer, J.*	F	28/28	Vienna	Housewife(H)	4	2
Bettauer, C.*	M	22/32	Prague	Social Scientist(B)	4	2
Leischner, F.*	M	72/66	Vienna	Physician(R)	2	0
Leischner, A.	F	66/60	Vienna	Housewife(H)	2	0
Riedl, I.*	F	88/62	Vienna	Housewife(H)	2	0
Mandl, L.	F	28/28	Vienna	Teacher(E)	4	2
Mandl, P.	M	35/7	Vienna	Salesman(E)	4	2
Schieder, M.	F	34/34	Vienna	Housewife(H)	4	2
Schieder, G.	M	36/36	Vienna	Travel Agent(E)	4	2
Kurzweil, D.	F	28/28	Vienna	Executive(X)	1	0
Neubau, H.	M	57/51	Vienna	Journalist(E)	2	0
Klein, P.	M	59/53	Vienna	Editor(X)	2	0
Klein, I.	F	57/52	Vienna	Housewife(H)	2	0
Brunner, W.	M	56/56	Vienna	Supervising Engineer(E)	3	1
Brunner, S.	F	55/34	Vienna	Interpreter(E)	3	1
Linz, T.	M	61/53	Vienna	Executive(X)	2	0
Baier, P.	M	35/35	Bonn	Executive(B)	4	2
Ehn, G.	F	23/23	Vienna	Biologist(E)	1	0
Böhm, K.	F	23/23	Vienna	Teacher(E)	1	1
Kleinburger, H.	F	25/25	Vienna	Secretary(E)	1	1
Hautmann, R.	F	27/27	Vienna	Secretary(E)	1	1
Renner, B.	F	21/21	Vienna	Law Student(S)	5	2

E–Angestellte (employee); W–Arbeiter (worker); I–Freiberufler (self-employed); X–Executive; B–Beamte (government worker); R–Pensionist (retired); S–Student

Note: An asterisk indicates that a quotation from this informant was used in the text of this study.

In 1970, a second large sample time budget study was mounted by the same department. It was structured identically with the Twelve Nation Study on the Uses of Time, organized by Alexander Szalai, Philip Converse, Erwin Scheuch, and Philip Stone through the European Coordination Center for Research and Documentation in the Social Sciences (the Vienna Center) (Szalai 1972).[2] Although preliminary results were published almost immediately (Mündel 1971), the complete analysis was not available until 1979 (Mündel et al 1979). The sample included 2,012 respondents selected from the addresses of the Viennese members of the Arbeiterkammer. The survey was conducted in two sections. All of the respondents filled out a multipage questionnaire structured in a similar fashion to the 1961 study, while a smaller sample (approximately one hundred) were asked to keep activity logs for a week (Mündel 1976, personal communication). The responses were analyzed as ranks, and the distribution of responses among a category range was reported. Thus, we learn what percentage of the respondents stopped work at 3:00–4:00 P.M., 4:00–5:00 P.M., and so on. The time logs were not available to me, although I hope to have a chance to look at them someday. These logs were analyzed in terms of the percentages of respondents engaged in a particular activity on each of the seven days. This format was useful for describing the shift in activity patterns between weekday and weekend, and for observing the variation in, say, shopping trips, within the weekly round.

The categories of the respondents are more sophisticated in the 1971 study, with more discrimination among extended households, educational experience, and marriage status. It is interesting to note that the conclusion of the preliminary results in 1971, at the height of the debate about the effectiveness of the work-time-reduction policy, was that people were spending more of their newly won time on recreations. The conclusion of the 1979 report, published at a time when the momentum for further reductions had stalled, was that people who worked variable shifts had substantially less time for recreation, even if they worked the same number of hours per week as people who had regular shifts. The attention of the policy planners had clearly changed its focus toward that of protecting part-time employed women from variable shifts. To my knowledge this is the last of the time budgets mounted by the Arbeiterkammer.

The 1981 time budget study was conducted by the Austrian Central Statistical Bureau as part of the Sonderprogram of the 1981 Mikrozensus. This was a census of national scope in which Vienna represented only 14.3% (4,433 people). It was structured as a simple one-page questionnaire that asked people to record the beginning time of their activities in the order in which they happened. The respondents were supplied with a list of forty-seven categories of activities that they were to use. The returned questionnaires indicated a relatively even distribution among the seven days. Saturday, which had to be recorded on Sunday, had the lowest representation (12.7); Tuesday had the highest (15.0). The data was arranged by the average amount of time (hours, minutes) the respondents spent among the forty-seven categories. Respondents were also asked if they were on vacation, on a day off, bedridden, or ill but not bedridden. Those who answered affirmatively were grouped and subtracted from the main group. This left a main group whose responses reflected their ordinary routine. The sequence in which the activities occurred produced tables that described the number of people engaged in an activity at specific hours of the day. These are exceptionally useful arrangements of the data. In the 1984 report, the editors provided only the daily rhythm graphs for gender and work status—employed, unemployed, retired, or dependent housewife (Simhandl, Riess and Riha 1984, 247-82).

In the figures that follow, I have graphed the daily rhythm tables on gender and employment/educational status of *Arbeiter* (hourly workers, including apprentices), *Facharbeiter* (skilled workers), *Angestellte und Beamte* (all salaried employees), *Angestellte und Beamte mit mittlerer Schulbildung* (salaried clerical employees), and *Angestellte und Beamte mit Hochschulbilding* (highest educated salaried employees, including primarily self-employed professionals, executives, and managers). These daily rhythm graphs represent the entire national sample, and not Vienna alone. The component of the public schedule that derives from federal law is considerable and greatly reduces variation across the country among wage earners and shop owners. All seven days are averaged together, which creates a number of distortions, primarily because of the shifting of work within the household to Saturday morning by households in which all of the adult members

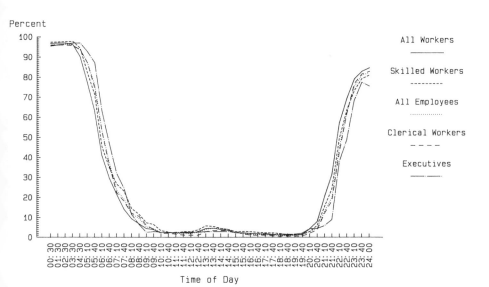

FIGURE 13: Sleep Segment for All Workers, 1981. *Source: Simhandl, Riess, and Riha 1984.*

are wage earners. In spite of these difficulties, these graphs are the best available picture of how the different provisions of the public schedule create variation among households in Vienna.

The activity categories are not all equally constrained by the differences in the work schedules. The Viennese sleep segment is the same for all categories of employment and for men and women. In all of the other categories, there are apparent differences among types of workers and between genders. A number of clocks, both natural (the night) and social (television), tell the Viennese when it is time to sleep. The number of evening and night-shift workers is kept to the absolute minimum by trade-union policy.

The wage-earning work segment (Work Outside the Home) shows that most hourly and salaried workers follow essentially the same pattern, one hour apart. Female executives have much less homogeneous work segments. Teachers are included in this group, and since they have a short workday, they distort the pattern during the morning portion of the segment. Female executives are likely to use their increased control over the pace of work to engage in many different kinds of nonworking activities during the work segment.

The housework segment has a morning and an afternoon peak. Since the data include Saturday activities, the morning peak can be understood to refer primarily to Saturday morning housework segments. Looking at the weekday afternoon housework segment, female executives and male clerical workers are the least

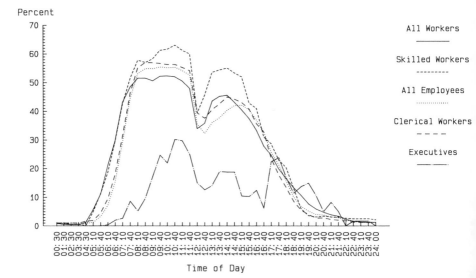

FIGURE 14: Work Outside the Home for Women, 1981. *Source: Simhandl, Riess, and Riha 1984.*

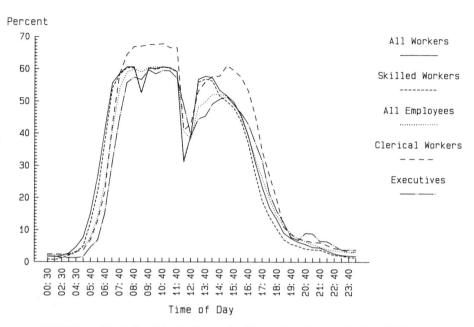

Percent

All Workers

Skilled Workers

All Employees

Clerical Workers

Executives

Time of Day

FIGURE 15: Work Outside the Home for Men, 1981. *Source: Simhandl, Riess, and Riha 1984.*

frequently involved, suggesting that they are the most likely to postpone housework until Saturday. The norm among other workers seems to be to fulfill housework responsibilities immediately after work.

Recreational activities are highly consistent. The norm appears to be that a daily recreation segment occurs after the housework segment on weekdays. The deviations among male and female executives refer to weekend activities. Not even executives can give over portions of the work segment to play during the week. This pattern suggests that while all Viennese play on weekends, higher-educated and higher-salaried workers tend to devote a greater portion of their weekends to play than do other residents.

The patterns of food consumption (mealtimes) reflect the three-meal pattern. Some evidence of the five-meal pattern remains in the small peak among hourly, skilled, and clerical workers at 9:10 (Gabelfrühstück) and the smaller peak at 16:10 (Jause). Executives, especially female executives, have the most varied mealtimes. Hourly workers and salaried employees have their breakfast peaks one hour apart, reflecting the different starting time. It is impossible to tell from the data whether these food-taking activities are social meals or individual snacking.

Socializing with friends and relatives overlaps with the recreation segment on weekdays and weekends. The lateness of the socializing is due to weekend evening amusements. The graph for females shows the greatest differences among the

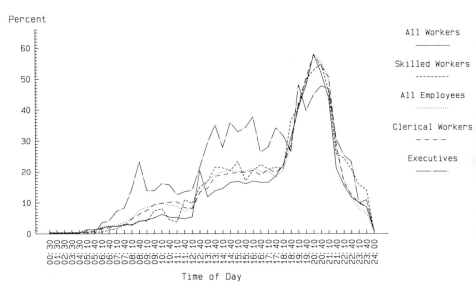

FIGURE 16: Recreation Activities for Women, 1981. *Source: Simhandl, Riess, and Riha 1984.*

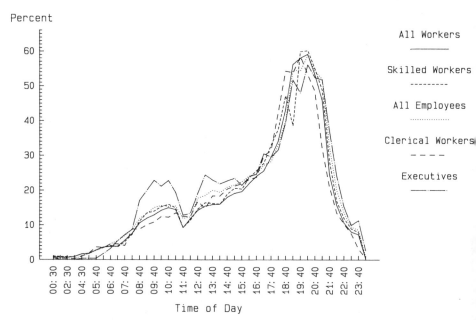

FIGURE 17: Recreation Activities for Men, 1981. *Source: Simhandl, Riess, and Riha 1984.*

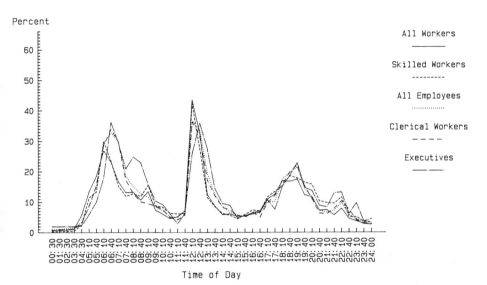

FIGURE 18: Meal-taking Activities for All Workers, 1981. *Source: Simhandl, Riess, and Riha 1984.*

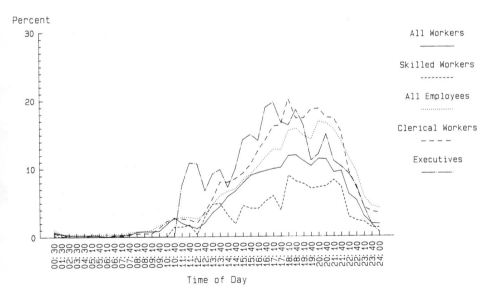

FIGURE 19: Socializing Activities for Women, 1981. *Source: Simhandl, Riess, and Riha 1984.*

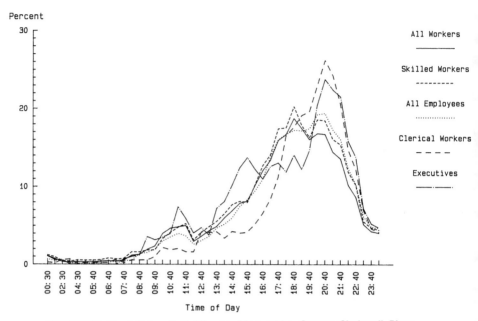

FIGURE 20: Socializing Activities for Men, 1981. *Source: Simhandl, Riess, and Riha 1984.*

employment groups of any activity studied. This is probably the result of geographic variation within the data, and not any constraint on socializing imposed by work schedules.

NOTES

1. Population figures are quoted from the most recent sources available for each category. These include the Microcensus of June 1982, the National Census of May 1981, and the Microcensus of June 1979 (Magistratsabteilung 66 1980, 1983)

2. This study also produced the data on French urban households that Johnson used in his comparison of French urban and Machiguenga village uses of time (1978).

NOTES

1. In order for the uptown visits to outnumber the downtown visits nine to one, the waiting time for the uptown train must be nine times longer than the waiting time for the downtown train. If the interval for each train is ten minutes, the downtown train arrives one minute after the uptown train leaves and the uptown train arrives nine minutes after the downtown train leaves. If the man is arriving at the platform at random times, there is a nine in one chance that the first train to arrive will be the uptown train.

2. The combination of local and supralocal forces in the creation of urban experiences was first described by Redfield and Singer (1954). Wolf observed that power differences affect all social relationships in state societies (1966). Leeds determined that supralocal forces dominate local ones through institutionalized power differences in urban societies specifically (1973). My understanding of metropolitan knowledge grows out of these seminal observations.

3. Smith identifies three different types of irregular development: primate cities, feeder systems, and top-heavy systems. All three can be identified with metropolitan experiences historically. Vienna, for example, was a primate city region immediately after World War I severed it from its former empire. Subsequent development has enabled the region to evolve into a top-heavy system. Smith (1976, 261) defines top-heavy systems as follows: "High production diversity, and advantages of scale, capital and infrastructure in a region that is partly underdeveloped lead to top-heavy central place systems (which reinforce the determining variables), and top-heavy central-place systems in turn lead to concentrated growth, monopoly control, and internal stratification in the top-heavy marketing area (which reinforce the determining variables)."

4. Penzing, the middle-sized Fourteenth District from January to February 1975; Fünfhaus, the middle-sized Fifteenth District from February to May 1975; Josefstadt, the small Eighth District from February to June, 1976; on the boundary between Wieden, the small Fifth District, and Favoriten, the large Tenth District from September to October, 1976; Donaustadt, the large Twenty-second District from October 1976 to January 1977; the suburban Lower Austrian town of Perchtoldsdorf during summer 1980 and in December 1981.

5. Johann Pezzl will be introduced in the next chapter. Anton Josef Gross-Hoffinger was a Bohemian-born, Viennese geographer living in Leipzig in the late 1820s and 1830s. He was well known for his German-language geographical writings and traveler's guides to the lands of the Danube River Valley, a popular travel and trade route. He was the author of the book *Wien wie es ist*, a kind of *Fodor's Guide* for Germans intending to visit the imperial capital. I have discussed the particular problems of using such traveler's guides as ethnographic sources elsewhere (Rotenberg 1986).

6. Population figures are quoted from the most recent sources available for each category. These include the Microcensus of June 1982, the National Census of May 1981, and the Microcensus of June 1979 (Magistratsabteilung 66 1980; 1983).

7. The data introduced here come from the May 12, 1981, House and Apartment Census (Magistratsabteilung 66 1983, 280). The conversion from Viennese room units to American bedroom units is not easy. In Vienna rooms are counted exclusive of kitchens, balconies, bathrooms, or entry halls. However, apartments can have two or more living rooms. Thus, a two-room unit would probably be a one-bedroom apartment, while a four-room unit could be a two-bedroom apartment.

8. The amount of space available in these housing units has also increased from an average of 53 square meters per unit in 1961 to 64 square meters per unit in 1981. The new housing has also increased the availability of three- and four-room units. Most of this new housing includes both public and private apartment complexes built in the large outer districts of the city, especially the Twenty-first and Twenty-second, on the east side of the Danube (over 100% increase), and a group of four districts (Tenth, Eleventh, Twelfth, and Twenty-third) along the southern rim of the city (51% to 100% increase). The inner-city districts have experienced either a less than 20% increase, or, in the Seventh, Eighth, and Fifteenth, even a net loss of housing units (Kainrath 1978, 4).

9. These figures are from 1971 (Magistratsabteilung 66 1979, 25). Figures on commuting were not published in the 1981 census.

1. The 1923 edition of Pezzl's *Skizze von Wien* was used for the translation because it provided the clearest orthography and spellings. The text of the chapter is identical with the 1792 edition. I am grateful to Jolanta Zalud for her help with this translation. I have included explanatory remarks in brackets if the reference in the text would be unclear to a modern reader.

2. The areas Pezzl refers to as suburbs are in fact small village parishes within half an hour to an hour's walk from the central district. In the eighteenth century, these areas provided the primary location for new craft workshops and the first factories. In the nineteenth century, they were already too crowded to absorb the new immigrant factory laborers or the new factories. These were forced to locate farther away, in the belt more than an hour's walk from the city center. These eighteenth-century suburbs were incorporated as municipal districts in the 1880s.

3. The Viennese ate four meals a day from at least the 1500s to the mid-nineteenth century. Then a fifth, mid-afternoon meal was added. The current norm of three meals began after World War I. This midmorning meal, Gabelfrühstück, was eaten in public houses or brought from home. It traditionally consisted of a thick soup, or bread and sausage. Schoolchildren and mothers who stay home are most likely to still eat this meal. The coffeebreak in offices is not the midmorning meal of old. The old meal lasted at least a half-hour and was eaten outside the office, usually in a pub. The impact of industrialization on mealtimes is discussed in detail in chapter 5.

4. The Prater is Vienna's largest park. During Pezzl's lifetime, it was primarily the private reserve of the nobility, although commoners traditionally used the northern corner of the park, the Wurstlprater. Today, the park is a public one.

5. The traditional middle- and upper-class Viennese midday meal was the main meal of the day and included three courses: soup, entree, and dessert. The poorer classes simply ate bread, a thin soup, and potatoes. Meat was quite scarce, as were the time and fuel to prepare it.

6. These locations are either suburban districts surrounding the central district, parks, or famous gardens. The particular group of places he names suggests that in the late afternoon in spring or autumn, the city residents seek the outdoors in settings that remind them of the countryside. Chapter 7 explores the role of rural settings in Viennese play in more detail.

7. External corroboration of this feature of preindustrial Vienna is provided by Lichtenberger's study of the housing stock of the First District between the six- teenth and eighteenth centuries (1977, 42–97). She shows that all economic classes lived within the walls of the city. The villages beyond the walls were neither

bedroom communities nor ghettos. Instead, they were independent economic units oriented toward agriculture and cottage crafts. When the villagers came into the city, it was as peddlers and marketeers. Since the entire length of the old city today can be traversed in twenty minutes, even with heavy automobile traffic, home was never very far away from work.

8. A series of graphs based on my analysis of this study is provided in the appendix. Also contributing to my understanding of the variety of activity paths in the contemporary city is the interview material contained in chapter 4.

9. Joseph II in that year successfully promulgated a Sunday Closing Law for administrative offices and offices under state contract. The law was widely ignored in the suburbs (Pezzl 1923, 220).

CHAPTER 3

1. Paul Rabinow's *French Modern* (1989) became available only as I was in the final revisions of the manuscript. This work explores the ideas of French social modernists in a similar fashion. Rabinow cites Gombrich's distinction of the emergence of the modern taste in opposition to the classical as a continuing dialectic in the history of art. For me, social modernism is not the appropriation of an art-historical term, but a recognition that both the art-historical and the social-historical phenomena emerge from a dialectic in the cultural apprehension of time in all places and in all epochs. The default condition is the classical/traditional only because it requires the least effort. The challenge is to explain why the energetic, radical taste of modernism should emerge to dominate the symbolic production of a society for a period of time. I agree with Rabinow that crises devalue the classical/traditional and open the door for modernist activism. But, following Benjamin (1977), I locate the origin (*Ursprung*) of the crises, not in the problem of representations in the nineteenth century, but in the states of emergency that begin in the seventeenth century and continue through the present.

2. The shape of the boulevard was influenced by the military considerations of rapid troop movement in the event of urban warfare, a principle of urban design that had been popularized by Haussmann in his redesign of Paris. The imperial army had been frustrated by the narrow, crooked streets of the central district, which inhibited their movements during the 1848 revolution, and welcomed a means for efficient access to all sides of the central district.

3. This translation comes from Schorske's essay (1981, 63).

4. The translation of Wagner's remarks in this paragraph comes from Schorske's essay (1981, 74).

5. Leon Trotsky, for example, made the following observations (quoted in Wil-

son 1972, 502): "The Viennese leaders of the Social Democracy used the same formulas I did, but one had only to turn them five degrees around in their own axis to discover that we gave quite different meanings to the same concepts. Our agreement was a temporary one, superficial and unreal."

6. In 1977, when double-digit inflation was the rule in most industrial countries, Austria's inflation rate was 5.7%, and dropping from a high in 1975 of 8.4% (Bundesministerium für Finanzen 1977, 67).

7. Peasant craft production was particularly important in the growth of the textile trade. This trade was built on the traditional skills and production tools of the rural population.

8. Christoph Bettauer, an informant, related having once read the diary of a great-grandfather who had been a buyer of textiles under the Kaufsystem in Northern Bohemia in the 1840s. He would sit on a chair in a peasant market as producers brought cloth for him to inspect. At the end of the day, he would buy the best-quality textiles by having the producers bid against each other to offer him the lowest price. He later was able to invest his profits from this activity by building the first textile mill in that district.

9. The first charters sought to revive the city's reputation as a producer of luxury items. The first one was granted to an Italian silk finisher in 1697. The privilege charter was itself developed from the system of *Privativa,* workshops that were created specifically by the emperor and were independent of guild oversight. Privativa charters were extended to an entrepreneur whom the emperor wanted to entice to work in Vienna. One such early industrial, J. J. Becker, brought considerable international experience and training with him when he built the Manufakturhaus auf dem Tabor in 1675 (Hatschek 1886).

10. The reinstitution of restrictions on internal migration and occupations helped the landed gentry to consolidate the second serfdom in the eastern provinces. Prior to absolutism, the peasantry could escape a repressive lord by fleeing to the cities. After absolutism, the lords controlled the cities and flight was fruitless. Within the cities, this absolutism ensured that economic change could occur only from above.

11. The Church, while not particularly effective as an advocate for working-class interests, continued to work for enforcement of free Sundays and a thirteen-hour limit to work shifts on moral grounds (Gordon 1975).

12. The Monday was called *Krugtag* or *Blauer Montag,* because the drinking activities that occupied craftsworkers on Sunday were paid for with hangovers on Monday (Kramer 1975, 26–28). E. P. Thompson gives evidence of the wide distribution of this pattern among European artisans, noting that English weavers

kept a Saint Monday, and sometimes Tuesday as well, to make up for working on Friday and Saturday nights (1963, 338).

13. Unlike the English situation described by E. P. Thompson (1967), churchmen did not participate in this process of socialization in the industrializing provinces of the Habsburg Empire. After the Wars of Religion, protestant groups were persecuted and the dominant Catholic clergy were not interested in workplace problems unless they threatened the morality of the community with drunkenness and the impoverishment of families (Gordon 1975).

14. Gross-Hoffinger applauds as diligent a working-class family of his acquaintance in which the father is a woodchopper, the mother washes laundry, and the children work in a factory (1832, 50). An 1831 edict, the first attempt to regulate the working standards of the new factories, guaranteed that children could spend Sundays with their parents free from factory work. It did not apply to adults.

15. The suburban and outlying districts were incorporated into the municipal administration as follows: Second through Tenth districts in 1880, Eleventh through Nineteenth in 1890, Twentieth in 1900, Twenty-first in 1910, Twenty-second in 1938, and Twenty-third in 1948.

16. Rudolph has calculated the decade-by-decade growth rates of the major European industrial powers. They show that Austria as a whole grew at a slower initial rate than France, Germany, and England. When the rate did surpass growth in these countries after 1861, it was not sufficient to catch up with the early spurt of its competitors (1976).

CHAPTER 4

1. *The Workingman:* We have a bed/ We have a child/ Dear wife!/ We also have work/ and all we need/ and the sun/ and the rain and wind/ and we lack only a trifle:/ To be as free as the birds are/ In time!

2. One persistent issue, first raised by Galbraith in *The Affluent Society* (1958), is whether industrialism reduces work time. Galbraith, focusing on the differences in work time between the early factories and current standard work laws in developed societies, believes it does. Harris, surveying a highly problematic set of time-allocation studies in the anthropological literature, sees work time as increasing geometrically from food collecting through horticulture and intensive agriculture to industrialized agriculture (1975, 204–18). Johnson has made an effort to resolve these two views by applying Becker's neoclassic models of measuring the value of time allocations in households (1965) in a Machiguenga village (1975), and comparing the results to those of French urbanites (1978). He concludes that the Amazonians work fewer hours. Minge-Klevana summarized the available eth-

nographic data on time allocations cross-culturally and concluded that work time neither increases nor decreases with industrialism. Instead it is reallocated through existing role relationships. The most important change is the loss of child labor to the household as a result of school schedules (1980, 287). I agree with Minge-Klevana's reading, but would add that it is misleading to focus artificially on daily units when trying to understand this redistribution. Industrialism makes possible both the increase and the decrease of the work segment as workers and managers make choices among competing priorities within a framework of culturally attributed meanings of the work experience.

3. This example pertains to those workers with forty-five-hour weeks in 1969 only (about 50%). The formula for calculating paid break time varied for people working forty-four hours and forty-three hours with a base of one hundred minutes of break time (twenty minutes per day) and forty-five hours with a base of three hundred minutes of break time (one hour per day). Cf. Kinzel 1969, 28–29 for a summary of these formulas.

4. The issue of time organization among the pensioned and disabled is an important one, but outside the scope of this work. Time budget studies of the daily activities of the pensioned segment of the population were included in the initial social gerontological studies in Vienna. A significant feature of their activities is their social isolation. These results and a discussion of the social networks and household relations of this significant segment of the population can be found in the works of Rosenmayr and Koecheis (1962, 1965a, 1965b).

5. Tenure protection is the extension of full civil service job protection to employees, whether they are employed by the state or by a private firm. Not all private firms are required to provide this status for their Angestellte unless the state has a financial interest in the firm. This includes most of the largest employers in the country. It is an administrative action that is taken after varying periods of provisional job status. For all intents and purposes it is a guarantee of life tenure.

6. For a description of the entire interview group and the relationship of its characteristics to those of the city in general, see the Appendix.

7. These schedules were elicited in the following way: the informants were asked to recall and describe everything they had done "yesterday" from the time they awoke to the time they retired, making as many references to clock time as possible. The responses were recorded on tape and written notes were also taken. Informants were allowed to go into as much detail as they wanted. I would occasionally ask for more information about a particular activity, or a reference to clock time. Otherwise, the informants were not interrupted or interrogated. Some informants spoke better English than I spoke German. In those cases, the interviews

were conducted in English. Otherwise, the interviews were in German. In the case of Herr Ulrich, the interview was conducted in English.

The taped responses were translated with the help of a professional German/ English simultaneous translator who is also a native speaker of the Viennese dialect of German. This translation process ensured that the nuances of the informants' speech were retained as much as possible. The responses were edited so that the details of the activities were in balance with each other. No references to activities were deleted. When appropriate I have included the specific words used by the informant. The American voice in some of these accounts results from my efforts to smooth out an otherwise rough translation.

8. This interview was conducted in German.

9. The "filling" process refers to the most central manufacturing task in the factory: the production of dishwashing detergent. What are being filled up are tanks of liquid raw material which is then mixed by machine and distributed into two-liter plastic containers.

10. This interview was conducted in German.

11. This interview was conducted in English. Frau Hartinger lived in England for a number of years and speaks English without hesitation.

12. This interview was conducted in English. Herr Doktor Schönthal lived in England for a number of years and speaks excellent English.

13. This interview was conducted in German.

14. The wash package is a box of goods for newborns provided free by the city. It includes information on infant care, special disinfectant soaps for laundry, rubber pants, and a few cloth diapers.

15. This interview was conducted in English. Frau Doktor Bettauer has lived in both England and the United States and speaks an educated English.

16. This interview was conducted in German.

17. In households with two working spouses, this creates problems of supervision. So-called *Schlüsselkinder* (latch-key children), who must sit in an empty house until their parents come home from work, are a continuing problem for both parents and educators.

CHAPTER 5

1. The Viennese are not alone in naming five mealtimes. The expansion of mealtimes from two or three to five took place in a variety of European commercial cities in the eighteenth and nineteenth centuries. Within Austria-Hungary, residents of Prague name a midmorning (*Přesnídávka*) and midafternoon (*Svačina*) meal, in

addition to breakfast, lunch, and supper. Residents of London have their "elevenses" and, of course, afternoon tea. Florence, too, has a tea time in the afternoon, but has no specially named midmorning meal. Instead, the midmorning and early morning meals share the same term, *Colazione,* but the earlier meal requires the addition of *prima* in order to avoid confusion. The mealtimes of imperial capitals were copied in the colonies, distributing the five-meal pattern as a feature of elite behavior to Africa, South America, and Southeast Asia. The pattern is almost exclusively an urban one. The farther one moves from these commercial centers, the fewer the mealtimes.

2. This distinction between meals and snacks emphasizes the social focus of the activity. In doing so, it differs from Mary Douglas's article on food meanings in which the major contrast is drawn between meals and drinks, solids or liquids, rather than meals and snacks (cf. Douglas 1972). Such differing emphases are inevitable, given the importance and multivocality of food-taking for people. Douglas is looking at the rules which underlie meal composition, while I am interested in the process which determines meal attendance and how this custom changes over time. Hence she and I are dealing with different senses of the word *meal.*

3. Both of these older informants had spent considerable time in English-speaking communities. The interviews were conducted in English.

4. The word Jause comes from the Slovak *justina* (meal), but an older German term, *Vesperbrot,* was also in use at the turn of the century (Jakob 1929, 92). Hauenstein also gives the term *Imbiss* (snack) as a synonym. The term referred to any *Zwischenmahlzeit* (between-meal snack). Thus, there was also a *Zehnerjausn* in dialect that was a synonym for Gabelfrühstück (1972, 40). Today the term is used exclusively for the afternoon snack.

5. The Kaffeehaus is thought to have originated in 1685. By 1747, there were only eleven in the city. But by the time of Gross-Hoffinger (1832), there were one hundred and fifty, twenty-five of them within the walled city alone. In 1910, the popularity of the concessions for eating Jause was well established, and 1,202 Kaffeehäuse were in operation (Brandstätter, Treffer, and Lorenz 1986, 133).

6. Preparation times were established experimentally, using the recipes and techniques described in Maier-Bruck (1975).

7. Those accustomed to thinking of long-simmering soup stocks may find this statement surprising. Poorer Viennese families prepared an *Einbrenn,* or an *Einmach* soup. These were essentially thin white sauces. In the Einmach soup, the roux was only cooked a short time before the water, milk or cooking liquid from boiled vegetables was added to form a thin, translucent consistency. In Einbrenn soups, the roux was cooked until the flour was colored a deeper brown. Oftentimes,

the primary flavoring was a handful of caraway seeds added to the roux and briefly softened before the liquid was added.

8. Fewer than 10% of Viennese households are so composed. This description is a combination of two families' suppers. Familie Mandl provided the choreography, while Familie Schieder provided the particular meal contents.

CHAPTER 6

1. Urban markets differ from peasant markets in that urban markets are specifically designed to accommodate non-food producers. They are more likely to have evolved a money economy of some sort, allowing consumers to better transfer their labor credits to purchasing credits. This does not preclude the existence in cities of peasant-style barter markets in which goods and services are exchanged directly without use of tokens. During a crisis, "second," or "black," markets based on barter will evolve spontaneously. In such cases, the value of institutional tokens is lost or seriously eroded.

2. The specific processes involved in the creation and development of these central places were initially formulated by Christaller (1966) and elaborated on by Lösch (1954). The theory of central places and their location forms the basis of urban economic geography. For a detailed discussion of the importance of such geographic considerations in economic anthropology, cf. the introduction to regional analysis chapter in Smith 1976.

3. In 1976, there were nineteen officially sanctioned farmers' markets in the city. They are a collection of wooden stands which occupy a city street during shopping hours and then disappear at 6:30 P.M. They range in size from the huge, semi-permanent Naschmarkt in the Fourth District, the Augustina Markt in the Third, or the Viktor Adler Markt in the Tenth, to small two-day-a-week markets, such as the Per Alban Hansan Siedlung Markt in the Tenth District and the Barmaullistrasse Markt in the Twenty-second.

4. Bakeries were even allowed to open two hours earlier in the morning in recognition of the importance of fresh bakery goods to Viennese households and the traditional early morning work schedule of bakers. Bread is ready to sell at 5:30 A.M. No other retail shop was considered to have as compelling a need for its goods to reach the public in a timely fashion.

5. When the Landeshauptmann from Salzburg Province allowed shopkeepers to keep their stores open on Saturday, December 8, a few years ago to keep their customers from driving over the nearby border to do their Christmas shopping in Bavaria, the federal government sued him in Constitutional Court. The court up-

held his power to make this decision. Federal law eventually changed to allow stores to remain open all day on the four "golden" Saturdays before Christmas.

6. This was actually the case for less than one year: March 15, 1959, to January 1, 1960. But I could find no evidence in the newspapers from that period of the public outcry I was hearing at the time of the interview.

7. For an excellent discussion of the power and class issues involved in the experience of waiting in urban societies, cf. Schwartz 1975.

8. The market basket for this comparison contains half a loaf of rye bread, four tomatoes, ten decagrams (approximately 1/4 lb.) of Swiss cheese, ten decagrams of hard salami, fifteen decagrams of sliced ham, ten decagrams of liver paté, and two half-liter bottles of beer. The price is based on early autumn shopping when the tomatoes are at their yearly average price. The greatest savings between Kleingeschäfte and Supermarkte are in the meat prices, and are a clear indication of the discounting available to chain Supermarkte.

9. The differences between men's and women's work-segment boundaries are provided in the Appendix.

10. The value added tax was a national sales tax established in the early 1970s. It required retail owners to collect not only the portion of the tax that was created by their sale to customers, but also the portion entailed by the sale of those products from producer to wholesaler and wholesaler to retailer.

11. Preliminary results of this survey were previously reported in Rotenberg and Hutchison 1980.

12. There are two provisions in the variances created by the Bürgermeister and the Landeshauptmann that might influence merchants' choices: the extension of store hours in Lower Austria during daylight savings time; and in the wine-growing villages of Mödling county, including Perchtoldsdorf, a locality-specific variance that grants food stores an extension to 11:00 P.M. if they provide readymade take-out foodstuffs for visitors to the Heurigen located in and around these towns. To compensate for the first provision, the survey was conducted in December, after the variance was no longer in effect. To counter the second, the two shops in Perchtoldsdorf that were identified as having extended their hours were excluded from the sample of fifty-eight stores. There were no such stores in Mödling.

13. Of these, the most important is the national health service offices and clinic. The office administering motor vehicle registration and driving tests, as well as other kinds of licenses, is also in Mödling.

14. These percentages were established by weighting non-food-shop hours by a factor of 0.6 and food-shop hours by 0.4, and then computing the simple mean for the locations.

CHAPTER 7

1. These influential ideas come from an essay on the relation between work and play written for Rothacker's *Festschrift* (1958, 94–101). Similar efforts to analyze the function of play activities by Central European theorists can be found in Weber (1963) and Kramer (1975). These later works are strongly influenced by Habermas.

2. The word *Erholung* comes from the verb *erholen*, to make whole, to recuperate. It extends the notion of returning to wellness, to completeness from the sphere of medical conditions to the conditions of everyday life. There is a participatory, as well as a restorative, flavor to the activity. Recuperation is something individuals must actively do for themselves. *Vergnügung* comes from the verb *vergnügen*, to amuse or enjoy oneself. It is similar to *Erheiterung*, and both words can be translated as amusement. Erheiterung includes the sense of brightening the disposition and changing one's mood for the better. Vergnügung connotes a more enduring sense of pleasure and enjoyment.

3. This ceremonial calendar was ratified in 1957 and is fully described in section 2, paragraph 1, clause 1 of the Feiertagsruhegesetzes, BGBL. Nr. 153/1957. The Nation Day date was established on June 28, 1967. Cf. Nationalfeiertag BGBL. 263/1967 (Haubeneder 1971, 63).

4. As E. P. Thompson points out, it was not that sports did not exist before industry, but the notion of organized competition between villages, factories, or nations coincides with the destruction of traditional village and workshop relationships, and may have produced a substitute identity for the moribund preindustrial collectivity. In other words, organized sport is the industrial version of the lost commons and playgrounds. It becomes the only legitimate outlet of the playful impulses among coworkers that are otherwise repressed by work discipline (1963, 448).

5. Acquaintanceship in Vienna is a variety of instrumental friendship (Wolf 1966). In an early article, I discuss the dynamics of these relations in greater detail (Rotenberg 1979).

6. There are even older forms of using pronouns to create social distance that are very difficult to find today. These include children using the third person plural when addressing their parents and adults acknowledging class differences through the use of the third person singular.

7. Nothing is more confounding to the non-native speaker of Viennese German than the pronoun rules. It is not simply a matter of power and solidarity (Brown and Gilman 1960). Issues of gender, generation, marital status, educational status, context, and *Sympathie* (emotional congeniality) can override differences of power

and negate claims of solidarity. When asked, the Viennese will say that it is safest to always use the polite pronoun, Sie. On a number of occasions, my adherence to this practice has actually offended people who could not understand why I was trying to remain so aloof. On other occasions, what seemed to me to be a clear case of social solidarity dictating the easy use of du resulted in embarrassed laughter. Efforts to wait to hear how people addressed me often led to sustained practice in composing sentences without any personal references. The conclusion I finally arrived at is that it is one's inclusion or exclusion in a network of intimates that determines how the pronouns are used when people are first introduced. Thus, if I was introduced to someone and the person making the introduction was per du with both of us, then we were per du with each other. In any other combination, we would be per Sie. However, I am sure there are exceptions to this rule, as well. This is one more indication of how important the Bekanntenkreise are as units of social organization.

8. This prefix means tree trunk and is found in expressions of kinship and lineage, such as one's original home, *Stammhaus*, or family tree, *Stammbaum*.

9. The tradition of creating a moral polarity in space with the rural at the sacred end and the urban at the profane end is quite ancient. In the fourth century B.C.E. Akkadian epic of Gilgamesh, Enkidu loses his capacity to speak with animals after having sex with an urban temple harlot sent by urban king Gilgamesh to seduce him and strip him of his natural strengths. Hebrew prophets, especially Amos, continually apostatized the cities. Ibn Khaldûn equated the settling down of the Bedawi into the cities of the Magreb with their corruption. Philosophical utopians, from Plato to More and Bacon, constructed alternative urban places freed from moral decay. Closer to the cultural memories of the Viennese were the agro-romantics of the nineteenth century, Rushkin and Morris, Kropotkin and Tolstoy, Bellamy, and especially Theodore Hertzka. His book, *Freiland* (1890), pictured German-speaking metropolitans setting up a utopian socialist colony in the middle of Africa. For Hertzka, the source of moral decay in the cities was private property. In a manner similar to popular reaction in the English-speaking world to Bellamy's *Looking Backward* (1888), hundreds of Freiland societies were established throughout Germany and Austria to study the feasibility of his model.

10. The basis for the often observed xenophobia of Viennese is older than the Industrial Revolution. Gross-Hoffinger (1933, 48) offers the following explanation in 1832: "The Viennese street people (*Pöbel*) hate all foreigners because they have found that all foreigners hate them. He [*sic*] derides, curses, and insults them as if he believed that they, in their own places, give him the same treatment. But there is one difference. In the other places, people of all classes despise the Viennese, while in Vienna only the street people return the favor."

11. Wild grapes of the *silvestris* variety are indigenous to the valley, having spread

there from the Black Sea. The domesticated *vinifera* variety was introduced to the area in the first millennium B.C.E. Spontaneous hybridization between the two varieties produced a hearty white grape on which the Vienna Basin wine industry is based (Zohary and Speigel-Roy 1975, 321–23).

12. The problem of socializing children to alcohol drinking is a significant one in societies, such as those of the European Alpine region, in which alcoholic beverages were once an important source of calories during some parts of the year. While this nutritional problem is no longer pressing, the custom of socializing children to social drinking continues to occupy the Viennese. However, the rates of alcoholism are rising. This suggests that arenas for teaching children to drink, such as Heurigen, are less effective today than they once were. For a fuller discussion of this problem, and of Heurigen in general, cf. Rotenberg 1984.

13. Buschenschank is the common spelling of the word and the spelling that most closely approximates the Viennese pronunciation (Hauenstein 1972, 21). An Ausschank is a tap. However, the root verb for dispense is *schenken* and the word *Weinschenke* (wine tap) is also commonly used to refer to Heurigen. Jakob even offers Buschenschenken in his 1929 dictionary of Viennese dialect (1929, 44).

CHAPTER 8

1. Melbin describes the social relations between urbanites after dark, and especially late at night, as substantialy different than during the day. He has suggested that nighttime behaviors reflect lower interactional densities, mimicking those of a "frontier" social experience (1978).

2. Zerubavel suggests that a necessity of planning exists in industrial societies and that it constitutes a fourth dimension, which he calls duration (1976, 88–90). Lauer has argued that Moore's dimension of rate is actually two separate dimensions: rate of recurrence, which he calls periodicity, and rate of intensity, which he calls tempo (1981, 28–35). The difference between the two rates is the duration of time over which the recurrence is observed (periodicity), and how many intervening activities there are between the occurrences (intensity). These later models are testimony to the pervasive influence of Moore's functional positivism in theorizing about social time.

3. This tradition has a long history in social science beginning in 1797 with Eden's *State of the Poor*, and including the case studies of LePlay (1871) and Engels (1934). The success of these studies in demonstrating that poverty was not a result of household mismanagement tended to promote budget studies beyond the scope of microeconomics to questions of social and psychological import (Szalai 1966, 3).

4. In technical terms, money provides a ratio scale, a statistical appraisal of the precision of the numbers that provides for powerful statistical inference. Minutes are often assumed to be on a ratio scale in terms of the analytical techniques employed, but in fact, the numbers reflect only an ordinal scale. This means that the best information one can retrieve from counting minutes is a ranking of differences. The actual values of the differences in durations, be they minutes, hours or days, are meaningless except when used to generate the ranking.

5. Lee has demonstrated quite convincingly that even without clocks, people experience the variability of time units throughout the world. In this case, the San day is experienced as having a variable length depending on the work activity the day contains (1979, 253–54; Cf. Draper 1976 for the same experience among women's activities in the Kalihari). Among the Bemba, busy-season activities are reflected in the number of days devoted to a task, not the number of minutes in the day. In fact, the busier these agriculturalists get, the shorter the times they spend at their work activities each day (1939). In the Middle Ages, so-called temporal hours divided daylight and night each into twelve equal portions regardless of the season, generating hours of unequal duration from day to day (Bilfinger 1969). Parkinson's Law is a recognition of the variable length of minutes (1957).

6. Sleep provides both the end point and beginning point of schedules. Although the physiological basis of the activity is not yet fully understood, sleep is a universal human activity. At least one group, the Semai, considers sleep and the dream world it makes available at least as important as the activities of the waking world (Denton 1979, 51–54). All other societies schedule only waking activities. Sleep cannot be postponed indefinitely, thereby limiting the total length of the schedule and the total duration of obligatory activities.

7. Cf. Zerubavel 1985, for an extended discussion of the origin of weekly and daily units, and Landes 1983, for the origin of smaller units.

8. The term *technical order* was first used by Redfield to demonstrate that all societies had a moral order and to show how the same moral principles could produce different behaviors under differing technological conditions: "generally speaking a people desperately concerned with getting a living cannot develop a rich moral or esthetic life (1953, 18)." He defines technical order as "that order which results from mutual usefulness, from deliberate coercion, or from mere utilization of the same means. In the technical order, men are bound by things, or become things. They are organized by necessity or expediency (1953, 21)." He goes on to contrast the civilized and primitive in terms of the emphasis given to the technical and moral orders. Among the civilized, the technical order dominates. I find it useful to think of technical order in a narrower sense, namely as the relations between people that arise as people make decisions about how to use technology to achieve desired ends (Rotenberg 1987, 134). I see it as a feature of the moral order

as that develops under specific conditions, rather than something altogether separate. Thus, industrialism is a technical order. Mercantilism and bureaucratic centralism are technical orders, too. We may not immediately think of technology when we hear such labels, but these social formations represent the use of technology (transportation, guild production, literacy, communication, military, etc.) to achieve desired ends.

9. These categories overlap with the system-wide characteristics of mode of production in which the cities are embedded. By mode of production, I mean the patterns for mobilizing the labor of others around specific legitimating appeals: the market in the case of the capitalist mode; obligations of marriage and descent in the case of the kin-ordered mode; and political domination in the case of the tributary mode (Wolf 1982). A ceremonial city is a specialized arena within a tributary state. Administrative, trade, military, colonial, and manufacturing cities are specialized arenas within capitalist states. There are no cities in the kin-ordered mode, but colonial cities often confront kin-ordered organizations of time. I discuss the relationship of time to mode of production in detail elsewhere (Rotenberg 1991).

10. The division of the temporal hours is only equal on the spring and autumn equinoxes. Although made obsolete by the mechanical clock, the system was still used in some parts of Eastern Europe until the seventeenth century.

11. This system was also adopted in Bohemia, Poland, and some areas of Eastern Germany. Clock faces that use the Italian hours put the XXIV mark at 3:00. This allows midnight to occur in the bottom position and midday at the top, thus simulating the movement of the sun.

12. On June 23, the day had sixteen hours and the night eight. One hour would move periodically from day to night, until on December 21, the night would have sixteen hours and the day eight. This system, also known as the great clock hours, was common throughout southern Germany.

13. In England, Sunday was established as a work-free day by Oliver Cromwell, but on the Continent, Sunday continued to be a workday well into the 1890s. In Vienna, for example, Sunday was first granted as a work-free day to warehouse workers in 1911. Earlier, many pious work-givers did insist upon Sabbatarian observance among their workers and provided a free day (or at least a free morning) to that purpose. But the economy-wide observance of a free Sunday was late in coming. When it did come, it signaled the beginning of the industrial weekend, a period of scheduled leisure that in some economies extends across three days.

14. Richards chose to focus on the organization of time in her study of the Bemba in part to counter the claims of colonial administrators that the natives were unfit for civilized labor. In the last chapter of that study, she explodes that myth,

pointing out that there are simply two differing approaches to the relation of work to time between the two cultures (1939).

15. The first official rantings against *Müssigkeit* (idleness) began in the early 1700s. Abraham a Sancta Clara, a cleric who was a favorite among the nobility and whose witty sermons form part of the folk wisdom of the Viennese, denounced idleness in a poem that reads in part: "Eating, Drinking, Walking/ Singing, Whistling, Annoying People/ Mis-using Time and thereby losing/ the Power that Many must answer for (Sancta Clara 1709, 373; translation mine)." In the Resolution of 1763 for the support of enterprises, Maria Theresa seeks to establish the opportunity for the "idle masses to work and support themselves, and at the same time to insure that those idlers who have not the will to do so can be imprisoned in a workhouse (Pribram 1907; translation mine)."

BIBLIOGRAPHY

Ackerknecht, Erwin
    1958   *A Short History of Medicine*. New York: Ronald Press.

Anderson, Perry
    1974   *Lineages of the Absolutist State*. New York: NLB.

Arensberg, Conrad M.
    1963   The Old World Peoples: The Place of European Cultures in World
            Ethnography. *Anthropological Quarterly* 36 (3): 75:99.

Bach, Maximilian
    1898   *Geschichte der Wiener Revolution, 1848*. Wien. Cited in Peter
            Zeisel, Die Geschichte der Arbeitzeitregelungen. Master's thesis,
            Hochschule für Welthandel, Vienna, 1971.

Barea, Ilsa
    1966   *Vienna, Legend and Reality*. London: Saecher and Warburg.

Becker, Gary
    1965   A Theory of the Allocation of Time. *The Economic Journal* 75:
            493–517.

Bellemy, Edward
    1888   *Looking Backward, 2000–1887*. Boston.

Benda, Peter H.
    1960   *Die Industrie und Gewerbebetriebe in Wien*. Wiener Geographische Schritten. Wien: Verlag Ferdinand Berger.

Benjamin, Walter
    1977   *The Origins of German Tragic Drama*. London: Verso (NLB).

Berend, Ivan T., and Gyorgy Ranki
1974   *Economic Development in East Central Europe in the 19th and 20th Centuries.* New York: Columbia University Press.

Berman, Marshall
1982   *All That Is Solid Melts into Air: The Experience of Modernity.* New York: Simon and Schuster.

Berry, Brian J. L.
1971   City Size and Economic Development: Conceptual Synthesis and Policy Problems with Special Reference to South and Southeast Asia. In L. Jakobson and V. Prakash (eds.), *Urbanization and National Development*, 111–55. Beverly Hills: Sage Publications.

Bilfinger, Gustav
1969   *Die Mittelalterlichen Horen und die Modernen Stunden: Ein Beitrag zur Kulturgeschichte.* Reprint of the 1892 edition. Wiesbaden: Dr. Martin Sändig oHG.

Bloch, Marc
1961   *Feudal Society.* Vol. 2, *Social Classes and Political Organization.* Chicago: University of Chicago Press.

Bobeck, Hans, and Elisabeth Lichtenberger
1978   *Wien: Bauliche Gestalt und Entwicklung seit der Mitte des 19. Jahrhunderts.* Wien-Köln: Verlag Hermann Böhlaus Nachf.

Bock, Philip K.
1966   Social Time and Institutional Conflict. *Human Organization* 25: 96–102.

Bourdieu, Pierre
1984   *Distinction: A Social Critique of the Judgment of Taste.* Richard Nice (trans.). Cambridge, Mass.: Harvard University Press.

Brandstätter, Christian, Günter Treffer, and Anna Lorenz
1986   *Stadtchronik Wien: 2000 Jahre in Daten, Dokumenten, und Bildern.* Wien, München: Verlag Christian Brandstätter.

Braverman, Harry
1974   *Labor and Monopoly Capital: The Degradation of Work in the Twentieth Century.* New York: Monthly Review Press.

Brown, Roger W., and A. Gilman
1960   The Pronouns of Power and Solidarity. In T. Sebeok (ed.), *Style in Language.* Cambridge, Mass.: M.I.T. Press.

Bundesministerium für Finanzen
1977   *Erfolge, Probleme, Chancen: Oesterreichs Wirtschaft zur Mitte 1977.* Wien: Österreichische Staatsdruckerei.

Carlstein, Tommy
1982   *Time Resources, Society and Ecology.* Vol. 1, *Preindustrial Societies.* London: George Allen and Unwin.

Catlin, George
1857   *Illustrations of the Manners, Customs, and Conditions of the North American Indians.* 9th edition. Vol. 1. London: Henry G. Bohn.

Christaller, Walter
1966   *Central Places in Southern Germany.* C. W. Baskin (trans.). Englewood Cliffs, N.J.: Prentice-Hall.

Coe, Michael D.
1971   *The Maya.* Harmondsworth, England: Penguin.

DeGrazia, Sebastian
1963   *Of Time, Work and Leisure.* New York: Doubleday.

Denton, Robert K.
1979   *The Semai: A Non-Violent People of Malaya.* New York: Holt, Rinehart and Winston.

Deutsch, Julius
1908   *Geschichte der Österreichischen Gewerkschaftsbewegung.* Wien: Verlag des Österreichische Gewerkschaftbundes.

Doggett, Rachel
1986   *Time: The Greatest Invention.* Washington, D.C.: The Folger Shakespeare Library.

Dorner, Peter
1975   Das Arbeitzeitgesetz. *Betriebs-Kurier* 53/53a (2): 5–35. Jänner 1975.

Douglas, Mary
1972   Deciphering a Meal. *Deadalus* 101 (1): 61–82.

Draper, Patricia
1976   Social and Economic Constraints on Child Life among the !Kung. In R. Lee and I. Devore (eds.), *Kalihari Hunters and Gatherers.* Cambridge, Mass.: Harvard University Press.

Ehmer, Josef
    1980   Produktion und Reproduktion in der Wiener Manufakturperiode. In
            Banik-Schweitzer et al, *Wien im Vormärz*. Wien: Verein für Ge-
            schichte der Stadt Wien.

Ehrenberg, Richard
    1963   *Capital and Finance in the Age of the Renaissance: a Study of the
            Fuggers and Their Connections*. New York: Reprints of Economic
            Classics.

Engels, Friedrich
    1934   *Condition of the Working Class in 1844*. F. K. Wischnewetzky
            (trans.). London.

Fox, Richard G.
    1971   *Kin, Clan, Raja and Rule: State-Hinterland Relations in Preindus-
            trial India*. Berkeley: University of California Press.
    1977   *Urban Anthropology: Cities in their Cultural Settings*. Englewood
            Cliffs, N. J.: Prentice-Hall.

Fox, Richard G., and Allen Zagarell
    1982   The Political Economy of Mesopotamian and South Indian Tem-
            ples: The Formation and Reproductions of Urban Society. *Com-
            parative Urban Research* 9 (1): 8–27.

Galbraith, John Kenneth
    1958   *The Affluent Society*. Boston: Houghton Mifflin.

Geertz, Clifford
    1973   *The Interpretation of Culture*. New York: Basic Books.
    1980   *Negara: The Theater State in Nineteenth Century Bali*. Princeton:
            Princeton University Press.
    1983   *Local Knowledge*. New York: Basic Books.

Geissler, Hermann
    1959   Die Auswirkung der Arbeitzeitverkürzung von Standpunkt des Un-
            ternehmers. In K. Kummer (ed.), *Das Arbeitzeitproblem von
            heute*. Wien: Verein für Sozial-und Wirtschaftspolitik.

Glossy, Carl (ed.)
    1919   Wien, 1840–1848: Eine amtliche Chronik, Teil 2. *Schriften des
            literarischen Vereins in Wien* 24.

Godelier, Maurice
    1977   *Perspectives in Marxist Anthropology*. New York: Cambridge Uni-
            versity Press.

Goodenough, Ward H.
1963   *Cooperation in Change.* New York: Russell Sage Foundation.

Gordon, B.M.
1975   The Challenge of Industrialization: The Catholic Church and the Working Class in and around Vienna, 1815–1848. *Austrian History Yearbook.* Vol. 9/10. Houston: Rice University Press.

Groner, Richard
1965   *Wien, wie es war.* Reprint of 1922 edition. Wien and München: Molden.

Gross-Hoffinger, Anton Johann (a.k.a. Hans Normann)
1832   *Österreich wie es ist.* Erste Theil: Wien wie es ist. Leipzig und Löwenberg: Eschrich und Comp.

Gurvitch, Georges
1964   *The Spectrum of Social Time.* Dordrecht: D. Reidel Publishing Co.

Haas, Erich (ed.)
1979   *Arbeitzeitverkürzung: Eine Dokumentation.* Materialien zu Wirtschaft und Gesellschaft. Wien: Verlag der Kammer für Arbeiter und Angestellte für Wien.

Habermas, Jürgen
1958   Soziologische notizen zum Verhältnis von Arbeit und Freizeit. In G. Funke (ed.), *Konkrete Vernunft* (Rothacker Festschrift), 90–103. Bonn: H. Bonvier.

Halbwachs, Maurice
1947   La memoire collective et le temps. *Cahiers internationaux de sociologie,* 3–31.

Hammerl, Ernst
1976   Wann kauft Staris Frau: Politiker bestimmen den Ladenschluss— aber sie baden ihn nicht aus. *Kurier,* October 30, 1976, p. 3.

Hansely, Hans-Jörg, and Ottokar Indrak
1978   *Arbeitsmarkt: Probleme, Entwicklungstendenzen, Ziele.* Stadtentwicklungsplan Wien. Wien: Magistrat der Stadt Wien.

Harris, Marvin
1975   *Culture, People and Nature: An Introduction to General Anthropology.* 2d edition. New York: Thomas Crowell.

Hatschek, Hans J.
1886   *Das Manufakturhaus auf dem Tabor in Wien: Ein Beitrag zur österreichischen Wirthschaftsgeschichte des 17. Jahrhunderts.* Leipzig: Verlag von Dunker and Humblot.

Haubeneder, Max
1971   *Die Ladenöffnungszeiten im Einzelhandel unter besonderer Berücksichtigung der österreichischen Gesetzgebung.* Doctoral dissertation, Institut für Politische Ökonomie, Hochschule für Welthandel in Wien, Vienna.

Hauenstein, Hans
1972   *Wiener Dialekt: Weanerische Drahdiwaberln von Adadbei zu Zwirnknäullerl.* Wien: Karl und Otto Karner.

Haüsler, Wolfgang
1980   Von Manufaktur zum Maschinensturm. Industrielle Dynamik und sozialer Wandel im Raum Wien. In Banik-Schweitzer et al, *Wien im Vormärz.* Wien: Verein für Geschichte der Stadt Wien.

Hawley, Amos
1950   *Human Ecology.* New York: Ronald Press.

Hertz, Frederick
1970   *The Economic Problem of the Danubian States: A Study in Economic Nationalism.* New York: Howard Fertig.

Hertzka, Theodore
1890   *Freiland: Ein Soziales Zukunftsbild.* Leipzig: Duncker und Humblot.

Hill, C.
1964   The uses of Sabbatarianism. In *Society and Puritanism in Pre-Revolutionary England.* New York: Schocken Books, Inc.

Honigmann, John
1963   Dynamics of Drinking in an Austrian Village. *Ethnology* 2 (2): 157–69.

Huizinga, Johan
1955   *Homo Ludens: A Study of the Play Element in Culture.* Boston: Beacon Press.

I.F.E.S. (Institut für Forschung im Empirischen Soziologie)
1974   *Kultur in Österreich: Grundlagenforschung im Kulturellen Bereich 851/73.* Wien: Institut für Forschung im Empirischen Soziologie.

Jakob, Julius
1929   *Wörterbuch des Wiener Dialektes mit einer kurzgefassten Grammatik.* 1980 reprint of the 1929 edition. Dortmund: Harenberg Kommunikation.

Johnson, Allen
1975   Time Allocation in a Machiguenga Community. *Ethnology* 14: 301–10.
1978   In Search of the Affluent Society. *Human Nature* 1 (9): 50–59.

Johnston, William M.
1972   *The Austrian Mind: An intellectual and social history, 1848–1938.* Berkeley: University of California Press.

Kammer für Arbeiter und Angestellte
1961   *Freizeitgestaltung der Arbeiter und Angestellten Wiens.* Wien: Verlag der Kammer für Arbeiter und Angestellte.

Kann, Robert A.
1974   *A History of the Habsburg Empire, 1526–1918.* Berkeley: University of California Press.

Kinzel, Herbert
1969   *Kollektivvertrag betreffend die etappenweise Verkürzung der Arbeitzeit.* Wien: Bundeskammer der Gewerblichen Wirtschaft.

Kisch, Herbert
1981   *The Textile Industries of Selesia and the Rhineland: A Comparative Study in Industrialization.* In Kriedte, Medick, and Schlumbohm (eds.), *Industrialization before Industrialization.* Rural Industry in the Genesis of Capitalism. New York: Cambridge University Press.

Klenner, Fritz
1952   *Die österreichischen Gewerkschaften.* Wien: Verlag des österreichische Gewerkschaftbundes.

Klima, A.
1974   The Role of Rural Domestic Industry in Bohemia in the Eighteenth Century. *Economic History Review* 27 (1).

Kramer, Dieter
1975   *Freizeit und Reproduktion der Arbeitkraft.* Köln: Pahl-Rugenstein.

Kriedte, Peter
1981   The Origins, the Agrarian Context, and the Conditions in the World Market. In Kriedte, Medick, and Schlumbohm (eds.), *Industrial-*

ization before Industrialization. Rural Industry in the Genesis of Capitalism. New York: Cambridge University Press.

Kupka, Paul
1971   *Das Ladenschlussgesetz samt Landesregelungen.* Wien: Österreichischer Wirtschaftsverlag.

Lamel, Joachim
1975   Die Auswirkungen der Arbeitzeitverkürzung 1975 in der Industrie. Wirtschaftspolitische Blätter (January). In Haas (ed.), *Arbeitzeitverkürzung: Eine Dokumentation.* Materialien zu Wirtschaft und Gesellschaft, 90–95. Wien: Verlag der Kammer für Arbeiter und Angestellte für Wien. 1979.

Landes, David S.
1983   *Revolution in Time: Clocks and the Making of the Modern World.* Cambridge, Mass.: Harvard University Press.

Lapidius, Ira M.
1967   *Muslim Cities in the Later Middle Ages.* Cambridge, Mass.: Harvard University Press.

Lauer, Robert H.
1981   *Temporal Man: The Meaning and Uses of Social Time.* New York: Praeger.

Le Goff, Jacques
1980   *Time, Work and Culture in the Middle Ages.* Chicago: University of Chicago Press.

Le Play, Frédéric
1871   *L'Organisation de la famille selon le vrai modèle signalé par l'histoire de toutes les races et de tous les temps.* Paris: Téqui, bibliothécaire de l'Oeuvre Saint-Michel.

Leach, Edmund
1976   *Culture and Communication: The Logic by Which Symbols are Connected.* New York: Cambridge University Press.

Leaf, Murray
1983   The Organizations of Cities. Paper read at the 11th International Congress of Anthropological and Ethnological Sciences. Quebec City. August 14, 1983.

Lee, Richard B.
1979   *The !Kung San.* Cambridge, England: Cambridge University Press.

Leeds, Anthony
    1973   Locality Power in Relation to Supralocal Power. In A. Southall (ed.), *Urban Anthropology*; 15–42. New York: Oxford University Press.

Leitich, Anna Tizia
    1941   *Wiener Biedermeier*. Bielefeld und Leipzig: Velhasen und Klasing.

Leitner, S.
    1976   "Lasse mich nicht festlegen": Handelsminister Staribacher und die Zukunft des Ladenschlussgesetzes. *Kurier*, November 19, 1975, p. 3.

Lewis, David J., and Andrew J. Weigert
    1981   The Structures and Meanings of Social Time. *Social Forces* 60: 432–62.

Lichtenberger, E.
    1977   *Die Wiener Altstadt: Von der mittelalterlichen Bürgerstadt zur City*. Wien: Franz Deuticke.

Lohrmann, Klaus
    1981   Die Kuenringer und Wien. In H. Wolfram and K. Brunner (eds.), *Die Kuenringer: Das Werden des Landes Niederoesterreich*. Wien: Amt der niederoesterreich Landesregierung (Abt. III/2-Kulturabteilung).

Lösch, August
    1954   *The Economics of Location*. W. F. Stolper (trans.). New Haven: Yale University Press.

Lowie, R. H.
    1935   *The Crow Indians*. New York: Farrar and Rinehart.

Magistratsabteilung 66
    1912   *Statistisches Jahrbuch der Stadt Wien*. Wien: Magistrat der Stadt Wien (Jugend und Volk Verlagsgesellschaft). Vol. 1911.
    1961   *Statistisches Jahrbuch der Stadt Wien*. Wien: Magistrat der Stadt Wien (Jugend und Volk Verlagsgesellschaft). Vol. 1960.
    1965   *Statistisches Jahrbuch der Stadt Wien*. Wien: Magistrat der Stadt Wien (Jugend und Volk Verlagsgesellschaft). Vol. 1964
    1970   *Statistisches Jahrbuch der Stadt Wien*. Wien: Magistrat der Stadt Wien (Jugend und Volk Verlagsgesellschaft). Vol. 1969.
    1975   *Statistisches Jahrbuch der Stadt Wien*. Wien: Magistrat der Stadt Wien (Jugend und Volk Verlagsgesellschaft). Vol. 1974.
    1979   *Statistisches Jahrbuch der Stadt Wien*. Wien: Magistrat der Stadt Wien (Jugend und Volk Verlagsgesellschaft). Vol. 1978

1980	*Statistisches Jahrbuch der Stadt Wien*. Wien: Magistrat der Stadt Wien (Jugend und Volk Verlagsgesellschaft). Vol. 1979.
1981	*Statistisches Jahrbuch der Stadt Wien*. Wien: Magistrat der Stadt Wien (Jugend und Volk Verlagsgesellschaft). Vol. 1980.
1983	*Statistisches Jahrbuch der Stadt Wien*. Wien: Magistrat der Stadt Wien (Jugend und Volk Verlagsgesellschaft). Vol. 1982.

Maier-Bruck, Franz

1975   *Das Grosse Sacher Kochbuch: Die Oesterreichische Küche.* München: Schuler Verlagsgesellschaft.

Marschall, Karl

1957   *Grenzprobleme des Arbeitsrechts.* Wien. Cited in Peter Zeisel, Die Geschichte der Arbeitzeitregelungen. Master's thesis, Hochschule für Welthandel, Vienna, 1971.

Marx, Karl, and Frederick Engels

1974   Manifesto of the Communist Party. (Samuel Moore trans.). In D. Fernbach (ed.), *Karl Marx: The Revolution of 1848*, 62–98. New York: Vintage.

Matis, Herbert

1968   Die Ansätze zur Industrializierung in Niederösterreich im Spiegel einer zeitgenössischen Reisebeschreibung. In *Tradition, Zeitschrift für Firmengeschichte und Unternehmerbiographie*. 13: 119–32.

Maurice, Sigrid, and Klaus Maurice

1980   Stundenangaben im Gemeinwesen des 16. and 17. Jahrhunderts. In K. Maurice and O. Mayr (eds.), *Die Welt als Uhr: Deutsche Uhren and Automaten 1550–1650*. Munich: Bayerisches National-museum.

Meissl, Gerhart

1980a   Industrie und Gewerbe in Wien 1835 bis 1845. Brachenmässige und regionale Strukturen und Entwicklungstendenzen im Spiegel der Gewerbeausstellungen von 1835, 1839, und 1845. In Banik-Schweitzer et al, *Wien im Vormärz*. Wien: Verein für Geschichte der Stadt Wien.

1980b   Industriearbeit in Wien 1870–1913. *Jahrbuch des Vereins für Geschichte der Stadt Wien*. 36: 174–229.

Melbin, Murray

1978   Night as Frontier. *American Sociological Review*. 43 (1): 3–22.

Michelson, William

1978   Retrospective Observations on the Use of Time-Budgets in the

Analysis of Housing Implications. In Michelson (ed.), *Public Policy in Temporal Perspective*. The Hague: Mouton.

Mikalson, Jon D.
1975   *The Sacred and Civil Calendar of the Athenian Year*. Princeton: Princeton University Press.

Minge-Klevana, Wanda
1980   Does Labor Time Decrease with Industrialization? A Survey of Time Allocation Studies. *Current Anthropology* 21 (3): 279–98.

Ministerium für Soziale Verwaltung
1968   *50 Jahre Ministerium für Soziale Verwaltung, Festschrift 1918– 1968*. Wien: Ministerium für Soziale Verwaltung.

Mischler, Ernst
1905   Arbeitsschutz. In E. Mischler and J. Ulbrich (ed.), Österreichisches Staatswörterbuch. 2d. edition. 1: 206 ff.

Moore, Wilbert
1963   *Man, Time and Society*. New York: Wiley.

Mündel, Wilfred, A. Auer, H. Brachmeier, F. Endlicher, E. Hindler, G. Jersabek, O. Nitsch, M. Pfiel, E. Scholl, L. Sejkot, H. Stage, G. Stemberger, and K. Weber
1979   *Das Freizeitverhalten der Wiener Arbeitnehmer*. Wien: Verlag der Kammer für Arbeiter und Angestellte für Wien.

Mündel, Wilfried
1971   Der lange Weg zu den 40,000 Stunden. *Arbeit und Wirtschaft* (December): 2–6.

Nekula-Benton, M. P.
1967   *Karl Pick: aus seinem Leben, aus seinem Werk*. Wien: Verlag des Österreichischen Gewerkschaftsbundes.

Nelkin, Dorothy
1970   Unpredictability and Life-style in a Migrant Labor Camp. *Social Problems* 17 (Spring): 472–87.

Neumann, A.
1958   Das Wiener Stadtgebiet in Ur- und Frühgeschichtlicher Zeit. In Lettmeyer (ed.), *Wien um die Mitte des 20sten Jahrhunderts*, 244– 65. Wien: Verlag Jugend und Volk.

Nieuwalt, Simon
1957   *Die Funktionele Gliederung von Wien*. Doctoral dissertation, Philosophical Faculty of the University of Vienna.

Österreichischer Gewerkschaftsbund
1956   *Tätigkeitsbericht.* Individual volumes for years 1956–1968. Wien:
        Oesterreichischer Gewerkschaftsbund.

Österreichisches Statistisches Zentralamt
1972   *Statistisches Handbuch für die Republik Österreich.* Jahrgang
        XXIII, Neue Folge. Wien: Österreichische Staatsdruckerei.

Oswald, I., J. Merrington, and H. Lewis
1970   Cyclical "On Demand" Oral Intake by Adults. *Nature* 225: 959–
        60.

Parkinson, Northcote
1957   *Parkinson's Law.* New York: Ballantine Books.

Petermann, R. E.
1927   *Wien von Jahrhundert zu Jahrhundert.* Vol. 1. Wien: Gerlach und
        Wiedling.

Pezzl, Johann
1923   *Skizze von Wien: Ein Kultur- und Sittenbild aus der josephinischen
        Zeit.* G. Gugitz u. A. Schloffar (eds.). Reprint of the 1792 edition.
        Graz: Lehkam Verlag.

Plattner, Stuart
1989   Preface. In Stuart Plattner (ed.), *Economic Anthropology.* Stan-
        ford: Stanford University Press.

Preminger, Otto
1977   *Preminger: An Autobiography.* Garden City, N. Y.: Doubleday.

Press, Irwin
1979   *The City as Context: Urbanism and Behavioral Constraints in
        Seville.* Urbana: University of Illinois Press.

Pribram, Karl
1907   *Geschichte der österreichischen Gewerbpolitik von 1740 bis 1860.*
        Bd. 1. Leipzig.

Rabinow, Paul
1989   *French Modern: Norms and Forms of the Social Environment.*
        Cambridge, Mass.: MIT Press.

Rabl, Peter
1976   Ladenschluss: Es steht. 52:41. *Kurier,* December 4, 1976, p. 3.

Ragucci, Antoinette T.
 1981   Italian Americans. In Alan Harwood (ed.), *Ethnicity and Medical Care*, 211–63. Boston: Harvard University Press.

Rauscher, H.
 1976   Haie, Kleine Fische und die liebe Gott: Der Stadt der "Shopping City Süd" in Vösendorf. *Kurier*, September 23, 1976, p. 3.

Redfield, Robert
 1953   *The Primitive World and Its Transformations.* Ithaca, N.Y.: Cornell University Press.

Redfield, R., and M. Singer
 1954   The Cultural Role of Cities. *Economic Development and Culture Change* 3: 53–73.

Richards, Audrey
 1939   *Land, Labor and Diet in Northern Rhodesia.* London: Oxford University Press.

Riggs, Fred W.
 1964   *Administration in Developing Countries: The Theory of Prismatic Society.* Boston: Houghton Mifflin.

Rodgers, Daniel T.
 1978   *The Work Ethic in Industrial America: 1850–1920.* Chicago: University of Chicago Press.

Rotenberg, Robert
 1979   Intraregional Conflicts in Public Schedules in Austria. *Urban Anthropology* 8 (1): 73–94.
 1981   The Impact of Industrialization on Mealtimes in Vienna. *Ecology of Food and Nutrition* 11: 25–35.
 1984   Viennese Wine Gardens and their Magic. *East European Quarterly* 18 (4): 447–60.
 1986   Pseudonymous Accounts as Texts: A Case from 19th Century Vienna. *Ethnohistory* 33 (2): 149–58.
 1987   Community, Time and the Technical Order. In Steven E. Goldberg and Charles R. Strain (eds.), *Technological Change and the Transformation of America*, 133–44. Carbondale and Edwardsville: Southern Illinois University Press.
 1988   Boundaries in Time: The Dynamics of Schedule Constraints on Household Consumption in Vienna, Austria. In Benjamin Orlove and Henry Rutz (eds.), *The Social Economy of Consumption*. Studies in Economic Anthropology, Vol. 4. Lanham, Md.: University Press of America.

1992 Power and Temporality in Cross-Cultural Perspective. In Henry Rutz (ed.), *The Politics of Temporality*. American Ethnological Society Monograph No. 4. Washington: American Ethnological Society.

Rotenberg, Robert, and E. Ray Hutchison
1980 Social Organization of Time in a Small City: A Case Study from Mödling, Austria. In Robert P. Wolensky and Edward Miller (eds.), *Proceedings of the Third Annual Conference on the Small City and the Regional Community*, 345–54. Stevens Point, Wis.: University of Wisconsin Press.

Rudolph, Richard L.
1973 Austrian Industrialization: A Case Study in Leisurely Economic Growth. In *Sozialismus, Geschichte und Wirtschaft*. Vienna: Europa Verlag.
1976 The Pattern of Austrian Industrial Growth from the Eighteenth to the Early Twentieth Century. *Austrian Historical Yearbook*. Vol. 11, 3–43. Houston: Rice University Press.

Sancta Clara, Abraham a
1709 *Hundert Ausbündige Narren*. Reprinted 1978. Wien.

Sandford, John
1976 *The Mass Media in the German Speaking Countries*. London: Oswald Wolff.

Schilder, S.
1921 The Manufacturers of the Republic of Austria. In C. L. King (ed.), *Present Day Conditions in Austria*. Annals of the American Academy of Political and Social Science. Vol. 27, 53–55.

Schlumbohm, Jürgen
1981 Relations of Production—Productive Forces—Crises in Proto-industrialization. In Kriedte, Medick and Schlumbohm (eds.), *Industrialization Before Industrialization. Rural Industry in the Genesis of Capitalism*. New York: Cambridge University Press.

Schorske, Carl
1981 *Fin de Siècle Vienna: Politics and Culture*. New York: Vintage Books.

Sheehan, James J.
1978 *German Liberalism in the Nineteenth Century*. Chicago: University of Chicago Press.

Simhandl, G., R. Riess, and R. Riha
1984   *Tagesablauf: Regencies des Mikrozensus September 1981*. Bei-
        träge vom Österreichischen Statistik. Heft 707. Wien: Österreichis-
        chen Statistischen Zentralamt.

Simmel, Georg
1950   The Metropolis and Mental Life. In Kurt Wolff (trans.), *The So-
        ciology of Georg Simmel*. New York: Free Press.

Sinhuber, Bartel F.
1980   *Das Grosse Buch von Wiener Heurigen*. Wien: Verlag ORAC.

Sitte, Camillo
1909   *Der Stadtbau nach seinen künsterlerischen Grundsätzen*. Reprint
        of the 4th edition (1983). Braunschweig/Wiesbaden: Friedrich
        Vieweg & Sohn.

Sjoberg, Gideon
1960   *The Preindustrial City*. New York: Free Press.

Slicher von Bath, B. H.
1963   *The Agrarian History of Western Europe: A. D. 500–1850*. New
        York: St. Martin's Press.

Smith, Carol
1976   *Regional Analysis: Volume One, Economic Systems*. New York:
        Academic Press.

Solidarität
1970   Zwei Stunden Gewonnen. *Solidarität* 8 (February): 490–95.

Sorokin, P. A., and R. K. Merton
1937   Social Time: A Methodological and Functional Analysis. *Ameri-
        can Journal of Sociology* 42 (5): 615–29.

Szalai, Alexander (ed.)
1966   Trends in Comparative Time-Budget Research. *American Behav-
        ioral Scientist* 9 (9): 3–8.
1972   *The Use of Time: Daily Activities in Urban and Suburban Popu-
        lations in Twelve Countries*. The Hague: Mouton.

Tedlock, Barbara
1982   *Time and the Highland Maya*. Albuquerque: University of New
        Mexico Press.

Thompson, E. P.
1963   *The Making of the English Working Class*. London: Penguin
        Books.

1967   Time, Work-Discipline and Industrial Capitalism. *Past and Present* 38: 46–97.

Thompson, J. W.
1965   *Economic and Social History of Europe in the Later Middle Ages 1300–1530*. New York: Frederik Unger Publishing.

Thorington, R. W.
1970   Feeding Behavior of Nonhuman Primates in the Wild. In R. S. Harris (ed.), *Feeding and Nutrition of Nonhuman Primates*. New York: Academic Press.

Traxler, Hans
1981   *Wien and Wir*. Wien: Öesterreichischer Wienwirtschaftsfond.

Tremel, F.
1969   *Wirtschafts- und Sozialgeschichte Österreichs*. Wien: Franz Deuticke Verlag.

Wagner, Otto
1911   *Der Grossstadt: Eine Studie über diese*. Vienna: A. Schroll.
1914   *Die Baukunst unserer Zeit. Dem Baukunstjünger ein Führer auf dem Kunstgebiet*. Nachdruck der 4. Auflage (1979). Vienna: Löcker Verlag.

Weber, Ernst
1963   *Die Freizeit Problem: einer anthropologische-pädagogische analyse*. München, Basel: Reinhardt.

Weihsmann, Helmut
1985   *Das Rote Wien: Sozialdemokratische Architektur und Kommunalpolitik 1919–1934*. Wien: Promedia.

Weiszenberg, Gerhard, and Josef Cerny
1970   *Arbeitzeitgesetz*. Wien: Österreichischer Wirtschaftsverlag.

Williams, Raymond
1973   *The Country and the City*. New York: Oxford University Press.

Wilson, Edmund
1972   *To the Finland Station*. New York: Farrar, Straus and Giroux.

Wolf, Eric
1966   Kinship, Friendship, and Patron-Client Relations in Complex Societies. In Michael Blanton (ed.), *The Social Anthropology of Complex Societies*. New York: Methuen.
1982   *Europe and the People without History*. Berkeley: University of California Press.

Wolff, Kurt et al
    1969   *Untersuchung über die Probleme der Arbeitzeitverkürzung.* Beirat für Wirtschafts- und Sozialfragen. Wien: Carl Überreuter Druck u. Verlag.

Yang, Lien-Sheng
    1955   Schedules of Work and Rest in Imperial China. *Harvard Journal of Asian Studies* 18: 301–25.

Yazaki, Takeo
    1968   *Social Change and the City in Japan: From Earliest Times through the Industrial Revolution.* David L. Swain (trans.). Tokyo: Japan Publication, Inc.

Zeisel, Peter
    1971   *Die Geschichte der Arbeitzeitregelungen.* Master's thesis, Hochschule der Welthandel, Wien.

Zerubavel, Eviatar
    1976   Timetables and Scheduling: On the Social Organization of Time. *Sociological Inquiry* 46 (2): 87–94.
    1977   The French Republican Calendar: A Case Study in the Sociology of Time. *American Sociological Review* 42: 868–77.
    1981   *Hidden Rhythms: Schedules and Calendars in Social Life.* Chicago: University of Chicago Press.
    1985   *The Seven Day Cycle: The History and Meaning of the Week.* New York: The Free Press.

Zohary, D., and P. Spiegel-Roy
    1975   Beginnings of Fruit Growing in the Old World. *Science* 187: 319–27.